D0094726

Appalachian Mountain Club
River Guide
MASSACHUSETTS
CONNECTICUT
RHODE ISLAND

Third Edition

APPALACHIAN MOUNTAIN CLUB
BOSTON

Cover Photograph: Scott Underhill
Book Design: Eva Ruutopõld

Copyright 2000. Appalachian Mountain Club. All rights reserved.

Distributed by the Globe Pequot Press, Guilford, CT.

Published by the Appalachian Mountain Club. No part of this publication
may be reproduced or transmitted in any form or by any means, electron-
ic or mechanical, including photocopying and recording, or by any information storage or retrieval system, except as may be expressly permitted by
the 1976 Copyright Act or in writing from the publisher. Requests for permission should be addressed in writing to Appalachian Mountain Club
Books, 5 Joy Street, Boston, MA 02108

Library of Congress Cataloging-in-Publication Data
Appalachain Mountain Club river guide : Massachusetts, Connecticut,
Rhode Island — 3rd ed.
        p.   cm.
        Includes index.
        ISBN 1-878239-75-9 (alk. paper)
        1. Canoes and canoeing—New England—Guidebooks.
        2. Rivers—New England—Guidebooks. 3. New England—
        Guidebooks. I. Appalachian Mountian Club.

GV776.N35 A68 2000
797.1'22'0974—dc21   00-040124

The paper used in this publication meets the minimum requirements of
the American National Standard for Information Sciences—Permanence
of Paper for Printed Library Materials, ANSI Z39.48-1984.

Due to changes in conditions, use of the information in this book is at the
sole risk of the user.

Printed in the United States of America.

Printed on recycled paper using soy-based inks.

10 9 8 7 6 5 4 3 2   02 03 04 05

Contents

Preface

This Massachusetts/Connecticut/Rhode Island river guide is the first since the significant improvement in the water quality in most rivers. Wildlife is returning. Trash has been removed from many rivers. Watershed advocacy organizations have sprung up across the region. Our rivers are recognized now as a public resource, and are no longer the fetid industrial sewers they once were.

These improvements are largely due to the federal Clean Water Act, enacted more than a quarter century ago, and concerned citizens who have brought pressure to governments and polluters to clean up the rivers. Now federal and state regulations have mostly eliminated dumping into the rivers—in Massachusetts, state law restricts development along them.

Our rivers are now more attractive, and cleaner, than they have been any time since the 1850s. In many locations you can have a delightful experience on the river, whether in a deep forest, a coastal estuary, among historic mill buildings, or in whitewater.

This guide's purpose is to bring current information about these rivers to those who would like to enjoy them. The descriptions here are most often very similar to those in previous editions. This should come as no surprise. The rivers themselves change very little, if at all, in 10 or 25 years. Rapids do not change location. What does change, however, and what gives rise to this revision, is human management of the rivers. Access points have changed, dams have washed out, new bridges have been built, and the water is cleaner. Please keep in mind that specific details may change between the time this information was compiled and the time when you use this book.

As recreational use of our rivers increases, the awareness to continue to clean them up becomes more widespread. There is still much work to be done. You are an important member in the community of those who care about the rivers. People like you are helping make our rivers cleaner and more fun for all.

John Fiske
March 2000

Acknowledgments

Special thanks to the people and organizations that contributed to the River Guide. If your name should be here and it is not, our apologies.

Matthew Adiletta, American Whitewater, George Arthur, Boston Harbor Islands, Charles River Watershed Association, Chicopee River Watershed Council, Albert Clark, Russ Cohen, Peter Davis, Deerfield River Watershed Association, Rod Dore, Farmington River Watershed Association, Polly French, Ed Himlan, Hoosic River Watershed Association, Roger Hunt, Ipswich River Watershed Association, Rob Kibler, Charles H. Lewis, Gale Lyman, The Map Shack, Beverly Martin, Massachusetts Watershed Coalition, Neil Menschel (Nashoba Paddler), Merrimack River Watershed Council, John Monroe, Narrow River Preservation Association, Nashua River Watershed Association, National Park Service Rivers & Trails Commission, Neponset River Watershed Association, New England Power, Bernie Noonan, North and South Rivers Watershed Association, Ron Perry, Quinebaug-Shetucket Heritage Corridor, Quinnipiac River Watershed Association, Robert Rauseo, Cynthia and James Reik, Stew Sanders, Saugus River Watershed Council, Richard J. Schmidt, Jane Sergi, Dave Shephard, Douglas H. Smith, Lauren Stevens, SuAsCo Watershed Coalition, Taunton River Watershed Alliance, Cassis Thomas, William Tinglay, Edmund Toomey, Jeff Tubman, Paul Von Protz, Westport River Watershed Alliance, Dave Williams, Wood-Pawcatuck Watershed Association.

Introduction

Four major drainage basins in southern New England account for most of the rivers described in this guidebook. The Housatonic River drains western Massachusetts and western Connecticut, offering a variety of trips both on its main stem and on its pleasant tributaries. The Connecticut River drains central Massachusetts and central Connecticut and offers flatwater on its main stem. Outstanding tributaries of the Connecticut include the Millers, the Deerfield, the Westfield with its branches, the Farmington, and the Salmon. The Thames River drains eastern Connecticut and a small portion of Rhode Island and Massachusetts. The best paddling in this area is found on the Willimantic and the Natchaug. And finally, the Merrimack River drains northeastern Massachusetts and central New Hampshire. There the Concord and Sudbury offer interesting flatwater trips.

The area between major drainage basins offers mostly flatwater trips. Suggested trips are on the Wood, Bass, and Parker Rivers.

Many rivers in these watersheds have not been included. Remember, every square inch of land is drained; it is impossible to describe every stream in a book this size. Not surprisingly, a river may have different names in different sections and on different maps. Gathering up-to-date information for this book was not easy. If you want to try a stream not described here, try talking with local people to learn about it it. You'd be amazed at the depth of local knowledge—that knowledge contributed to this revision.

Safety

Although this book was prepared with care, no guidebook should be used on blind faith. Along with a map, this book is a very helpful companion to have when you run a river, but it will not solve every problem.

This book will not protect you from yourself. Managing a boat in current is a learned skill. The nature of the river will place different demands on your skills. Maneuvering with style and finesse is considerably different from simply paddling hard. Be realistic about your abilities and do not underestimate the power of moving water or the difficulty of a river. The Safety Code of the American Whitewater Affiliation is included in the appendix; it contains many good suggestions for safe boating.

This book also will not protect you from unexpected rapids or obstacles. Many permanent changes in rivers have taken place within the last few decades, and they have often occurred when dams were washed out. New England still has many old dams that could collapse and expose whatever the millponds covered. There is always the possibility of encountering temporary or seasonal obstructions. Snowmobile bridges and ice dam nets have become a noteworthy ice dam hazard on some small quickwater streams. Low and often awash, they usually block a river even more effectively than a fallen tree.

And lastly, this book is not a guide to sudden changes in water level. A moderate spring or autumn rainfall will significantly affect a river with a large, mountainous watershed. In a matter of hours, the river can rise several feet and become more difficult and hazardous. Unanticipated releases from dams can have the same effect.

Boating as a sport involves certain risks, which can be minimized with the proper training, forethought, caution, and equipment.

Be Considerate of Landowners

Many put-ins, takeouts, and portages are open for public use. Others require that you cross private property. You will note that many landowners whose property borders popular canoeing rivers have posted signs on their property against trespass. Paddlers can prevent additional closings by being thoughtful. Ask permission where it is possible, don't damage vegetation, park cars out of the way so they don't block roads, and pick up litter. Make your portage expeditiously and leave; don't hang around picnicking and making a disturbance. Don't expect local residents to be responsible for rescuing you and your canoe. Dumping boats and getting them pinned on whitewater rivers happens to the best of us, and paddlers should prepare before launching by having suitable equipment, clothing, and a large enough group. Access to put-ins and takeouts is the right of a private landowner, and only the privilege of the user. Access is becoming limited on some rivers, so it is increasingly important to maintain good relations with property owners.

Using the River Guide

Organization

Each chapter begins with a list of the rivers described. The tributaries of each river are listed below it. The principal river is described first, then its tributaries in descending (downstream) order.

Format for River Descriptions

Each description starts with general information about the river as a whole. Longer rivers are then broken into sections of reasonable length for a canoe trip and omit unrunnable sections of rivers. These sections are introduced in most cases by a table summarizing significant information about that segment, such as what kind of water you can expect; the recommended water level for paddling that section and the season or conditions at which that level is most likely to occur; the kind of scenery the river passes through; maps to reference and directions and distances for portage; and total distances to be covered, in miles.

On rivers that have not recently been checked, we recommend you scout drops and other obstacles before running that section.

The tables codify the information usually required to plan trips. In the descriptive text following the tables, cumulative distances from the section starting point are within parentheses.

Table Format

Description:	(Difficulty of the river in this segment)
Date checked:	(Last date that information was verified as being correct)
Navigable:	(Recommended water levels and seasons)
Scenery:	(What you will see from the boat)
Maps:	(U.S. Geological Survey quadrangles and other maps)
Portages:	(Where to, when to, and how far to carry)

Starting Point ➤ Ending Point   Total Miles

Terminology: Difficulty of River

The following terms appear opposite the "Description" heading in the summary table and describe the difficulty of the water to be paddled:

Lake The segment being described flows through a lake, or it is necessary to paddle across a lake to reach the beginning of a river.

Flatwater There is little or no current, and the river's surface is smooth and unbroken. Paddling upstream is easy.

Quickwater The river is fast. Its surface is nearly smooth at high water levels but is likely to be choppy at medium water levels and shallow at low water levels.

Marsh/swamp Vegetation often obstructs the river. Paddling may be slower than the distance alone would indicate.

Class Difficulty of rapids in a segment is rated according to American Whitewater Affiliation classifications I, II, III, or IV. *See the appendix for a description of these classifications.*

When two or more terms appear together opposite the "Description" heading in the summary table, expect to encounter all of those conditions in that segment of the river.

Judging the difficulty of rapids is subjective. Of course, the difficulty of the water depends on the type of boat you use, how well you read the river, and how skillfully you maneuver your boat.

The difficulty of rapids changes with the water level. A given stretch of rapids may become easier or harder when there is more water in the river. Water level affects parts of the same river differently. As a general rule, more water washes out a river with low gradient and small rocks, but it generates larger waves and more turbulence in a river that drops steeply through large rocks.

As water level rises, current picks up. Be aware of this. If the river is high and the air and water are cold, increase the rating by at least one and possibly two classes.

On small rivers, fallen trees present a greater hazard than do rapids, especially since their location cannot be documented in advance. In rural areas, barbed-wire fences frequently cross rivers and are hard to spot. Be alert and have your boat under control.

Terminology: Water Levels

The following terms appear opposite the "Navigable" heading in the summary tables. They describe the water level recommended for paddling a particular segment. The dates and conditions most likely to produce the recommended water level follow in parentheses.

Low Water There is a clearly defined shoreline below the bank. Small rocky rivers will be uncanoeable, but flatter stretches and rapids in large rivers will be navigable.

Medium Water The river extends to the bank; soft vegetation along the shore may be underwater. Marshy areas may be wet. Larger whitewater rivers, depending on the type of rapids, will be navigable at this water level. Dodging rocks will be the major entertainment.

High Water The river is near the top of its defined bank; alders along the shore may be underwater. This is an acceptable water level for small whitewater rivers.

Very High Water Large trees or clumps of smaller ones have their roots in the water. Reaching shore may be difficult or impossible. This water level is recommended only for experts who are familiar with the particular river and its problems.

Flood The river overflows its bank and makes pillows on large trees. This stage is dangerous for everyone.

Levels lower than those recommended do not necessarily mean that the river is not runnable. A river for which high water is recommended may be traveled in medium water, but it is likely to be scratchy, and you may have to wade down some sections.

Terminology: Scenery

The following terms are used in the tables to describe the territory through which the river flows.

Wild Long sections of semiwilderness with no more than a few isolated camps and occasional road access. Dirt roads may parallel the river within sight or sound, but only for short distances, and they do not noticeably alter the semiwilderness atmosphere of the trip. These roads may in fact be closed to the public or otherwise impassable.

Forested Banks on both sides of the river look densely wooded, but there are good dirt and asphalt roads that follow along the river or not far from it. These roads may frequently approach or cross the river. There may be farms and houses nearby, but not many of them are visible from the water.

Rural Farms are visible from the river, and some fields may extend down to the water.

Towns Small and isolated towns border the river. Aside from their effects on water quality, these towns have little impact on the trip.

Settled Many houses or small buildings are within sight or sound of the river.

Urban Multistoried buildings are visible. The shorelines are frequently unattractive.

Maps

Each chart includes pertinent topographic maps in 7.5-minute series unless followed by "15" to indicate that they are in the 15-minute series.

Topographic maps available at many outdoor-equipment retail stores. Check to see if what you need is in stock.

Another source is the USGS itself, on the web. Maps, aerial and satellite photographs, and volumes of other fascinating information are easily available from the USGS website: http://ask.usgs.gov/.

Maps are also available from the USGS by phone or mail: Map Distribution, USGS Map Sales, Box 25286, Federal Center, Bldg. 810, Boulder, CO 80225, 1-888-ASK-USGS (275-8747).

Portages

Portages are unavoidable carries, typically at dams, waterfalls, and difficult sections not runnable because of insufficient water. The chart lists these portages. In addition, some rapids are listed as portages if the rapids are significantly more difficult than the rating for that portion of the river. Some portages, such as lift-overs to pass fallen trees, may not be listed. There may also be additional carries around rapids you do not wish to run. Portages listed within parentheses are at the end of the river segment being described; only if you plan to paddle farther down the river would you make these portages.

Abbreviations

The following abbreviations are used in the summary tables and trip descriptions:

ft	foot, feet
mi	mile, miles
yd	yard, yards
L	left
R	right
e	either
cfs	cubic feet per second
USGS	U. S. Geological Survey

Example: How to Read a Summary Table

Smithville ➤ Brownville	3.75 mi
Description:	Class I-II
Date checked:	1999
Navigable:	High water: April to early May
Scenery:	Forested
Map(s):	USGS Waitsfield
Portages:	1.5 mi L dam 15 yd
	2 mi L two ledges 100 yd

Smithville ➤ Brownville The starting point for this imaginary segment is Smithville. The end point is Brownville.

3.75 mi The total distance to be covered is 3.75 miles.

Description: Class I-II Paddlers will encounter Class I and II whitewater on this segment. Most of the segment is Class II.

Date checked: 1999 The description here was verified as accurate in 1999.

Navigable: High water (April to early May) The river is runnable at high water levels, which are most likely to occur during April and the first part of May.

Scenery: Forested You'll paddle between wooded banks. Access roads may exist in the woods, close to the river.

Map: USGS Waitsfield The topographic map for this segment is the U.S. Geological Survey's Waitsfield 7.5-minute quadrangle.

Portages: 1.5 mi L dam 15 yd
2 mi L two ledges 100 yd

You will have to carry for about 15 yards around a dam about 1.5 miles from Smithfield. The best route for the portage is on the left as you face downstream. There is another portage in 0.5 mile, two miles from the starting point at Smithville. The best route is also on the left, and paddlers will have to carry their boats about 100 yards to avoid two ledges. The last portage is not the takeout point for the end of this section, however. If it were, it would appear in parentheses to indicate that only those wanting to continue downriver need to complete that portage.

Security

Crime is common. At put-ins for some popular rivers, close to 100 percent of the parked cars are burglarized. To discourage this, do not leave money, cameras, or other valuables in cars. The first place thieves look is in your bag of dry clothes; leave your wallet at home. Take only the cash and cards you will need, and carry them in a waterproof folder in your pocket. If this is not possible (for example, on an extended trip), pay to park your car at a gas station or at a house.

Time

It's impossible to realistically estimate the time a canoe trip will require. Too many factors influence how long it will take: the water height, which affects the speed of the current, and whether you pursue paddling as an athletic endeavor or prefer to float quietly with the current are only two factors. A small, well-qualified party may scout nothing, while an instruction trip may scout everything. You might want to stop to take pictures, or you may have to negotiate blowdowns. On a large river with the current and wind favorably behind, the miles whiz by. On a small stream blocked with alder thickets and fallen trees, it might take hours to travel a single mile. It is good practice to select alternate end points for a trip beforehand, especially on an unfamiliar river.

River Levels in New England

The water-level information given in the summary tables for individual rivers includes approximate dates, which are subject to wide variation from year to year. Some of the factors that influence water levels are discussed here.

Snow depth, temperature, rainfall, and transpiration are four seasonal factors that affect river levels. The farther south you go in New England, the less important the first two become, because there is usually less snow. As the snow cover disappears, temperature becomes less important, although runoff is greater and swifter when the ground is frozen. Once the leaves are out, surface runoff decreases substantially, because plants of all sizes use a great deal of water. Conversely, the fall foliage season invariably signals a rise in water levels. Significant rainfall is also more likely in autumn than it is in summer.

Terrain also must be considered. A river flowing from steep-sided hills and mountains will quickly collect the runoff from rainfall and melting snow. On the other hand, lakes, swamps, and gently rolling hills buffer the spring runoff, and the result is an extended canoeing season in spite of the weather. Knowledge of New England's topography will be as helpful to you as familiarity with its weather.

You must also take into account the nature of the river itself. If a river is flat, weather matters little as far as canoeability is concerned. If the river is steep and full of rapids, then heavy snow, warm temperatures, and moderate rainfall all may be necessary to keep the river runnable. You also must consider the size of the river—a large river generally will peak and ebb more gradually, and have a much longer season than a small stream.

Many New England rivers have just enough quickwater and easy rapids to make high or medium water necessary for good passage. In early March, rivers all over central and southern New England become runnable. Farther north, access to the water in early spring is hindered, first by snow and later by mud. Furthermore, ice shelves along the banks are hazardous in rapids and inconvenient elsewhere.

If you wish to run rapids in early March, Connecticut is the place. By late March the season in that state for good Class II and Class III rapids is fading, and you will probably be limited to some of the larger rivers. By May the rivers of northern New England, which are fed by melting snow deposits in the high mountains, are usually at optimal levels. Sometimes they are passable through Memorial Day, but there have been years when the whitewater season is over in late April.

Many of New England's rivers have gauges that have been set up by the U.S. Geological Survey. USGS district offices collect daily gauge readings for some of these rivers. This book contains occasional references to these gauges and other water-level indicators, but comprehensive and detailed information about their use is not included. Some gauge readings are now on the Internet, and web addresses are included as appropriate.

River levels can vary tremendously from season to season, and unusually heavy rainfall can make any river passable at any time. If you do enough canoeing and kayaking, you will probably eventually meet someone who will defend winter boating, claiming that the canoeing season includes any sunny day when the temperature is above freezing.

Over a period of several years, a person who runs a lot of rivers develops a sense of river levels. Just as those who fish the ocean acquire an instinct for the tides, and those who live off the land can almost smell the weather, so it is with river people. After a while they get to know when a river runs and when it does not.

Water Releases

Many of New England's rivers are passable for only a few weeks in the spring or after an unusually heavy rainfall, but on some rivers water releases can extend the paddling season. Increasingly—and for paddlers, happily—there are now more releases for recreation than ever before.

Generally speaking, there are power-generation releases, drawdown releases, minimum-flow releases, and recreational releases.

Recreational releases are scheduled. Call the Deerfield River/ Connecticut River hotline, 888-FLO-FONE, for updated release information on those rivers.

Power-generation releases come from dams used in connection to hydropower. The Bear Swamp (Fife Brook) section of the Deerfield features power-gen releases, as well as about 115 recreational releases per year, providing Class II water.

Drawdown releases, which are often coordinated with paddling clubs, are annual drawdowns of lakes that are primarily used for summer recreation. The drawdown of the Otis Reservoir, for example, offers two weekends of Class II and Class III-IV paddling every October on the upper Farmington.

Minimum-flow releases are intended to keep water levels below a dam at an accepted minimum. They may be for sewage dilution, power generation, or fish-habitat protection. Tariffville Gorge on the Farmington benefits from this type of constant release. Releases cost the power company money. Any water let over the dam without generating electricity, or generating it at a wrong time, is, well, water over the dam. It's gone. New England Power deserves credit.

Recreational releases are more and more common. Dam owners have agreed to provide recreational releases as a condition for relicensing. The Deerfield has been the benificiary of such an agreement, and the river is once again an outstanding location for sport whitewater paddling. There are also U.S. Army Corps of Engineers recreational releases every spring on the Millers, Tully, and Westfield Rivers.

Rentals

Many places rent canoes in New England, and they are easy to find. Begin your search on the web or in the Yellow Pages under "canoes." Many outdoor-equipment retail stores also rent canoes.

Rivers Omitted from This Guide

We are always compiling information for future editions of this book. If you have new or updated material to offer, please send it to: AMC River Guide Committee, 5 Joy St., Boston, MA 02108.

Suggested Rivers with Flatwater and Quickwater Canoeing

Suggested Rivers with Easy Rapids

[1] below 2.0 on MA-9 gauge

State	Miles	Portages	Lake	Flatwater	Quickwater	Class I	Passable at all levels
MA	10.5			•			•
CT	7.25			•	•		•
MA	8						•
MA	7			•	•		•
RI	13.25	5	•	•	•	•	•
CT	14.75		•	•	•		

State	Miles	Portages	Short Rapids	Long Rapids	Continuous Rapids	Flatwater	Quickwater	Class I	Class II	Class III
CT	16		•	•		•	•	•	•	•
CT	27.5		•				•	•	•	•
CT	5.25			•	•				•	
CT	4.75	1	•					•	•	
MA	8.5	1		•	•			•	•	•
MA	7.5			•	•				•	•
MA	10			•	•				•	•

Suggested Rivers with Class III Rapids

[1] below 4.5 on gauge
[2] below 5.0 on gauge

Suggested Rivers with Class IV and V Rapids

[1] above 10 on gauge

	State	Miles	Portages	Short Rapids	Long Rapids	Continuous Rapids	Class V
....	MA	6			•		
....	MA	5		•			
....	CT	1.5		•			
....	MA	3			•	•	•
....	MA	5.25	1	•			

	State	Miles	Portages	Short Rapids	Long Rapids	Continuous Rapids	Class V
....	MA	4.5	1		•	•	•
....	MA	9.5	2		•	•	
....	CT	3.25		•			•
....	CT	4			•	•	
....	CT	1		•			
....	VT	3	1		•	•	•
....	CT	4			•	•	

CHAPTER 1

Connecticut
Coastal Watersheds

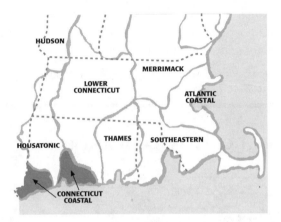

Three major rivers reach the sea in Connecticut: the Housatonic, the Connecticut, and the Thames. These and their tributaries drain a major portion of the interior, leaving little area to be drained by the coastal rivers. Thus the latter tend to be short, with nice tidal sections.

Tidal streams are of particular interest for their flora and wildlife, which are more visible there than in most places, especially if you are alone and moving quietly. Be sure to watch the tide so as not to be caught on mud flats when the tide goes out.

Two of the best rivers on the Connecticut coast are the East and the Hammonasset.

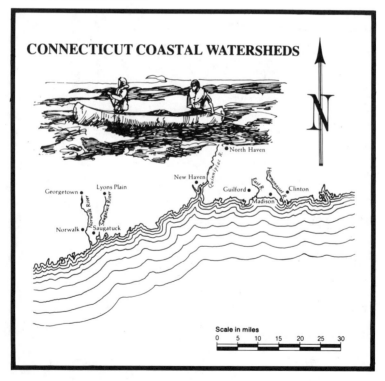

CONNECTICUT COASTAL WATERSHEDS

Scale in miles
0   5   10   15   20   25   30

Norwalk River

The Norwalk River is paralleled by US 7 and flows into Long Island Sound at Norwalk. In spite of its length it is small and shallow, and it can be run only when there is a heavy runoff. A fair amount of the upper river is enjoyable but not necessarily scenic. Much of the lower section through Norwalk is unattractive. See the USGS Norwalk North sheet.

One possible 7-mile run begins at Old Mill Road about a mile below Georgetown. From there to the bridge in Cannondale, there are Class I rapids and the river is occasionally blocked by debris. From Cannondale to the takeout just a few yards south of the Norwalk-Wilton line, the difficulty reaches Class II. Below the Norwalk-Wilton line the rapids are considerably more difficult.

Saugatuck River *CT*

Maps: USGS Westport, Sherwood Point

The Saugatuck River flows south into Long Island Sound at Saugatuck in Westport. It is best to canoe the river early in the year, in March and early April.

Lyons Plain ➤ Saugatuck   9 mi

Put in at Lyons Plain in Weston. It is a pleasant, 7-mile paddle with easy current through woodlands to tidewater, 0.5 mile above Westport. There are a few small dams with short carries. Take out at the bridge at tidewater, continue another 0.5 mile to Westport, or continue an additional 1.5 miles to Saugatuck, where you can take out near US 1. There are no good takeout spots near the mouth of the river.

Quinnipiac River *CT*

The Quinnipiac River, only 38 miles long, rises in a red maple swamp in Farmington, forms a channel near the border of New Britain and Plainville, and flows south through Southington, Cheshire, Meriden, Wallingford, North Haven, Hamden, and New Haven before ending its journey in New Haven Harbor. Its watershed is densely populated and urbanized, with a variety of land uses including residential, commercial, industrial, recreational, agricultural, and undeveloped land. At various points along its course, the river channel has been culverted, dammed, and otherwise modified.

The river is generally navigable from mid-Plainville to its mouth. However, numerous deadfalls may cause blockages through some stretches, particularly in Wallingford and North Haven, and many stretches are not passable during low-water conditions. The tidal influence of Long Island Sound extends as far north as Wallingford, about 14 miles from the river's mouth.

Deadwood Swamp ➤ Plainville ➤ Southington Line   2.5 mi

Description:	Flatwater
Date checked:	1995
Navigable:	Medium to high water
Scenery:	Forested, towns
Maps:	USGS New Britain, Bristol, Southington, Meriden

Put in at the Shuttle Meadow Road Access and take short trips to the north and south. Certain stretches are canoeable only in the spring.

Mill Street, Southington ➤ CT 322   4 mi

Description:	Flatwater
Date checked:	1995
Navigable:	Medium to high water
Scenery:	Town
Map:	USGS Southington
Portage:	3 mi L Plants Dam

The stretch from Mill Street to West Main Street (1 mi) is channelized, relatively shallow and narrow (20 ft). Below West Main Street the Eight Mile River enters, effectively doubling the Quinnipiac's volume. The channel meanders until it reaches Plants Dam in Plantsville (3 mi). Use caution when approaching the 4-foot dam. Portage on the left. Below the dam the river passes under CT 10 and enters a series of tight S-curves. Following its confluence with the Ten Mile River, the Quinnipiac meanders gently to the CT 322 bridge.

CT 322 ➤ Hanover Pond, Meriden   5 mi

Description:	Flatwater, Class I
Date checked:	1995
Navigable:	Medium to high water
Scenery:	Town
Maps:	USGS Southington, Meriden
Portage:	3.5 mi L Carpenter's Dam

Put in at CT 322. Paddling is generally easy throughout, with some maneuvering around, over, and through the many tree-falls and assorted quick turns, especially during extreme high and low water levels. The short whitewater stretch between Carpenter's Dam and Red Bridge (4.5 mi) is a good place for fastwater practice. Hanover Pond is shallow and an excellent area for learning and teaching general canoeing skills.

Hanover Pond ➤ CT 68, Wallingford   5 mi

Description:	Flatwater
Date checked:	1995
Navigable:	Navigable at all water levels
Scenery:	Town
Maps:	USGS Meriden, Wallingford
Portages:	0 mi R Hanover Pond
	5 mi R Brittania Spoon Company Dam

Put in at Donnin Beach on Hanover Pond. Portage steeply on the right around the dam at Hanover Pond. It's an easy 2.5- to 3-hour trip to the old dam at Brittania Spoon Company. The dam was breached in 1997. You may be able to run it, otherwise portage on the right. In either case, stay right; the dam is difficult to see, especially in high water. The CT 68 bridge is 0.5 mile below the dam.

CT 68 ➤ Toelles Road, Wallingford ➤ North Haven   5.25 mi

Description:	Flatwater
Date checked:	1995
Navigable:	Navigable at all water levels
Scenery:	Town, roads
Maps:	USGS Wallingford, New Haven
Portage:	2.5 mi R spillway

The river in this stretch is generally slow moving in a meandering and relatively flat channel. Shortly downstream of CT 68 the channel splits around a large island. The left channel is the more passable of the two, but it is generally shallow and you may have to drag canoes over sandbars at various locations, especially at low water. A now washed-out dam at Hall Avenue held back Community Lake, a vestige of which remains today. There is a movement afoot to replace the dam and bring the lake back. The river cuts channel several feet deep in fine sand and silt. The segment from the Quinnipiac Avenue crossing to Toelles Road may be difficult to negotiate due to several large blockages, mostly downstream of the Wallingford sewage treatment plant.

Toelles Road ➤ Sackett Point Road, New Haven		5.5 mi
Description:	Flatwater	
Date checked:	1995	
Navigable:	Navigable at all water levels	
Scenery:	Town, roads	
Map:	USGS New Haven	

Put in on the left, upstream side of the Toelles Road bridge. From here to Banton Street (3 mi), downed trees and logjams may require portages. The Red Sandstone Railway bridge is passable at high tide through the right side openings. At low tide proceed with caution, as the bottom is lined with bricks and pilings. The river begins to widen as it approaches Sackett Point Road.

Sackett Point Road ➤ Grand Avenue, New Haven		6 mi
Description:	Tidal	
Date checked:	1995	
Navigable:	Navigable at all water levels	
Scenery:	Town, roads	
Map:	USGS New Haven	

This section is an estuary with a wide, deep channel and slow-moving water, which is affected by wind and tide. High tide at Sackett Point follows New Haven Harbor by two hours. Plan to put in an hour before high tide at Sackett Point Road to ensure adequate water for side trips.

Much of this area is the state-owned Quinnipiac Meadows Wildlife Area. Nesting osprey may be observed on the left bank in an old light tower downstream of the abandoned Cedar Hills railroad yards, and on two osprey platforms erected by the Quinnipiac River Watershed Association (QRWA).

East River *CT*

Nut Plains Road ➤ Long Island Sound	6 mi
Description:	Tidal
Date checked:	1989
Scenery:	Forested, rural
Map:	USGS Guilford

This river, which forms a part of the boundary between Guilford and Madison, is one of the nicest tidal streams along the Connecticut coast. It provides a pleasant and easy 6-mile paddle as it flows through woods to farmland, past some houses, and then out into the salt marshes. The houses are attractive, some are very old, and none are obtrusive. Most of the salt marsh is owned and preserved by the state or the Audubon Society.

Access upstream is from the upper end of Nut Plains Road, which is east of CT 77 and north of the Connecticut Turnpike (I-95). Near the ocean there is access at the US 1 bridge, the Guilford town dock, and the state launching ramp at the end of Neck Road in Madison.

Hammonasset River *CT*

The Hammonasset River runs south into Long Island Sound between Clinton and Madison. It is a pretty stream, and the Madison Land Trust has been acquiring land along the upriver part in order to protect it. Dredging and filling at US 1 have ruined many acres of salt marsh, but there are still long stretches to the north and south of the highway where none of this is visible.

If you plan to paddle in the tidal portion immediately below the old fish hatchery, plan your trip for mid-tide or higher, or be ready to carry and drag over some rocks where the stream is too shallow. Tides run about a half-hour earlier than Boston.

Off CT 79 ➤ US 1   7.25 mi

Description:	Flatwater; quickwater, Class I-II; tidal
Date checked:	1998
Navigable:	High water: needed above Green Hill Road, early March
	Medium water: passable below Green Hill Road, spring and fall
Scenery:	Forested, settled
Map:	USGS Clinton

Follow Chestnut Hill Road northeast from CT 79 in Madison. Just before the bridge, turn north up Summer Hill Road and put in where it follows along the river.

At first the river drops gradually in easy Class II rapids. Just around the bend below Chestnut Hill Road there is a foot-bridge, which can be passed on the right if the water is too high for you to pass under it. After about 0.5 mile of rapids, the stream runs for a while through a swamp and then into a pool above a broken, runnable dam. Green Hill Road is about 100 yards farther.

Below Green Hill Road (1.5 mi) there is a long stretch that is flat, deep, and meandering. A broken, washed-out dam by the Connecticut Turnpike (I-95)—at the site of an old fish hatch-ery—marks the beginning of tidewater.

Salt marshes begin at a bridge just above the Connecticut Turnpike (5.5 mi) next to Exit 62, where there is a road on the left. Paddle through salt marshes the rest of the way to US 1 (7.25 mi). In another mile the river opens into Clinton Harbor (8.25 mi).

CHAPTER 2

Hudson
Watershed

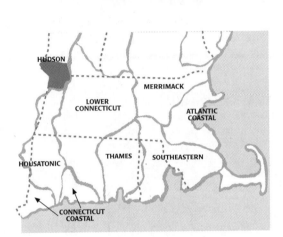

The Taconic Mountains of western Massachusetts and Connecticut force most runoff toward the east, the Housatonic watershed, and Long Island Sound. An exception is the Hoosic River, which, unlike the majority of rivers in New England, lies in a pre-glacial riverbed and flows southeast to northwest through a breach in the Taconic and Green Mountains. The Hoosic River crosses the southwest corner of Vermont and continues northwesterly to the Hudson River.

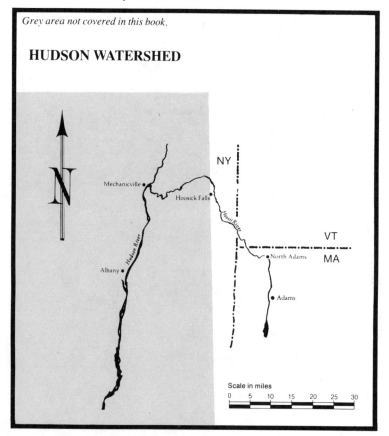

Grey area not covered in this book.

HUDSON WATERSHED

Hoosic River *MA, VT, NY*

The Hoosic River rises in Lanesboro, Massachusetts; flows north to North Adams; turns west to Williamstown; and then takes off northwesterly across a corner of Vermont into New York, where it again turns north to make a big loop to meet the Hudson River near Mechanicsville. The flood-control works in Adams and North Adams have reduced the threat of flooding and have also eliminated the canoeing in Adams and North Adams, as the river drops sharply between high retaining walls. Boating is not only illegal there, it is suicidal.

The upper sections are passable only in high water, but below North Adams much of it can be done later in the year.

Cheshire Reservoir ➤ First Adams Dam   4.5 mi

Description:	Quickwater, swamp
Date checked:	1998
Navigable:	Medium or high water
Scenery:	Swamp, forested, towns
Maps:	USGS Cheshire, Windsor
Portage:	(4.5 mi e dam 100 yd)

You can paddle the reservoir from the roadside rest area on MA 8 at the north end of the lake, but paddling below the dam at the outlet of the reservoir is not recommended because the river is shallow, narrow, and obstructed by branches. You can put in at MA 8 at the outlet of the Cheshire Reservoir. After the the first mile, to the first bridge, it starts to diffuse into a wide area, meandering back and forth, coming into a small open area by a farm and passing under a small bridge before coming to a dam. This bridge is reached by turning east from MA 8 onto the first road (obscure) downstream of Fast View Drive.

First Adams Dam ➤ MA 8 Bridge   1 mi

Description:	Class II
Date checked:	1998
Navigable:	Medium to high water
Scenery:	Town
Map:	USGS North Adams

This run is delightful, although short. Take out at the park at the low bridge immediately downstream of the high MA 8 bridge.

Through Adams   3 mi

Below the next MA 8 bridge (0.5 mi), the river starts a steeper drop to the flood-control channels, which extends through Adams. Canoeing in this area is both dangerous and illegal: the river drops over dams confined within cement retaining walls.

Adams ➤ North Adams   4 mi

Description:	Quickwater
Date checked:	1998
Navigable:	Medium to high water
Scenery:	Town
Map:	USGS North Adams

Put in at the Lime Street bridge at the north end of Adams, at the end of the dikes. The river size increases slightly here and the water quality deteriorates. This section has been prone to extensive logjams.

Take out at the MA 8A bridge (3 mi) or, with difficulty, a mile farther down at the start of the dikes.

Through North Adams   4.5 mi

The flood channels start well south of North Adams and continue all the way through town and on to the west. Portage by car.

North Adams ➤ North Pownal, VT   11.75 mi

Description:	Quickwater, Class I, II
Date checked:	1998
Navigable:	Medium water
Scenery:	Towns, rural, forested
Maps:	USGS North Adams, Williamstown, MA; North Pownal, VT
Portage:	11.25 miles R dam in North Pownal 0.25 mi

Put in below the last dam at the west end of North Adams, just west of the Protection Road bridge. The most convenient place is the old sewage-treatment plant on the north side.

Most of the distance is smooth, with only occasional rapids of moderate difficulty broken by stretches of quieter water between them. Pass two bridges close together in a little more than a mile. You then come to the bridge that carries the Appalachian Trail (3 mi), the US 7 bridge in Williamstown (4.25 mi), and the Massachusetts-Vermont line (6.25 mi). The bridge at Pownal crosses at 9 miles.

The dam at North Pownal is confined between cliffs and walls, so be sure to scout it in advance. Carry up the road on either side, although neither is easy. By the time you can see the factory chimney from the river you may be past the best takeout.

This is a beautiful stretch. You may want to consider continuing to Hoosic Falls, NY, which is 30.5 miles from North Adams.

CHAPTER 3

Housatonic
Watershed

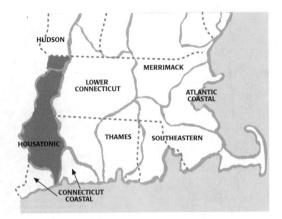

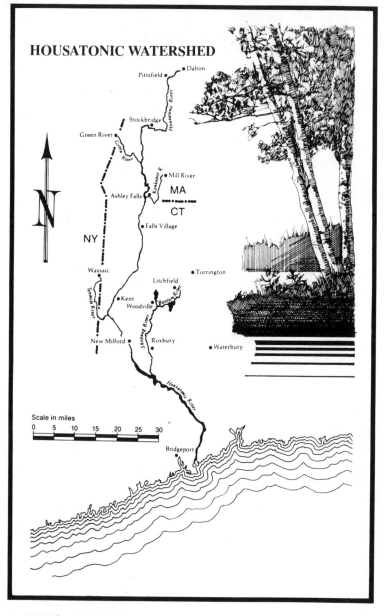

HOUSATONIC WATERSHED

N

NY

MA

CT

Dalton
Pittsfield
Stockbridge
Green River
Mill River
Ashley Falls
Falls Village
Wassaic
Torrington
Litchfield
Kent
Woodville
New Milford
Roxbury
Waterbury
Bridgeport

Housatonic River
Green River
Konkapot R.
Tenmile River
Shepaug River
Bantam River
Housatonic River

Scale in miles
0   5   10   15   20   25   30

Housatonic River _MA, CT_

Maps: USGS Pittsfield East, Pittsfield West, East Lee, Stockbridge, Great Barrington, Ashley Falls, South Canaan, Cornwall, Ellsworth, Kent, Dover Plains, New Milford, Danbury, Newtown, Southbury, Long Hill, Ansonia, Milford

The Housatonic River rises near Pittsfield, Massachusetts, flows south through the wide valley between the Berkshire Hills on the east and the Taconic Range on the west, and continues through Connecticut to the sea between Stratford and Milford. It is called by its Indian name, which means "river beyond the mountains." Its total length from Hinsdale, Massachusetts, to the sea is 142 miles.

Dalton ➤ Lenox   19 mi

Put in below the last dam in Dalton. The river is still at Pittsfield by the Pittsfield sewage plant, so this section is not particularly pleasant. Below Dalton, and all the way to Lenox, it is mostly a flat, winding river, but there are stimulating views of Mount Greylock from the meandering stream. This section is best canoed in the spring when the water is high, the current fast, and the pollution at a minimum.

Lenox ➤ Stockbridge   12 mi

Just below Lenox (0.5 mi) is a dam, and again at Lee (1.5 mi) there are two more dams. This part is flat, with some rapids. From here to Stockbridge the river is wilder and more attractive, as the stream winds through a swampy, overgrown section with some small rips.

Stockbridge ➤ Great Barrington   13 mi

The first few miles through the Stockbridge meadows to Glendale wind quite a bit, but at high water the current is fast. There are two dams below Glendale, with a bad rapid below the second. The river then widens into a lake for 1.5 miles to another dam. Just above Housatonic is a dam with a bad rapid below, then 1 mile of lake to the dam at Risingdale. The remaining

5 miles to the dam in Great Barrington are flatwater, with the Williams River entering from the right 1 mile below the dam.

Great Barrington ➤ Falls Village		25 mi
Description:	Flatwater; quickwater, Class I, II	
Date checked:	1999	
Navigable:	Passable at all water levels	
Scenery:	Wild, forested, rural	
Maps:	USGS Great Barrington, Ashley Falls, South Canaan	
Portages:	19 mi island dam W of Canaan	
	24 mi L dam above Falls Village 160 yd	

This stretch is mostly flatwater with only two dams. From the dam in Great Barrington it is 2 miles to the mouth of the Green River, which enters on the right. The Konkapot River enters on the left at Ashley Falls, just above the Connecticut line (17 miles). Another 2 miles brings you to the old dam west of Canaan. Portage river left. Five miles farther is the dam (24 miles) above Falls Village. Use extreme caution when running this section, due to old reinforcing rods under the surface. The safest run is far left. There was a gristmill at Falls Village as early as 1740, and the first bridge in this section across the Housatonic was built here in 1744. It was later known as Burral's Bridge.

Falls Village ➤ Kent (Bull's Bridge)		27.5 mi
Description:	Quickwater, Class I, II, III, IV	
Date checked:	1999	
Navigable:	Dam controlled (888-417-4837 for info)	
Scenery:	Forested, rural, towns, settled	
Maps:	USGS South Canaan, Cornwall, Ellsworth, Kent, Dover Plains	

Caution! The rapids described in this and the following section are technical drops, not to be attempted by beginners. Consult AMC's *Classic Northeastern Whitewater Guide* for detailed information.

To run the Class III-IV Rattlesnake Rapids above Falls Village, just below the Great Falls, put in river right. The rapids twist through granite ledges and end with an 8-foot plunge just above the bridge. A slalom course has been set up in this area.

The river below the hydroelectric station in Falls Village is a favorite one-day trip, with much smoothwater alternating with Class I and II water, and a more difficult rapid at the covered bridge in West Cornwall.

The water level is controlled at the powerhouse at Falls Village. Most paddlers put in at a rest area across from the powerhouse. There is a tricky corner just below, which novices should scout before starting. There are no particular problems, except for many small rips that can be dangerous in high water, until West Cornwall, 7.5 miles downstream. **Caution!** There is a long wooden bridge here, and one should pull out well above it to look over the 0.25 mile of rapids (Class II-III) that start just above the bridge and run down to the corner below. This can be dangerous (Class IV) at high water. For some miles below this point, the river runs beside Housatonic Meadows State Park. The next 9 miles to Kent are mostly quickwater except for a drop over a ledge about 1 mile below Cornwall Bridge, at the former site of Swift's Bridge. The remaining 5 miles to the dam at Bull's Bridge are flatwater. Most day-trippers from Fall's Village take out above the CT 341 bridge on a dirt road on the right side of the river.

Bull's Bridge ➤ Gaylordsville		3.25 mi
Description:	Class IV, V	
Date checked:	1998	
Navigable:	High and medium water: March, April	
Low water:	Summer releases	
Scenery:	Forested	
Map:	USGS Kent	

This section has the biggest water described in this guide. Put in at the covered bridge. For a Class V start, carry up above the bridge to the tip of the island. The staircase is the drop on the left and should be carefully scouted. The bottom is riddled with potholes. Several essential moves must be made in quick succession.

For a Class IV run, put in below the bridge. The flume lies immediately downstream. The flume must be run on the right, but the water coming from the right side of the island pushes you left. The drop 0.5 mile below should be scouted from the left; there is a nasty hole on the right.

The rapids get slightly easier after the Ten Mile River enters from the right. The Appalachian Trail crosses the Ten Mile at this point on a footbridge. There are two more heavy rapids before the takeout, but they are not as difficult as the earlier ones. These two rapids often are run in conjunction with a trip on the Ten Mile. It is also possible to put in below the Funnel by following the Appalachian Trail downstream on the right bank. Take out at the US 7 bridge in Gaylordsville.

Gaylordsville ➤ Long Island Sound		45 mi
Description:	Quickwater, flatwater, tidal	
Date checked:	1998	
Navigable:	Navigable at all water levels	
Scenery:	Forested, rural, towns, urban	
Maps:	USGS New Milford, Danbury, Newtown, Southbury, Long Hill, Ansonia, Milford	
Portages:	10 mi dam at New Milford	
	20 mi Shepaug Dam	
	28 mi Stevenson Dam	
	33 mi Shelton Dam	

We do not recommened any of these portages. Instead, the lakes between the dams may be done as separate trips. The 10 miles to the dam at New Milford is mostly strong current. The Shepaug Dam backs the river nearly to New Milford; the Stevenson Dam backs the river nearly to the Shepaug Dam; the Shelton Dam backs water nearly to the Stevenson Dam. The remainder of the river is tidal.

Green River NY AND MA

Maps: USGS State Line, Egremont, Great Barrington

The Green River rises in Austerlitz, New York, and flows southeastward to enter the Housatonic just below Great Barrington. It is a beautiful, clear, limestone brook with NY 71 following it most of the way. It is small and must be canoed during freshet or after heavy rains.

Green River ➤ Housatonic River   12 mi

You may start at Green River village, but the first 1.5 miles to a bridge on the side road off NY 71 are extremely rough. The going then becomes easier for 2 miles to the NY 71 bridge. This section is all quickwater with numerous short rapids and some very shallow places. The valley is all open farmland. After crossing the New York-Massachusetts border it is only two miles to North Egremont, passing two bridges along the way. **Caution!** Watch for barbed wire in the lower part of this river. Pass through broad meadows and lift over occasional logs for the 2 miles from North Egremont to the Egremont Plains Road bridge. The current continues strong for another 2 miles to the MA 23 bridge. The remaining 2 miles to the US 7 bridge, where the river joins the Housatonic River, are through broad meadows.

Konkapot River MA, CT

The Konkapot arises in Lake Buel in Monterey and flows south across the Connecticut line, where it turns west and north, recrossing into Massachusetts to flow into the Housatonic at Ashley Falls.

Mill River ➤ Konkapot Road   4 mi

Description:	Class II, III, IV
Date checked:	1998
Navigable:	High water: March, April
Scenery:	Rural, settled
Maps:	USGS Great Barrington, Ashley Falls

This is a small, narrow whitewater stream running through a mixture of pastures and small towns. Numerous small broken dams could create hazards at higher water levels, but at lower levels they are Class II-III and do not require scouting if approached with caution.

Put in just below a milldam in the hamlet of Mill River on Hayes Hill Road just off MA 57. One-half mile downstream is a washed-out dam; Class III at low levels, Class IV at high levels. Scout on the left. The best run is left center over an exposed ledge. No other scouting is required at low to medium levels. Take note of a scenic waterfall (Umpachene Falls) 0.25 mile below the second bridge for an enjoyable short hike and a good picnic spot.

Be aware of a fence stretched across the river 0.5 mile below the falls. It is not a problem at low to medium levels. Line boats on the left. Strainers may be present at any corner, so be alert as you paddle.

There is an excellent takeout at a small sandy beach on the right just below the Konkapot Road bridge, off Southfield Road.

Ten Mile River NY, CT

The Ten Mile River rises in Salisbury, Connecticut, where it is known as Webatuck Creek. It flows southwest into New York, where just below Wassaic it is joined by Wassaic Creek and becomes known as the Ten Mile River. It then flows south and finally turns east to meet the Housatonic just below Bulls Bridge in Connecticut. Although it starts and ends in Connecticut, most of the running on the river is in New York. This river has a number of difficult rapids and should not be attempted by novices, especially at the lower end. It is best run during medium water levels; at high water some pitches can be difficult, and at low water it's impassable.

Wassaic ➤ Webatuck   14 mi
Maps: USGS Amenia, Dover Plains

Put in about a mile below Wassaic, near the bridge at the Wassaic State School. At high water you can put in a mile farther upstream near South Amenia. Two difficult pitches lie just below the start, then it is fast, smooth current around sharp turns in the meadows for 5 miles to Dover plains, where there is a dam that must be carried. Just below is a broken dam which can usually be run, followed by 8 miles of easy, pleasant running to the dam at South Dover. For the next 5 miles from here to the Housatonic, the stream is deeper and more sporting where it cuts through the hills. There are some rough turns 1 mile below the bridge at South Dover and again at Webatuck.

Webatuck ➤ Gaylordsville		4.75 mi
Description:	Class II-III	
Date checked:	1998	
High water:	January-May	
Low water:	October-December and June	
Scenery:	Farmland, forested	
Map:	USGS Dover Plains, NY	

Put in at Webatuck, NY. There's a dirt pulloff on the right about 200 yards west of the NY 22 and NY/CT 55 intersection in Webatuck. The Ten Mile is a beautiful run for the beginner paddler looking for a easy run with a few drops to enhance skills. The river at the put-in is about 20 yards wide. For the first 2 miles the river meanders through the low hills and farmland on the New York-Connecticut border, with several Class II-II+ rapids.

On river right a white house close to the river signals the beginning of the Class II-III section of the Ten Mile. In the next 0.25 mile you approach State Line rapid. State Line is recognized by the large pile of trees and debris on river right and a red house just below. At very high water this pile of debris can be a real hazard, but normally it is easily avoidable. The rapid consists of a narrow chute on river left. The river drops about 8 feet in the next 20 yards and ends in a pool. The drop can be scouted from river left. Please avoid scouting or stopping on the right shore, as this is private property. Below the pool is a set of waves that are good for beginners to play on. The next mile consists of several Class II-II+ rapids. All are easily negotiated and have several surfable waves. A wood and steel footbridge carries the Appalachian Trail over the Ten Mile to an AT campsite on river right. The bridge signals the end of the Ten Mile but not the end of the run. At this point the Ten Mile flows into the Bulls Bridge section of the Housatonic, creating Confluence rapid. See AMC's *Classic Northeastern Whitewater Guide* for a detailed description of the technical whitewater on the Housatonic.

Shepaug River CT

The Shepaug is a popular early-season whitewater run. A water-supply reservoir in its headwaters means the upper section is rarely runnable. Below Roxbury Station, the recommended takeout, lies the unrunnable Roxbury Falls. There is no easily accessible takeout just above the falls because it is located in a narrow gorge. This is an extremely dangerous spot.

Route 341 ➤ Romford Road		3.5 mi
Description:	Class III	
Date checked:	1998	
Navigable:	High water	
Scenery:	Forested	

This section, commonly referred to as the upper Shepaug River, flows out of a water supply reservoir, so it is rarely runnable. The put-in is located 1 mile north of CT 341 below the reservoir dam, just upstream of a small stone bridge over the Shepaug. A five-foot-high dam here can be run through a chute in the center. There should be at least 6 inches of water over the dam; if there is much less than that, the trip will be very scratchy. The river then passes under a bridge and enters some rocky Class II+ rapids. The river is narrow and twisty here, often splitting around islands into even narrower channels. The rapids are fairly continuous throughout the length of the run.

After the CT 341 bridge, the river enters several standing-wave rapids located in small turns. The river continues in this fashion for another mile, coming to a bridge that is in the middle of the state park. The next section has benefited greatly from cleanup work to remove the many fallen trees that crossed the river. Some of these trees may still be on the shoreline, and parts may be sticking into the main channel. Another mile of rapids follows. The last two rapids in this section are the hardest of the trip, consisting of an assortment of rocks and several sharp drops. The first place to take out is located at the Romford Road bridge. This road is often snow or ice covered and impassable during the early part of the season. In those conditions it is suggested that the run be completed down to CT 47 (Bee Brook).

Romford Road ➤ Route 47 (Bee Brook)   3 mi

Description: Class III
Date checked: 1998
Navigable: Medium water
Scenery: Forested

This section can be run as a continuation of either the upper Shepaug or the Bantam, or as a separate trip. The river is much larger here than in the upper section and has a longer season. This run consists of much Class II-III water interspersed with several harder rapids which can be up to Class III in medium to high levels.

A start can be made on the Romford Road bridge (upper Shepaug) or behind the Rumsey Hall School (Bantam River). From either place it is a short paddle to the confluence of these two rivers, where the river's size and current increase noticeably. Soon you come to a rock cliff on the right bank and the first rapid, consisting of a slight left turn with a strong current and standing waves at the bottom. Following this are several easier rapids. The next Class II+ rapid again consists mostly of a strong current and standing waves. There aren't many play opportunities here, or anywhere else in this trip. The river becomes less steep and flows through some quickwater and Class I rapids. It becomes very broad and shallow in places, requiring careful channel selection. The last rapid lies a short distance above the Route 47 bridge and consists of several rocks and standing waves in a right turn. Take out on the left above the bridge, where there is plenty of parking.

CT 47 (Bee Brook) ➤ Roxbury Station   9.5 mi

Description: Class II
Date checked: 1998
Navigable: High and medium water: March
Scenery: Forested
Maps: USGS New Preston, Roxbury

The section from Washington Depot to Roxbury is one of the most attractive whitewater runs in Connecticut. Beautiful, steep, hemlock-covered banks rise 300 to 500 feet above the river; in a few places there are scenic cliffs. Evidence of civilization is minimal. The rapids are intermittent Class II, permitting easy running without the need for scouting.

Below the first CT 47 bridge (Bee Brook), the Shepaug is gentler than above. One and a half miles of Class II rapids lead past two more CT 47 bridges in Washington Depot. Then there are 6 miles of scenic Class II rapids through the "clamshell" area, a deep canyon and a bend in the river away from all roads. The river flattens out for the next two miles to Roxbury Station. Take out at Hodge Park on CT 67 (9.5 mi) where the road on the east bank is close to the river, 0.25 mile above a small roller dam.

Caution! Four miles below the dam at Roxbury Station is Roxbury Falls. It is a trap. The approach is blind, and many canoeists, caught in the swift current as they approached it, have been swept over it. The steep walls and strong current at the top make a safe landing and exit both difficult and unlikely. Below Roxbury Falls it is only a mile to the ponding in Lake Lillinoah.

Bantam River *CT*

The Bantam River is a small stream that rises in Litchfield and joins the Shepaug in Washington. It is one of the early whitewater runs in New England—the first weekends of March bring many groups to the Bantam. Because of the river's small size, it is sometimes plagued by fallen trees and dangerous ice ledges.

Litchfield ➤ Bantam   9.25 mi

Put in at the CT 25 bridge northeast of Litchfield. The pretty, narrow stream winds slowly through swampland to Bantam Lake (5.75 mi). It is about 0.75 mile along the north shore around a promontory to the outlet (6.5 mi), and then a little over 1.5 miles to the town of Bantam, where there is a dam.

Paddlers can put in where the river turns sharply left in Bantam (8.5 mi), but novice groups desiring whitewater would be better off farther down. The first 0.75 mile from Bantam to a bridge on Stoddard Road is Class III, with a high probability of tree obstructions.

Bantam ➤ Shepaug River   4.75 mi

Description:	Class I-II
Date checked:	1998
Navigable:	High water: March
Scenery:	Forested
Maps:	USGS West Torrington, Litchfield, New Preston
Portage:	2.25 mi L broken dam at West Morris 30 yd (optional)

The best start for an easy whitewater trip is at the Stoddard Road bridge, reached by going south on West Morris Road from CT 25 in Bantam and following the former until Stoddard Road leaves on the left. There are easy Class II rapids for 0.5 mile to the next bridge and another 1.75 miles of similar rapids to a broken dam and a bridge in West Morris. This dam can be run, but it should be looked over. It is generally carried.

Below West Morris (2.25 mi) there are 2 miles of more difficult Class II rapids to the steel bridge at Rumsey Hall School (4.25 mi). One-half mile more of rapids brings you to the confluence with the Shepaug River (4.75 mi). Take out either at Rumsey Hall School or at CT 47, which is 3 miles down the Shepaug.

CHAPTER 4

Lower Connecticut Watershed

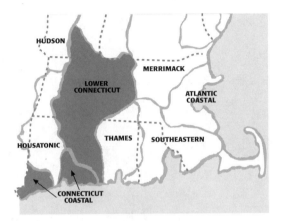

LOWER CONNECTICUT WATERSHED

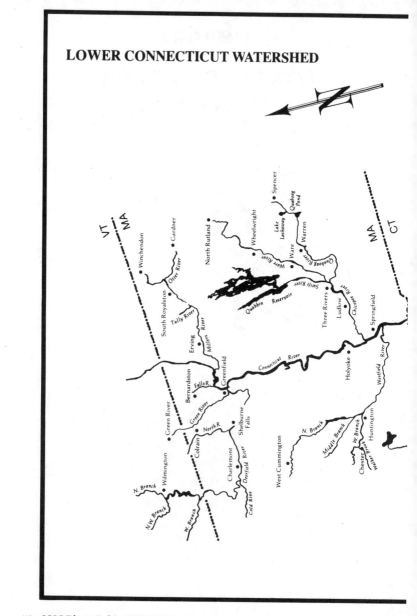

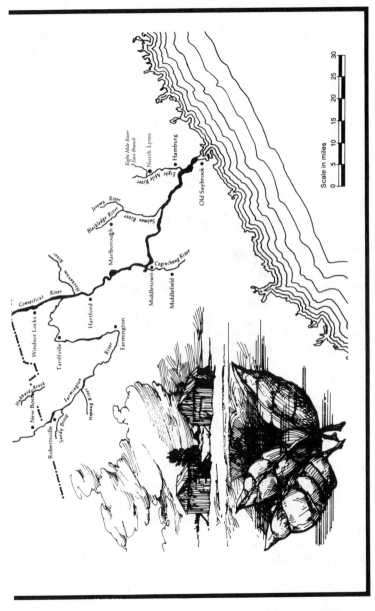

Map labels (top to bottom, along rivers):

Eight Mile River East Branch
North Lyme
Hamburg
Eight Mile River
Old Saybrook
Jeremy River
Blackledge River
Salmon River
Marlborough
Coginchaug River
Middletown
Middlefield
Hockanum River
Connecticut River
Hartford
Windsor Locks
Farmington
Tariffville
Hubbard Brook
Farmington River
Nepaug River
New Boston
Robertsville
Sandy Brook

Scale in miles
0 5 10 15 20 25 30

The Connecticut River, the largest river in southern New England, dominates New Hampshire, Vermont, Massachusetts, and Connecticut and receives much of the water that falls in these states. It is already a large river when it crosses from New Hampshire into Massachusetts.

Many of its best-known and frequently canoed tributaries lie to the north. Only those tributaries whose confluence lie south of the New Hampshire-Vermont line are included in this guide.

A complete boating guide to the Connecticut River is published by and available from the Connecticut River Watershed Council, 15 Bank Row, Greenfield, MA 01301 (413-772-2020).

Connecticut River MA, CT

Vernon Dam ➤ Turners Falls		21.5 mi
Description:	Flatwater, quickwater, Class I-II	
Date checked:	1998	
Navigable:	Navigable at all water levels	
Scenery:	Forested, rural, settled	
Maps:	USGS Brattleboro, Keene, Northfield, Millers Falls, Greenfield	
Portage:	(2.5 mi Turners Falls Dam, west side of Barton Dam state ramp)	
Campsites:	13 mi L Northeast Utilities, Munns Ferry Campground	
	19.5 mi R Northeast Utilities, Barton Cove Campsite	

Below the Vernon Dam the going is swift and may be rocky when the water is low. After a sharp turn, pass Stebbin Island (1 mi). At 2 miles you will see the mouth of the Ashuelot River on the left in Hinsdale, New Hampshire. During periods of low water you can paddle upstream on the Ashuelot into Hinsdale to obtain supplies. Below the confluence with the Ashuelot, you pass a small island, then a railroad bridge (3 mi). The Massachusetts border is crossed at 6.5 miles, and the MA 142

(Schell Bridge) is reached at 8.5 miles. Note the state-owned Pauchaug Brook public-access area on the left just above the bridge. The access ramp has a large, paved parking area. One-half mile farther is another railroad bridge (9 mi). The flatwater river continues along for some distance, but canoeists should exercise caution around powerboats, which travel south on this stretch of the river to the Turners Falls Dam. Powerboat use diminishes greatly during the weekdays.

The Munn's Ferry Boat Camping Area is on the left bank at 13 miles. Northeast Utilities provides water, shelters, campsites, and firewood free of charge to the boating public on a first-come, first-served basis. The campsite fills quickly during summer weekends. About a mile from the campsite, Riverview Picnic Area is on the left.

At 16 miles the intake/outlet of the famous Northfield Mountain pumped-storage hydroelectric facility is reached. Do not paddle past the line of floating buoy markers. From there it is five miles to the French King Gorge, at the upper end of which is a large rock (17 mi) in the middle of the channel. French King Rock may cause turbulence even when the rest of the river is calm. Choose a route close to either shore at this point. The current quickens as the river turns right after passing under the French King Bridge (MA 2) and the confluence with the Millers River on the left. At high water this section of the river can become extremely rough; under these conditions, some canoeists may prefer to take out at the bridge that crosses the Millers River at its mouth.

The current slackens after this section as the river enters the pool behind the Turners Falls Dam. Parts of the river here can be very deep. Eventually campsites can be seen on the right bank. Continuing, the river narrows and comes out onto Barton Cove (21 mi) and passes the tip of the peninsula that forms Barton Cove Campsite. The state boat ramp lies straight ahead and can be seen on the right. The campsite can be reached by turning right after the peninsula's tip and keeping the island on the left. Canoeists may wish to explore the ancient, rocky plunge pools and their hidden lagoons along the west shore of the campground peninsula.

At Turners Falls, take out at the public boat ramp on the west side of Barton Cove. Portage arrangements can be made by calling Northeast Utilities, Northfield Mountain Superintendent, Northfield, MA (413-659-3761). Call from the pay phone when you reach the boat ramp. The electric company truck will arrive in 10-15 minutes.

The section of river below the dam requires a 3-mile portage through Turners Falls to the Montague city bridge. There is very little water between these two points except during flood, when canoeing is not advised. Most of the water is diverted to the power canal, where canoeing is not allowed.

Turners Falls ➤ Northampton	21.5 mi
Description:	Flatwater, quickwater
Date checked:	1998
Navigable:	Navigable at all water levels
Scenery:	Rural, forested, towns
Maps:	USGS Millers Falls, Greenfield, Mount Toby, Mount Holyoke, Easthampton
Campsites:	0.5 mi Cabot Island
	7 mi Second Island

The 3.5 miles of river below the Turners Falls Dam to the Montague city bridge cannot be run even by experienced canoeists. Most canoeists, therefore, will make the long carry to put in at the Montague city bridge 3.5 miles below the dam, just below the confluence with the Deerfield River. Camping is possible a short distance upstream from the confluence along the Connecticut River on Cabot Island. The island is owned by, and sits opposite, Western Massachusetts Electric Company's Cabot Hydro Station. A nice side trip is possible upstream on the Deerfield River. Access points on the Deerfield are located at the MA 5 and US 91 bridges.

The next 21 miles to Northampton are easy paddling, with little interference from powerboats along most of the way. This section of the river is considered to be the most remote for canoeists. Although the way is through farmland, the 20-foot-high riverbanks generally block the view of the fields. As most of these fields are cultivated down to the riverbank, the best camping spots on this stretch are on the islands in the river. After passing a low, treeless island (1 mi) on the right, you will reach the B&M Railroad bridge (2.5 mi). Soon the Saw Mill River enters on the left. Third Island, owned by the Connecticut River Watershed Council, is on the right at 4 miles. Mount Toby is soon visible on the horizon. At the bend in the river, Cranberry Pond Brook enters on the left. If you land your canoe on the rocks at this point and take a short side-hike up the steep bank, you will be rewarded with a view of a scenic waterfall. Turning west here, the river affords a fine view of Mount Sugarloaf, and at 7 miles Second Island provides excellent primitive camping on town conservation land. It is another 3 miles to the MA 116 bridge in Sunderland. A public access on the left at 11 miles provides a small parking area. From here it is a very short walk into the village of Sunderland to obtain supplies. Across the river from this access is an unofficial access point where canoeists might tie down and enjoy a 1-mile side-hike on a blue-blazed trail to the summit of South Sugarloaf Mountain. The mountain affords a scenic, panoramic view of the Connecticut River valley.

For the next several miles the river runs through a wide valley. The setting is very rural and little can be seen of civilization. At 15 miles the river takes a sharp right turn where sandstone ledges on the left bank make a good picnic spot. A sandy beach on the right is good camping, but you have to obtain the owner's permission. The next 4 miles form a large oxbow around the town of Hadley. Powerboat activity increases at this point, but it generally does not pose a hazard. There is a public access ramp where Cow Bridge Brook enters on the right (16 mi). The river takes a straight course for the next 3 miles, passing the confluence of the Mill River on the left (17 mi). A small access area is located here. Once around Hadley, the river proceeds straight again, passing another Mill River on the right bank at 19 miles. The river takes a sharp U-turn left just after passing between Canary Island on the right and Scott Island on the left. Both islands are heavily used for camping by the powerboaters, now quite numerous at this point in the river. Stay close to either shore during weekends. The north tip of Elwell Island (20.5 mi) is reached at the end of the U-turn. The island is a popular camping spot for river users. A route along the channel on the right bank is better during busy days and offers total solitude for canoeists. After passing under an abandoned railroad bridge, you come to the MA 9 bridge. The Sportsman's Marina at the east end of the bridge offers a launching area and permits camping and car-spotting for a small fee.

Northampton ➤ Holyoke Dam		11 mi
Description:	Flatwater, quickwater	
Date checked:	1998	
Navigable:	Navigable at all water levels	
Scenery:	Rural, forested, settled, urban	
Maps:	USGS Mount Holyoke, Easthampton, Springfield North, Mount Tom	
Portage:	(11 mi L Holyoke Dam)	
Campsites:	0.5 mi Sportsman's Marina 2 mi Rainbow Beach	

The river now makes a large bend around Northampton. Below the bridge is the old Shepherd Island (2 mi) that has now been connected to Rainbow Beach by natural river action. The entire area on the right bank is state owned and allows for suitable primitive camping. This section of river is perhaps the most beautiful, but it is also the most heavily traveled by powerboats. A route close to either shore is advised, particularly on weekends.

Mitch's Marina (3 mi) on the left bank offers a launching area and picnic tables. Just after the marina is a privately owned island in mid-channel. Below that island, on the right, is the Mill River (4 mi), the scene of the great flood of May 16, 1874, in which 141 lives were lost. Just below this point is the entrance to the Oxbow created during the flood. You can paddle up this waterway 1.5 miles to Hulbert's Pond and the Arcadia Wildlife Sanctuary. The sanctuary hosts the headquarters of the Connecticut River Watershed Council. Oxbow Marina is located 0.5 mile farther on the Oxbow. From the Oxbow entrance the

river turns eastward for 1 mile and cuts through the Ho..
Range, with Mount Nonotuck and Mount Tom on the right a.
Mount Holyoke on the left. At 5 miles the Mount Tom power station is on the right and the scenic high cliffs of Titan's Pier are
on the left. Bachelor Brook enters on the left at 6.5 miles and
Stoney Brook at 7 miles. Brunnelle's Marina on the left offers an
opportunity for a vehicle portage around the Holyoke Dam,
which is located 4 miles downstream; call the Holyoke Water
Power Company (413-536-9458, 24 hours a day). If you prefer to
self-portage, you may continue downstream to the dam. It is
about 0.5 mile to the famous Dinosaur Tracks just above the
ledges where MA 5 comes close to the river on the right.

When the water is up in the spring, a surfing wave or hole forms
adjacent to the ledge at the Dinosaur Tracks. To take advantage
of it, park at the roadside pulloff and carry down the trail to the
river. Depending on the level, it can be either a large hole or a
series of very big waves. A large eddy downstream allows for
recovery. But keep in mind, this is really big water, sometimes
more than 100,000 cfs, packing an awesome force.

Continuing, the river narrows as it passes through a rocky gorge
where the water can be rough at times. As you near the dam, pull
out on the left bank at the southern end of a peninsula about
200 yards above the US 202 bridge. Ascend the steep 20-foot
bank to Canal Street and walk 0.25 mile past the MA 116 bridge.
Put in just beyond a playground under the bridge on an
unpaved public access.

Holyoke Dam ➤ Enfield Dam	18.5 mi
Description:	Flatwater, quickwater
Date checked:	1998
Navigable:	Navigable at all water levels
Scenery:	Rural, forested, settled, urban
Maps:	USGS Springfield North, Mount Tom, Springfield South, Broad Brook
Portage:	(18.5 mi R Enfield Dam)

At the dam, the river is shallow and quite swift. In 2 miles you
pass the B&M Railroad and MA 141/116 bridges. This is a heavily populated area with unattractive riverbanks, but as you leave

hind the landscape improves. There is a paved pub-
and parking area on the left just below the
etts Turnpike bridge (5.5 mi). At 6 miles the
River enters on the left. The North End bridge is
9 miles, and Bassett's Marina, just below on the left,
good launching spot. Soon the Conrail and the
Memorial bridges are passed and Riverfront Park becomes visible on the left. The Bondi's Island boat ramp is soon reached on
the right bank. After passing the Westfield River on the right in
0.5 mile, you reach the South End bridge. Here the Agawam
Yacht Club offers access on the right bank. From this point the
river flows southward with low banks through a mostly rural setting. A lengthy sandbar on the left bank indicates the location of
the Stebbin Wildlife Refuge, which extends about 3 miles to the
Massachusetts-Connecticut boundary. Two miles below the border is the dismantled CT 190 bridge at Thompsonville. There is
a town boat ramp just below the bridge abutments on the left
bank. From here it is only 0.75 mile, mostly through tobacco
fields, to the new CT 190 bridge and the Enfield Dam. On the
right bank is a state boat ramp in Suffield. Take out here to
portage the dam, which is immediately below the bridge. The
dam crosses diagonally, slanting downstream toward the right
bank. This 9-foot-high dam has been breached in several locations. Although it has been shot by experienced canoeists at low
water, it is not recommended.

Enfield Dam ➤ Wethersfield Cove	20 mi
Description:	Flatwater, quickwater, Class I
Date checked:	1998
Navigable:	Passable at all water levels
Scenery:	Rural, forested, settled, urban
Maps:	USGS Broad Brook, Manchester, Hartford North, Hartford South

Lift over the dam and run the 4.5 miles of easy rapids through
rough, wooded country to the canal outlet opposite Windsor
Locks. Most canoeists, however, use the canal.

Land on the west shore just above the lock, lift the canoe into the
canal, and paddle down to the lower lock, which should not be

approached too closely because of the currents. The lift back into the river is down a steep bank on the left, below the factory.

Re-enter the river 1 mile above the I-91 bridge. The remaining portion of this trip is in tobacco-farming country which becomes more urban as Hartford nears. In 3 miles the Scantic River enters on the left, and 2 miles farther is Windsor, with its interesting old houses. Here the Farmington River enters on the right. In another 4 miles the Podunk River enters on the left. Enjoy a fine view of the Hartford skyline on the right for the next 3 miles to the Charter Oak bridge, where the Hockanum River enters on the left and brings in a certain amount of pollution. In another 2.5 miles, the Wethersfield Cove opens up on the right under the I-91 bridge. There is a public landing on the south side of the cove, and some of the fine old houses of the town, which are open to the public, are well worth a visit.

Wethersfield Cove ➤ Middletown	15 mi
Description:	Flatwater, quickwater, tidal
Date checked:	1998
Navigable:	Passable at all water levels
Scenery:	Rural, forested, settled, urban
Maps:	USGS Hartford South, Glastonbury, Middle Haddam, Middletown

Although the lower part of this river is tidal, the tides have little effect until Middletown and are not really important until Hadlyme. In the 7 miles to the Rocky Hill ferry, the river meanders across a broad flood plain. The banks are generally low and sandy, with fields and woods offering good picnic or camping places. Just above Rocky Hill, below an abutment of large rocks, is the Hall's Landing marina. For the next 8 miles to Middletown the river's course is straighter and the countryside is hillier. Gildersleeve Island, 5 miles below the ferry, offers suitable camping spots, while Riverside Marine Park, on the right bank, has picnic tables and a launching area. In another 2.5 miles, just above the mouth of the Mattabessett River in Middletown, Wilcox Island offers campsites. At the CT 6A bridge there is a landing place on the right.

Middletown ➤ Old Saybrook · 27.5 mi

Description:	Tidal
Date checked:	1998
Scenery:	Forested, settled
Maps:	USGS Middletown, Middle Haddam, Haddam, Deep River, Essex, Old Lyme
Campsites:	6.75 mi L Hurd State Park
	11 mi L Gillette Castle State Park
	17.5 mi L Selden Neck State Park

Access points are listed here:

West bank	0 mi	Middletown launching area off CT 9
West bank	11 mi	Haddam Meadows State Park (south end) off CT 9A
East bank	ca. 11 mi	Haddam Neck nuclear plant
East bank	13 mi	Salmon River launching area off CT 149
East bank	13.75 mi	Goodspeed Opera parking lot off CT 149
West bank	16.5 mi	Chester ferry landing
West bank	22.25 mi	Essex town dock
West bank	27.5 mi	Mouth of South Cove in Old Saybrook from CT 154

For information and specific regulations concerning these access areas and campsites write well in advance to the Connecticut Department of Environmental Protection, Office of Parks and Recreation, Hartford, CT 06115. Ask for the "Canoe Camping" leaflet.

Below Middletown the river changes. It deepens and widens as it winds through the hilly country of southern Connecticut. The banks, high and ledgy, are more heavily forested. South of Middletown all property within the sight lines of the river is in the Connecticut River Gateway, an attempt by the state to maintain the scenic value of the river.

This lower part of the Connecticut River can be paddled any time of the year when it is ice free, but the best times are before Memorial Day and after Labor Day, when there are not as many powerboats.

Rather than follow the main river all the way, a more interesting route is to paddle the "back alleys" that parallel the river. They lie along the east side of the river in East Haddam, Lyme, and Old Lyme. In addition, there are several attractive coves in the same area. The most helpful maps for paddling behind the islands and in the coves are the USGS Deep River and Old Lyme sheets.

The back alleys along the east shore begin below the CT 82 bridge (13.75 mi). Keep to the left of Rich Island (14.5 mi), and enter Chapman Pond from the west and leave it at the south end. The next one begins below the ferry crossing and extends to the east of Selden Neck (17.25 mi) via Selden Cove and Selden Creek. The citizens of Essex hid their ships from the British raiding parties in Selden Cove during the War of 1812. There are more such passages above the Connecticut Turnpike/I-95 (25 mi) and below the railroad bridge.

The river can be idyllic at times, but summer weekends can be a madhouse, with heavy powerboat congestion. Many boaters do not observe river etiquette, and canoes are not given the right of way. Boat wakes in narrow stretches can mimic whitewater, and novices should beware. It is recommended that nonswimmers wear PFDs. The wind and tide can also be powerful adversaries. Tide times for Old Saybrook can be found in local newspapers. The tides at Essex, East Haddam, and Middletown follow Old Saybrook by approximately one, two, and five hours, respectively.

Millers River MA

The Millers River, whose water is naturally dark, flows west into the Connecticut River near Greenfield. Its several sections provide distinctly different types of canoeing. Above Royalston are many miles of smoothwater paddling; from South Royalston to Athol there are continuous, intermediate rapids. The stretch from Athol to Erving is mostly slack water, and from Erving to Millers Falls the river has a mixture of easy and heavy rapids.

Several miles of the river above Winchendon are probably canoeable in high water, but they are mostly through swamp. Through Winchendon, there is a series of millponds, dams, and rapids. The last dam is at Waterville on MA 202.

Waterville ➤ South Royalston   11 mi

Description: Flatwater, quickwater, Class I
Date checked: 1999
Navigable: High water
Scenery: Forested, towns
Maps: USGS Winchendon, Royalston
Portages: 9.5 mi flood-control dam (11 mi dam)

Put in just below the Waterville Dam on a side road; the first mile is obstructed by shallow rapids, a broken (but runnable) dam, and brush jams. Below the rapids, a branch enters from the north. It is small but canoeable in high water from State Line on MA 12, with some portages around dams and obstructions. Below this junction, the Winchendon sewage disposal plant is on the left.

The recommended starting point is the bridge at Hydeville. The next bridge is on New Boston Road, 5 miles downstream. The river winds through swamp and woodlands with almost no current, but is fairly pleasant if the water is not too low. All of this section is in the reservoir of the Birch Hill Flood Control Dam, in which the Massachusetts environmental officials are pursuing an extensive fish and wildlife management and improvement program. One mile below New Boston Road, the Otter River enters from the south, and 2 miles farther, the Birch Hill Dam is reached. It is another 1.5 miles to the dam at South Royalston.

South Royalston ➤ Athol   6 mi

Description: Class III
Date checked: 1999
Navigable: High water: late March, early April
                     Medium water: late April
Scenery: Forested
Maps: USGS Royalston, Athol

This popular whitewater run, known as the Upper Millers, consists of a number of Class III rapids. The amount of water in this section is controlled by the Birch Hill Flood Control Dam, and a check on the volume can be made by calling the Birch Hill

Dam (978-249-4467). A scratchy run can be made with as little as 500 cfs, but more water is really desirable. At 1200 cfs an open boat, singly paddled, is still suitable; it is estimated that 1600 cfs would require a heavy-water boat.

You may put in at the green MA 68 bridge, but there is a broken dam just above the next bridge in Royalston which can be rocky and dangerous at the wrong water level. Look it over carefully.

The better put-in is from a side road 0.5 mile below the MA 68 bridge on the right. Rapids begin immediately and pass around islands, then the pace slackens briefly before plunging into a wavy Class III drop at the first railroad bridge (1 mi). Another short, flat stretch leads into a sharp left turn and a mile of continuous Class III rapids.

There is a right turn and some smooth water under the second railroad bridge (3 mi). Just below is the site of the old Bear's Den bridge. The easy rapids that follow include a little drop next to the railroad bridge. In the next mile, the rapids increase through Hemlock Gorge, a Class III section. The rapids then moderate, gradually flattening out in the pool above the dam in Athol (6.75 mi).

A rough takeout is necessary on the right bank—through the brush and along an old woods road to a side road. To continue downstream you must portage three dams in Athol.

Athol ➤ Orange
Maps: USGS Athol, Orange

6 mi

This is a pleasant trip with lots of wildlife. There are several places to put in, with the easiest on river right off North Orange Road, off MA 2A, just below the confluence with the Tully River. On its way to Orange, the river flows with no particular difficulties through a flat valley. Some stretches are quite scenic, with an abundance of wildlife including otters, great blue herons, and wood ducks. Osprey and bald eagles are likely visitors in the spring and fall. Take out at the public boat ramp on river left 0.5 mile above the dam in Orange.

Orange ➤ Erving   5 mi
Maps: USGS Orange, Millers Falls

Put in at the Orange Sewage Treatment Plant on river right. Below Orange, the river leaves the flat valley and flows between steep hills. There are a few Class II rapids and quickwater associated with turns and bridges. A Class III rapid is at Erving Paper Mills dam, which is broken. Scout from the left. Rapids up to Class II+ and quickwater continue to the railroad bridge below Erving. Takeout is on river right on MA 2.

Erving ➤ Millers Falls   6 mi
Description: Class II-IV
Date checked: 1999
Navigable: High water: March, April
                     Medium water: May
Scenery: Forested, settled
Map: USGS Millers Falls
Portage: 3.25 mi E Funnel 150 yd (optional)

This popular whitewater run is referred to as the Lower Millers. It can be run late in the spring when other nearby rivers are too low, and often even later in the season after heavy rains. The gradient is not as steep as the Upper Millers, but the waves are larger.

Put in along MA 2 at the railroad bridge. The start can be made at an old bridge on a side road in Erving or 1 mile below at a pull-off next to a railroad bridge. Heavywater Class II rapids lead from the railroad bridge to the old bridge at Farley (2.5 mi). There is a Class III rapid, best run on the left, just below the bridge. Class II rapids lead to another Class III rapid with large rocks on the left, followed by a pool.

If you want a bit more privacy, put in 1 mile upriver at the end of Arch Street. From the railroad bridge to the Iron Bridge in Farley where the USGS gauge (low water is 3.2) is located is Class II-II+. If you have had any difficulty to this point, take out! The river is just getting warmed up and there are no other possible takeouts until after all the heavy rapids. Farley Rapid is just below the bridge, Class III in medium water. Run it river left, except in high water when other routes are possible. One-quarter mile below is a good surfing wave. Two more significant rapids lead up to the Funnel, by far the hardest rapid of the trip, Class IV at most levels. There is a long pool above the Funnel. Watch for the river to "funnel down" from very wide to quite narrow with a serious horizon line. Take out at the tail of the pool and scout on river right. It is also possible to scout on river left, but portaging is normally done on the right. The left portage is shorter but has less of a trail and the put-in is harder. The Funnel is about 100 yards long and is a very busy rapid. There are routes on the extreme left, extreme right, and down the middle. Water level will determine which is best. Look at this from all angles before deciding to run it. It's an unforgiving piece of water with a nasty run-out. One last word of caution: the large flat rock under the power line below is undercut on the left.

Below the Funnel things calm down some until Rest Area Turn, a sweeping S-turn with very heavy waves near the bottom. A takeout here is possible but arduous, especially if it's icy. The broken dam at the Hammermill Paper Company (previously the Millers Falls Paper Company) has had the worst of the debris removed. Run it river center. From here to the first takeout the going is easy. Take out on river left just below the Paper Mill Road bridge. Alternately you can proceed downriver to the confluence of the Millers and Connecticut Rivers. The rapid below the MA 63 bridge is heavy and has some old industrial trash complicating things. There is one more good ledge/turn before the takeout, but in general this section is much less demanding than the earlier section and is usually skipped.

Otter River *MA*

Maps: USGS Templeton, Winchendon

The Otter River is a short stream rising in Templeton and flowing north into the Millers River above South Royalston. A water-treatment plant in Templeton has improved the quality of the water substantially in both rivers.

From the MA 2A bridge it is 3.75 miles of moderate current past the MA 101 bridge and through mostly wooded countryside to the broken dam just above the River Street bridge in Otter River village. Lift over the center of the 8-foot dam.

There is another dam above the Depot Street bridge (4.75 mi) in Otter River village. Portage on the right or paddle along the canal on the left and carry out to the street. There are a few rapids to the US 202 bridge in Baldwinville (6.5 mi). The remains of an old dam just below this bridge form a couple of small Class II-III drops.

In the last 3.25 miles to the Millers River (9.75 mi), there is a fair current with no hazards. The river flows mostly through meadows to the ponding area of the Birch Hill Flood Control Dam (11.25 mi) on the Millers River.

Tully River MA

Maps: USGS Royalston, Athol

The Tully River is a tributary of the Millers River just west of Athol. It is mostly smooth water with some Class I and II rapids. Start a trip by going about 2.5 miles north of Athol on MA 32 and turning west onto Fryeville Road.

Begin at the bridge over the East Branch. The first 0.25 mile below Fryeville Road is narrow, shallow, and rapid, passable only at high water. The next mile to a broken dam is swamp and may not be navigable. The broken dam can be run, or it can be portaged on the right. Then there is fast current for 200 yards to the Pinedale Avenue bridge (1.25 mi). The West Branch joins below, and there is mostly flatwater to the Millers River (3.5 mi). Take out on the Millers at North Orange Road, 200 yards below the confluence.

Falls River MA

Maps: USGS Bernardston, Greenfield

The Falls River is a small stream that rises in Guilford, Vermont, and flows south through Bernardston to the Connecticut River at Turners Falls. Above Bernardston village it is too small for canoeing.

There are long stretches of dead water caused by dams in Bernardston and 1 mile below at Hoe Shop Road. The best part of the river is below this second dam, but even here the trip requires high water. No roads follow the river and the banks are steep and wooded. Much of the land on both sides is posted against trespassing, and the landowner at the takeout is hostile. Until this situation changes the river is best not run.

Bernardston ➤ Factory Village   4 mi

From the MA 10 bridge it is largely dead water to the dam 1 mile below. The next mile to Bascom Road is mostly rapid, but not difficult. Carry left around an impassable ledge 1 mile below the Bascom Road bridge. There are some good rapids a mile below here, near the Boy Scout camp on the right. Then the hills close in and form a small canyon. In less than a mile of easy paddling, you come to a picnic ground and a dam, which you portage on the right. Below the dam is 0.5 mile of fast current and easy rapids to the clearing above Gill Road. Caution! Proceed with care here, as the rapids increase to an impassable falls just above the bridge. Take out on the right. The gorge at the end, once regarded as unrunnable, has been run several times now.

Deerfield River MA

The Deerfield River rises east of the Green Mountains in southern Vermont and flows south into Massachusetts, where it turns east to join the Connecticut River near Greenfield. For many years the best whitewater locations on the Deerfield were dry because of the hydro dams. Now New England Power releases water for the benefit of paddlers (and others), and the Deerfield has become the premier whitewater spot in southern New England. Call the New England Power Company's toll-free dam-release line (888-FLO-FONE [888 356-3663]) for the release schedule.

Monroe Bridge ➤ Bear Swamp Reservoir   4 mi

Description:	Class IV
Date checked:	1999
Navigable:	High water: early spring, when other rivers are in flood
	Dam controlled: historically difficult to get information
Scenery:	Wild
Map:	USGS Rowe

This section of the Deerfield is for advanced and expert paddlers only. The rapids in this Class III-IV run are long, pushy, and technical, with short areas of flat moving water between rapids available for recovery. See AMC's *Classic Northeastern Whitewater Guide* for more complete information. The section is available only when water is released from the dam. Releases of 900-1,100 cfs are scheduled during the late spring, the early summer, and the fall, and occasionally after heavy rain. The schedule for the year is on the web at http://www.kayak.com/kayak/schedule.html. The release can be confirmed the night before by calling 888-FLO-FONE (select options: Deerfield, #5 Station Dam).

Put in on the left below the #5 Station Dam in Monroe Bridge. Because the put-in is down an extremely steep bank, you may need throw ropes. The first Class III drop is immediately below. Fine play spots continue for a mile to the harder section, where several Class IV drops appear in pool-drop succession to the reservoir. The steepest and pushiest drop is Dragon's Tooth rapids. It plunges straight ahead through a megahole and ends in either a fine pop-up spot or large standing waves, depending upon the water level. The portage is on the left. Below this are Labyrinth and Terminator. Because the reservoir rises and falls as much as 15 feet during the day, you may find the last drop drowned. Take out at the first grassy area that appears on the right. It is reached by an access road in the Dunbar Brook Picnic Area. Do not paddle below the takeout; the power company is required by their federal license to limit access to the reservoir.

Fife Brook Dam ➤ MA 2 Bridge   8.5 mi

Description:	Quickwater, Class I, II
Date checked:	1997
Navigable:	Medium water when released from dam
Scenery:	Forested, rural
Map:	USGS Rowe
Portage:	4.75 mi R Zoar Gap (optional)

This part of the river is beautiful. The river valley is quite steep in many places, with the Berkshire Hills rising from the river. There is a road, however, all along the river.

You should scout the portage takeout above Zoar Gap before putting in. The put-in is 1.25 miles above the Hoosac Tunnel and just a few hundred feet below Fife Brook. As River Road turns left at the crest of a short hill, go straight on the old river road. This area is reached from MA 2—the Mohawk Trail—by taking the River Road to Zoar at the east end of the MA 2 bridge, where it crosses over the Deerfield west of the town of Charlemont.

About 5 miles of quickwater, Class I and II, lead to Zoar Gap from the put-in. Zoar Gap is exceedingly difficult to recognize from above and has been the site of many serious accidents. It cannot be recognized by the sound of the rapids (nor can many other trouble spots, although people still keep trying!), and it isn't feasible to rely on signs. Portage to the Florida Bridge put-in (river left) after taking out (river right) above Zoar Gap.

Zoar Gap is a Class III-IV rapid extending about 50 feet, scout it from shore. It can be lined on the right shore. The easiest route to run is close to the right shore until you are even with the heavy hydraulics in the center; then shoot out to the center just below the hydraulics to avoid a rock hidden by heavy water close to shore on the right. Although you can run the gap in the center, you are likely to submerge an open canoe.

An alternate put-in at the power company picnic area is on the left, downstream. This makes a good lunch spot, or a put-in for a shorter trip if you want to avoid Zoar Gap. From here to the MA 2 takeout is easy Class II with some large rocks and ripples; the river is wide. The takeout is just below the MA 2 bridge on the left at the roadside rest area.

Take out on the left at the rest area just below the MA 2 bridge (where River Road starts). Note: there are a number of rest areas, so you could get confused with other MA 2 bridges.

MA 2 Bridge ➤ Deerfield #4 Dam   8.5 mi

Description:	Flatwater, quickwater, Class I
Date checked:	1997
Navigable:	Low water when released from Fife Brook Dam
Scenery:	Rural, towns
Maps:	USGS Rowe, Heath, Ashfield, Shelburne Falls, Colrain

The river is wide and shallow in this area. At a couple of points only one channel has enough water for a canoe, so the most difficult part of the trip is reading the river and finding the water. It is a good, easy river for beginning whitewater paddlers.

Put in west of the town of Charlemont at the rest area just before MA 2 crosses the river. From there the river provides an easy run with fine riffles. As you approach the center of Charlemont, you pass under the MA 8A bridge; MA 2—the Mohawk Trail—is close to the river all the way. As you near the takeout, the river becomes dead water held back by the dam at Buckland. The takeout is a public boat ramp on the left about a mile above the dam.

Through Shelburne   7 mi

From the public boat ramp above the first Shelburne Falls dam through Shelburne Falls there are several dams with no good boating water. Below Shelburne Falls are two dams with decent round-trip boating water between them. Access is down the dirt Wilcox Hollow Road, just east of Shelburne Falls on MA 2 (across from the Corvair quonset huts). Put-in is easy; then remove your car and park on the grassy area you saw just before the final leg of Wilcox Hollow Road.

There are Class II-III rapids below the third dam. The impoundment at the lower dam is very deep. This is a gorgeous, isolated flatwater area. The trip back can be strenuous at the Wilcox Hollow and if water is being released by the power company.

The portage at the lower dam is slick and unpleasant, although there are plans to improve it. The section from the dam down to Bardwell Bridge is shallow and often not navigable, and the bottom can be very slick underfoot. There is no road access to this area.

Bardwell Bridge ➤ Connecticut River		12 mi
Description:	Quickwater, Class I	
Date checked:	1997	
Navigable:	Medium water, dam controlled at Garner Falls	
Scenery:	Wild and then settled	
Maps:	USGS Shelburne Falls, Greenfield	

This section can be run in the summer as a swimming trip. It is mostly quickwater, with only one fun Class I rapid. Put in upstream of the bridge on river right at the ledges.

There are 4 river miles with a few rapids and riffles to the mouth of the South River on the right. The river continues unobstructed for another 3 miles in its narrow valley, with an average drop of 20 feet per mile. Near Wapping, it suddenly breaks out into open farmland and becomes mostly flat. The next 4 miles to the mouth of the Green River (on the left near Greenfield) and then another 2 miles to the Connecticut River make a good, easy paddle.

Eight Mile River (East Branch) CT

Darling Road ➤ CT 156		3 mi
Description:	Class II-III, flatwater	
Date checked:	1998	
Navigable:	Medium high water	
Scenery:	Rural	
Portage:	2.5 mi R dam	
Map:	USGS Hamburg	

The East Branch of the Eight Mile River provides an enjoyable run when the water is high. The river is small, rocky, and narrow. There are three long rapids on this run, each separated by a section of flatwater. Since there are a large number of swamps in the headwaters, the river tends to hold its water fairly well and can be run for several days after heavy rain in the early spring. To reach the put-in take Exit 19 off of CT 2 onto CT 11. Follow this to the end and take a quick right, then a left onto Darling Road. Take a right at the first stop sign and start anywhere that the river comes close to the road. The farther up you put in, the easier the rapids are.

The rapids start slowly, increasing to Class II at the first bridge. There are few eddies to be found in this section. Rapids consist mostly of standing waves up to 1 foot high and require maneuvering around an assortment of rocks, some of which may be sharp. Continuous Class II rapids continue for 1 mile as the river turns left, away from the road, and tapers to quickwater. When it returns back to the road, the most difficult rapids of the trip begin. This Class III-III+ rapid is narrow, steep, and full of boulders requiring many quick turns. Any hesitation could surely lead to a broaching situation. These boulders may be covered in high water, leaving a turbulent channel. The hardest parts are halfway down, where a large rock blocks the center, leaving a sharp stair-step drop on the left. Fifty yards below this is another sharp drop into a small pool. The rapids are continuous for 0.5 mile before slowing to the ponding behind a dam. Take out on the right, carry across the road, and put in below the bridge. Be courteous and prompt, since the surrounding land is posted. Class III rapids begin immediately and continue for 200 yards to the next bridge.

The river then flows quickly, with no rapids of consequence to the takeout, which should be made above a low bridge 50 yards above the confluence with the main branch. If the water is high, it may not be possible to pass beneath this bridge.

Deerfield River (North Branch) VT

Known locally as the Dover Branch, this stream rises in Dover, Vermont, and flows southwesterly through Wilmington to the northeast corner of Harriman Reservoir. It flows through scenic farm country with fine views of Haystack Mountain, and the water itself is sparkling clear.

This branch provides a fine early-spring run of moderate difficulty, mainly fast water with some Class II rapids and two Class III pitches of short duration. It is easier than the Northwest Branch.

Off VT 100 ➤ Harriman Reservoir	6 mi
Description:	Quickwater, Class I, II, III
Date checked:	1997
Navigable:	High water: late April through mid-May
Scenery:	Rural, town
Map:	USGS Wilmington 15

Put in 4.5 miles northeast of the center of Wilmington Village off VT 100, where a farm road leads down to the river across the end of a meadow below a bridge. The stream is narrow but clear, with a fast current. There are frequent riffles and mild Class II rapids. After passing under the cement bridge on VT 100 (3 mi), the stream swings to the right around a large meadow and, after bearing left at the edge of a sugar-maple orchard, descends over Class II rapids of moderate difficulty. These rapids are about 0.25 mile long and are best run on the left.

The river then levels off until entering the narrow, steep Class III chute that channels the river through the center of the village. There is a sharp turn to the left at the head of this rapid, then a straight run down to the bridge in the center of town. This run should be scouted before running.

Below the remains of an old milldam the stream becomes wider and swifter as it parallels VT 9. Some Class II rapids here require caution in very high water. A short distance above Harriman Reservoir (the distance varies depending on the height of the impounded water), another Class III pitch should be scouted carefully. Unless there is sufficient water to cover the boulder-filled run-out below this rapid, take out opposite the electric power relay station on VT 9 (6 mi).

Deerfield River (Northwest Branch) *vt*

Map: USGS Wilmington 15

This stream rises to the west of Somerset Reservoir and runs southerly to join the outlet of the reservoir a short distance above the lower dam where the penstock takes off to the Searsburg generating station. Take the road from VT 9 west of Wilmington toward the Somerset Dam, following the wooden penstock to the lower dam. Note carefully the conditions at the pond above this dam. Canoes must be taken out well above the lip of the dam, where the stream drops a sheer 120 feet. About 4 miles above, the road crosses the Northwest Branch, and this is a good launching spot.

The run from the put-in to the pond above the lower dam is about 5 miles of uninterrupted Class II and Class III rapids, making a fine whitewater run at the height of the spring runoff. The country here is wild and beautiful; the water is clear over a rocky bottom. Deer are common too.

Deerfield River (West Branch) *vt*

This is one of the most difficult whitewater runs in the Northeast. Gradient alone tells the story. The upper section drops 14 feet per mile, and the lower section drops 192 feet per mile. Not included in these calculations is the Class VI middle section, which drops 60 feet in 1,000 feet, better than 300 feet per mile. If you love horizon lines, technical rapids, horrible places to swim, and the biggest takeout high you've ever had, this is your river. See AMC's *Classic Northeastern Whitewater Guide* for detailed information.

Readsboro Falls ➤ Deerfield River		3 mi
Description:	Class IV, V, VI	
Date checked:	1997	
Navigable:	High water: March to early May	
Scenery:	Forested, settled	
Map:	USGS Wilmington	
Portage:	1.75 mi R Class VI section 500 yd	

The put-in is reached by traveling west on VT 8 about 3 miles to a gravel road on the left between a barn and a house. This is Readsboro Falls. Put in below the falls to avoid the strange hydraulic that causes boats to pencil up and down but not out. Just below the put-in is a 350-yard rapid. Stop under the bridge to scout the 5-foot drop and 50 yards of rapids that follow. Although the next drop looks unrunnable, it is run on the left. The river then drops to a pool and over a 3-foot drop, and comes up against a large boulder that splits the current. Avoid this drop on river left. From here to the pullover above the Class VI section on the right is an easy run. The Class VI section, called Tunnel Vision, has been run, but it is not recommended.

The lower section starts just after the river emerges from the tunnel under the road. After the first drop is a large waterfall on the right. The river splits here, with safe passage only on the left. From this point to a park on the right about 0.25 mile away, the river drops extremely fast and is very technical. Scout this section if you have any doubts about your abilities.

As you paddle into town, two rapids should get all of your attention—scout them both. The first, High Chair, is at the upper corner of the old wooden-chair factory. The big rock near the building where the river turns sharply right is undercut and poses problems in low water. Low Chair follows below the bridge. If you have any doubts about this one, do not attempt it. If you do decide to run it, start on the right, drop about 3 feet, and then cross to the left to hit the chute between the shore and the first big boulder. It can also be run on the right. The takeout is just below on the left above the Deerfield River.

The gauge is found at the bridge by the chair factory on the left (looking upstream). The river is barely runnable at 0, and is best at 5.

Cold River MA

The Cold River flows into the Deerfield near Charlemont. The Mohawk Trail (MA 2) follows the lower section, but most of the rapids are not visible from the highway. The river is known for its steep gradient and technical drops. It is runnable in the early spring or after heavy rains.

South County Road ➤ MA 2		6 mi
Description:	Class II, III	
Date checked:	1998	
Navigable:	High water: mid-March, April	
Scenery:	Wild	
Maps:	USGS North Adams, Rowe	

This is a beautiful section to paddle, with a very easy put-in. The takeout above the Class IV water, however, is difficult. Be prepared to portage around the occasional strainer. Although the gradient is 100 feet per mile, it is almost evenly distributed, so there are no big drops. At the takeout, be alert for the MA 2 guardrail high on the left. This is the end of the Class II-III section and the beginning of the Class IV section.

To find the put-in, drive west on MA 2 up the mountain to a small settlement. This is Drury. Turn south and continue straight until the road crosses a small stream. This is the Cold River.

MA 2 Dead Man's Curve ➤ Deerfield River		4.5 mi
Description:	Class IV	
Date checked:	1998	
Navigable:	High water: mid-March, April	
Scenery:	Wild	
Maps:	USGS North Adams, Rowe	
Portage:	4.25 mi R waterfall 20 yd	
	(runnable at higher levels)	

This section has been called one of the best whitewater runs in the East. The upper and lower sections have a gradient of 130 feet per mile, and the middle section has a gradient of 100 feet per mile. It is technical in nature and demands good boat control. See AMC's *Classic Northeastern Whitewater Guide* for additional information.

A gauge is located on the green bridge at the Mohawk Trail State Forest campground, on the downstream side of the left pillar. Low water is -1 to +2. Medium levels are 3 to 6, and high is 7+. When the gauge is in double digits, the Cold is Class V.

To reach the upper section of this run, travel west on MA 2 from the campground to a bridge. Drive up the mountain 1 mile to the hairpin curve, turn around where you can, then return to the hairpin. Unload the boats as fast as you can and leave. It is dangerous to linger in the road here. Use throw lines to lower your boats down to the river. The first big drop, High Anxiety, is where the river disappears in a left-hand turn. Scout on the right. Fifty yards below is a river-wide hole which must be run on the extreme left at high water; otherwise it becomes a keeper. The Savoy Shuttle leads to the bridge, the start of the middle section.

The first rapid in the middle section, Cuisinart, starts just after the bridge, and it is one of the longest and toughest on the river. An alternate put-in is just below this rapid, at a large parking lot. Several rapids below Cuisinart is Pinball, where several large boulders channel the water into a narrow sluiceway on the left. Stay left of the red rock. While it looks formidable, this is the easiest route.

The lower section starts at the green bridge. There is a large waterfall 0.25 mile below the bridge. Portage on the right, or run it on the right at high water. Watch out for Joe's Rock at the bottom of the drop.

A small stream entering on the right creates an eddy on the right. The best route for the next rapid is on the left. The last rapid is Landing Zone. Start on the left, cross over to the extreme right, and drop into the hole. Although this move looks impossible, it can be done.

North River VT, MA

The North River rises in southern Vermont and flows south into the Deerfield River. There are two Class V drops in Vermont, the lower of which is in Halifax Gorge. Do not put in on the flat stretch between the drops. The section above Halifax Gorge is too small for canoeing. MA 112 follows the river, providing many access points.

Halifax Gorge ➤ Colrain		7 mi
Description:	Class I, II, III	
Date checked:	1999	
Navigable:	High water: early spring, after heavy rains	
Scenery:	Forested, rural	
Map:	USGS Colrain	
Portage:	3 mi L dam	

Colrain ➤ Deerfield River	6 mi

It is possible to put in from VT 112 a mile north of the Massachusetts-Vermont state line where the road leaves the river and goes up a steep hill. The first three drops are Class III, and novices might elect to put in below them. The next 2 miles to the upper MA 112 bridge contains continuous Class II rapids. The 5 miles from the upper MA 112 bridge to the MA 112 bridge at Colrain is wider and, for the most part, gentler, with an occasional harder rapid.

Below Colrain, the river flows through an industrialized region and has less-attractive scenery. There are two portages and two Class III rapids as well as several Class II Sections.

Put in at a field just upstream of the MA 112 bridge at Colrain or at the school immediately downstream. A mile below at a sharp left turn is a broken dam and rapid that can be run with caution, Class III. There is a new concrete and steel bridge just below the broken dam.

For the next mile the rapids diminish. The covered bridge is gone (actually, it's sitting in a cornfield). The river soon enters the slack water of a large dam above Griswoldville. The West Branch enters on the right; it is small and steep, and is probably not canoeable. Portage river right 70 yards. In high water take out well above the dam. From here the next 2 miles are easy. In Shattuckville portage the falls on river left. Caution! The main falls may look like a relatively easy slide, but the ledge on the right is badly undercut. Below the falls a short pool empties into a Class III rapid. In low water, a left run is necessary, and in high water the center and right open up. From here to the Deerfield the rapids are Class II-II+, with several good play spots. There is a USGS gauge in Shattuckville, river right. A reading of 3.5 is low; 4-4.5 is medium.

Take out at the Deerfield River. This is private land, but public access is allowed. The road is too narrow for parking, however. It is best to park at a turnoff 100 yards north on MA 112.

Green River vt, ma

The Green River is a crystal mountain stream that descends a narrow valley through the hills north of Greenfield, Massachusetts, and empties into the Deerfield River near that city. Rising to the west of Governors Mountain in Guilford, Vermont, it is large enough to canoe in freshet by the time it reaches the Green River post office. There are excellent swimming holes and plenty of opportunities for trout fishing. It is an unusually beautiful stream and a delight to the nature lover. The chief difficulties are low water most of the season and numerous blowdowns. The river is quite isolated, especially in early spring, when the adjacent roads are marginal at best.

Green River ➤ West Leyden	6.25 mi
Description:	Class III
Date checked:	1999
Navigable:	High water: early April
Scenery:	Forested
Maps:	USGS Brattleboro, Colrain
Portage:	5.25 mi L dam

The access and car shuttle are as difficult as the canoeing on the Green River: the best water level for canoeing coincides with the last part of mud season. Although a dirt road follows immediately along the right bank, it is often a four-wheel-drive-vehicle-only road. The worst part is in the vicinity of the state line. The long way around continues north from the covered bridge past the turn to West Leyden. Avoid the dirt shortcut and take the turn 0.5 mile south of Guilford Center. Only the last mile down to the river is still unimproved.

A canoe can be launched a short distance above Green River. The usual start is on the dirt road on the right bank. All of the pitches can be run at ordinary high-water levels, but the river is small, steep, and full of ledges, particularly in the upper part where it rounds Pulpet Mountain. Proceed cautiously, checking each chute before you run it.

The Massachusetts state line is 3.25 miles. At Stewartsville the dam at the sawmill is best carried on the left.

West Leyden ➤ Water-Supply Dam	5.75 mi
Description:	Class I, II
Date checked:	1999
Navigable:	High water: early April
Scenery:	Forested
Maps:	USGS Colrain, Bernardston
Portage:	(7 mi L dam)

From West Leyden to the next bridge is a delightful run. Here the rapids are almost continuous but never severe. There are many clear, deep pools; beautiful banks; and steep, wooded hillsides. Canoes may be launched from the right bank just below the bridge at West Leyden. The most difficult drop is about halfway down and can cause trouble, especially at high water. Pull out 7 miles below on the left, just above the Greenfield water-supply dam.

Water-Supply Dam ➤ Greenfield	6 mi
Description:	Flatwater, quickwater, Class I
Date checked:	1999
Navigable:	Medium water
Scenery:	Forested, rural
Maps:	USGS Bernardston, Greenfield
Portages:	4 mi e dam 20 yd
	6.5 mi L dam 20 yd

A covered bridge marks the start of the run below the dam. Here the river leaves its narrow valley and curves through farmland and through the town. None of the rapids is difficult, but since the banks are soft, downed trees can be a real problem. Three dams must be portaged. The first, at the Greenfield town swimming hole (4 mi), is a short, easy carry on either side. The next is under the Mill Street bridge (6.5 mi), probably best carried on the left. The third dam is shortly below at an abandoned factory, also best carried on the left. The pool above the dam also offers a good takeout on MA 5 and MA 10, or you can continue to the Deerfield River.

Chicopee River MA

The Chicopee River begins with a short stretch of Class II and III rapids at the confluence of the Quaboag and Ware Rivers in Palmer and then flows a short distance into the Red Bridge impoundment. The river flows westerly 17 miles and drops 220 feet to where it empties into the Connecticut River in Chicopee. With six dams along its length, the river amounts to little more than a series of ponds. Due to the many dams and limited access, some river sections are rarely if ever traveled by boat or canoe. There are few free-flowing stretches. Dam operation can cause the river to fluctuate as much as two feet in less than an hour, and the river can completely dry up below dams when water is held back or diverted to power canals. A canoe trip the length of this river is more a logistical challenge for the hardy and is generally discouraged. But the river is not without interesting stretches, which can be explored in piecemeal fashion. Water quality is fair to good but becomes unacceptable in downstream urban stretches for several days following significant rain events.

Three Rivers ➤ Ludlow		8.25 mi
Description:	Flatwater, Class I-III	
Date checked:	1997	
Navigable:	Passable at most water levels	
Scenery:	Forested, urban	
Maps:	USGS Palmer, Ludlow, Springfield North	
Portages:	2.75 mi L Red Bridge Dam 100 yd	
	5 mi R dam at North Wilbraham 50 yd	

This section of Class III rapids should be looked over before running. Below this drop is a 2-mile-long impoundment that ends at Red Bridge Dam. In contrast to the questionable water quality, beautiful hemlock, white pine, and mountain laurel line the shores.

At Red Bridge (2.75 mi), take out on the left bank just above the dam, portage along Red Bridge Road, and put in from the right bank just below the powerhouse. There is a short Class II rapid and then more flatwater until you reach the dam at North Wilbraham (5 mi). Carry on the right bank. Below the dam is another brief Class II rapid, followed by flatwater to the third dam (8.25 mi) in Ludlow. Take out on the left bank on River Road near the point where the boundaries of Ludlow, Springfield, and Wilbraham meet.

Ludlow ➤ Chicopee

There are about a half-dozen dams in the remaining 8.5 miles to the Connecticut River in Chicopee, so the last half of the river is not appealing.

Ware River MA

The Ware River rises near Hubbardston and flows southwesterly to join with the Quaboag and Swift Rivers to form the Chicopee River. Much of it flows through a relatively unspoiled part of the state. The upper section is very overgrown. Water quality has improved in recent decades, making summer canoeing, which is generally possible below MA 32 in Barre Plains, more pleasant than it once was.

Barre Falls ➤ South Barre		6 mi
Description:	Flatwater, quickwater, Class I, II	
Date checked:	1998	
Navigable:	Ponds canoeable at most water levels	
Scenery:	Forested, settled	
Map:	USGS Barre	
Portages:	3.75 mi R Quabbin diversion 0.75 mi	
	(6 mi R dam)	

The river here might best be considered as two flatwater sections. The carry down from the road at Barre Falls Dam is steep and difficult, and the small stream is canoeable only at high water. The next downstream place you can reach the river is the covered-bridge site (1.75 mi). Find the covered-bridge site off MA 62 (heading east), the first left after the entrance to the flood control dam. At a large gambrel-roofed house, turn left and go to the end. Since the road is rough dirt and the next 2 miles of river are almost flat, in a wild area, it might be easier to paddle upstream from the access at the MA 122 bridge near Coldbrook Springs (3.75 mi).

Boating is not allowed above the Coldbrook Diversion Dam, so portage by car to below the second dam, if canoeing on the river, or to Powder Mill Pond, which lies between White Valley and the dam at South Barre.

South Barre ➤ Wheelwright		4.25 mi
Description:	Flatwater, Class I-II	
Date checked:	1998	
Navigable:	Passable at most water levels	
Scenery:	Forested, towns	
Maps:	USGS Barre, North Brookfield, Ware	
Portage:	4.25 mi L dam at Wheelwright 20 yd	

After a short rapid below the South Barre dam, the river divides, forcing you to choose the less-obstructed channel. The last 3 miles from Barre Plains and the MA 32 bridge (1.25 mi) are pleasant, as the river slows gradually to the paper mill dam at Wheelwright (4.5 mi).

Wheelwright ➤ Ware		10.5 mi
Description:	Flatwater, quickwater, Class II, III	
Date checked:	1998	
Navigable:	High or medium water: spring	
	Low water: passable for flatwater sections	
Scenery:	Forested	
Map:	USGS Ware	
Portage:	(10.5 mi L three dams in Ware 0.5 mi)	

This pleasant flatwater stretch of the Ware River is bifurcated by nearly 2 miles of rapids. Both flatwater and whitewater paddlers can arrange a trip to their liking.

In Gilbertville there is a gauge on the downstream side of the right abutment of the Upper Church Street bridge. At a reading of 11.5 and above, the rapids at Gilbertville are barely navigable. Note that on this particular gauge, higher numbers correspond to lower water levels.

From the Wheelwright dam, 2 miles of flatwater and occasional riffles lead to the bridge on the Barre Airport road. After a little drop underneath this bridge, there is smooth water for 0.5 mile to a railroad bridge (2.5 mi). Through wooded banks and mountain laurel the river flows gently for 1.25 miles to a side-road bridge (3.75 mi). Since there is no easy takeout right above the rapids, take out here if you are only interested in flatwater.

In another 2 miles you reach the third railroad bridge (5.75 mi), just below which Class II-III rapids begin. These rapids can be impassable in low water. On the whole, the rapids above the MA 32 bridge (6.5 mi) in Gilbertville are somewhat more difficult than the mile after this bridge. From the covered bridge in Gilbertville (6.75 mi) the rapids diminish, giving way to quickwater for the remaining distance to the Upper Church Street bridge (8.5 mi).

The last 2 miles to Ware are flat and somewhat wider. Grenville Park, 0.5 mile above the first dam (10.5 mi) in Ware, provides a number of takeouts with easy automobile access.

If you are continuing downstream, portage the three dams in Ware together. Under no condition should you put in below the first dam, since heavy rapids and concrete retaining walls make the stretch hazardous. For a carry on foot, pull out on the left just above the first dam, cross the bridge below the dam, continue through the center of town, turn left on West Street, and take the first alley on the left leading to the river (11 mi).

Ware ➤ Three Rivers   11.25 mi

Description:	Flatwater, quickwater, Class I, II, III
Date checked:	1998
Navigable:	Passable whenever ice free, except below dams
Scenery:	Forested, urban
Maps:	USGS Ware, Palmer
Portages:	8.5 mi L 1st dam at Thorndike 20 yd
	8.75 mi L 2d dam in Thorndike

From Ware to Thorndike there are 8.25 miles of fine quickwater canoeing with a strong current and several good riffles. The MA

32 bridge is 3.25 miles below Ware. At Thorndike (3.75 mi) are two dams, both of which should be portaged on the left. After the first dam and a road bridge, there is a short Class III rapid, which can be tricky in low water or heavy in high water.

The last 3 miles to Three Rivers contain a couple of Class II-III rapids, particularly right after the second dam in Thorndike. Below MA 181 (10 mi) the Swift River enters on the right (10.5 mi). Then it is 0.75 mile to Three Rivers, where the Quaboag and Ware Rivers meet to form the Chicopee River (11.25 mi).

Ware River (West Branch) *MA*

The Ware River is formed at the junction of the East and West Branches just above the Barre Falls Flood Control Dam. A large network of dirt roads winds through the area, but the dam is most easily reached from MA 62 by a paved road to the picnic area and canoe launch south of the dam. The river below the Barre Falls dam is rock strewn, and for most of the year it is too shallow to be passable.

Ware River (East Branch) *MA*

This is a small stream, barely a canoe-length wide and often obstructed by trees and bushes. While it has been run from the ponds above MA 62, even the section described below is not recommended except for adventure.

North Rutland ➤ Barre Falls	5.5 mi
Description:	Flatwater, quickwater, Class II
Date checked:	1998
Navigable:	Medium and high water: late March through May
Scenery:	Forested, town
Maps:	USGS Wachusett Mountain, Barre
Portages:	2.5 mi dam site at New Boston (5.5 L flood-control dam)

Put in below the last dam in North Rutland. The first 2.5 miles to New Boston provide interesting and varied running, but expect some brush. First is a good Class II rapid, which is easier in higher water. The current continues strong with some easy, intermittent Class II rapids followed by more strong current through swampy country. An easily run 1-foot dam and about a mile of smoothwater bring you to New Boston (2.5 mi). The milldam is gone, and you may have to carry the drop at most water levels. The river gradually becomes less steep and slows in the next 3 miles to Barre Falls Flood Control Dam (5.5 mi). **Caution!** Do not cross the log boom or in any way enter the intake channel for the 885-foot-long dam. There is no permanent lake behind this dam, and the stream is allowed to flow directly through a chute and tunnel in the dam. Five canoeists were injured here in 1975 when they were accidentally washed through or became hung up on the dam. Take out on the left.

Swift River MA

The runnable upper stretches of the Swift River and its branches have all been inundated by the Quabbin Reservoir, which supplies greater Boston with drinking water. The Metropolitan District Commission prohibits the use of canoes, sailboats, collapsible boats, and inboards on Quabbin. Therefore, boating is limited to the section of the Swift River below Winsor Dam.

The portion of the run immediately below the Quabbin Reservoir is the most attractive. The banks are heavily forested and the water is clear. There are several dams in Bondsville.

MA 9 ➤ Three Rivers		8.75 mi
Description:	Flatwater, Class I	
Date checked:	1998	
Navigable:	Passable at anytime after ice-out; Dam controlled	
Scenery:	Forested, towns	
Maps:	USGS: Winsor Dam, Palmer	
Portages:	1 mi R broken dam at West Ware	
	4.5 mi L 1st Bondsville dam	
	4.75 mi 2d Bondsville dam	
	5.25 mi R dam below MA 181	
	6.5 mi dam near Jabish Brook	

At the MA 9 bridge the current is strong and the water is clean. These conditions continue for a mile to the broken dam at West

Ware and a portage on the right. Four miles of smoothwater follow to Bondsville, with some old bridge abutments about halfway down and a low steel road bridge with a big parking lot 0.5 mile farther along on the right.

Canoeists are not allowed near the 12-foot dam in Bondsville (4.5 mi); take out 0.25 mile above it at a boat club on the left. This club is accessible from a road along the river. After putting in below the dam, a short paddle leads to a 3-foot dam just below.

Next are the MA 181 bridge (5 mi), then another dam and a short, easy Class II rapid. The Swift River then winds sluggishly to Jabish Brook (6.5 mi), where a milldam necessitates another easy carry. The river continues for another 1.5 miles through pretty country to its confluence with the Ware River. Take out either 0.5 mile up the Ware River at the MA 181 bridge or 0.75 mile downstream in Three Rivers (8.75 mi).

Quaboag River MA

The Quaboag River flows west from Quaboag Pond in Brookfield to Three Rivers, where it joins with the Ware River to form the Chicopee River. Its upper part provides a good flatwater trip, its middle section from Warren to Blanchardville is one of the best whitewater trips in central Massachusetts, and the lowest part is again smooth water.

Due to the large lakes in its watershed, the Quaboag holds its water remarkably well and is little affected by a single rain or short dry spell. It can always be run to the middle of June and frequently later.

The upper part of the Quaboag was used as a highway by the Indians. During King Philip's War, 1675–76, Brookfield was wiped out, and it was not re-established until 1686 when one of the original settlers returned.

The Bay Path, which extended across the territory of the Massachusetts Bay Company from Boston to Springfield, followed this valley and crossed the river by fords near West Brookfield and West Brimfield. Today, highways and a railroad follow the valley of the Quaboag.

For gauge information on the Internet, go to http:// h2o.usgs.gov. The readings are continuously updated, and they are accurate.

Quaboag Pond ➤ Warren		9 mi
Description:	Lake, flatwater, Class I	
Date checked:	1999	
Navigable:	Passable at most water levels	
Scenery:	Forested, rural	
Maps:	USGS East Brookfield, Warren	

This is an attractive flatwater trip that can be extended somewhat by beginning on the Brookfield River above Quaboag Pond. The Quaboag flows here in a broad valley in which towns and other built-up areas are hidden for the most part from the river. At the end of this section the valley narrows, forcing roads, railroads, and towns closer to the river.

Begin from the road along the north shore of Quaboag Pond. The river begins after about a mile of paddling west along the north shore. The 5.5-mile paddle from the pond's outlet to West Brookfield can be tedious in a head wind, as the river is fair sized and leads through marshy meadows. Near West Brookfield the river passes under a railroad bridge and the MA 67 bridge (6.25 mi), just below which the outlet from Wickahoag Pond enters from the right. This pond makes an interesting side trip. For those who wish to avoid all rapids, this bridge is a convenient takeout.

The last 2.25 miles to Warren have a stronger current and a few riffles. The first real rapid is just below the Old West Brookfield Road bridge (9 mi) at Lucy Stone State Park, a good access point.

Warren ➤ Blanchardville		10.25 mi
Description:	Quickwater, Class II, III, IV	
Date checked:	1999	
Navigable:	High or medium water: March through May, after fall rains	
Scenery:	Forested, settled, town	
Maps:	USGS Warren, Palmer	
Portage:	2.5 mi R dam at West Warren (difficult) 50 yd	

This section is often runnable when nearby rivers are not, due to the many lakes and swamps in its headwaters. The scenery is not pleasant, except for the gorge section, but the river offers a wide variety of rapids.

A gauge is located off MA 67 in West Brimfield, 0.75 mile upstream of the Massachusetts Turnpike bridge. A reading of 3.7 is considered the minimum, with 5.5 indicating high water. These readings translate to 0.3 and 1.3 on the gauge at the put-in.

The put-in is at Lucy Stone State Park north of Warren. One and three-quarter miles of intermittent Class II rapids follow to the broken dam above West Warren. Caution! Keep to the right, and scout from the right. The canal on the left, which looks very inviting from the water, leads to large tubes, which take the river below old walls. By the time you discover your error, it's too late! This could be a deathtrap. The far right of the dam is the location of the Mousehole, now collapsed. A channel exists just to the left of the Mousehole over the ruins of the dam. Scout this channel. A short rapid under a bridge leads to a pool above the railroad bridge. Do not scout the rapid from the bridge because the tracks have blind curves and the trains move fast; two people were killed by a train. You can easily scout it from the shuttle. If you must scout from the bridge, don't stand or walk in the tracks. Run either side of the center abutment, move to the right side of the left channel, and work your way through the rocks and holes at the end to a good recovery pool. A broken dam is next, followed by a rapid around an island. There is a difficult carry on the right (2.5 mi) at the dam in West Warren.

An alternate put-in lies around the corner on the left. The island is best run on the right. The next broken dam has an easy channel on the left, but it is very often completely blocked with trees and needs to be scouted. There is also a channel through the dam, about 20 feet from the right shore. Scouting is much easier from the right. If you decide not to run the dam, you can lift over for a short portage.

The river then passes a former outhouse overhanging the river, a sewage plant which increases the volume of the river, and a railroad bridge. The rapid below this bridge (variously known as

Railroad Rapids II and Angel's Field) contains large waves at high water but has an excellent recovery pool. The island below should be run on the right. Catch the right eddy below where the channel around the island rejoins the main channel in order to scout the rapid below.

This is the Devil's Gorge section, which contains three rapids of decreasing difficulty. Scout from the left, or eddy-hop down the left side if you're competent enough, and scout only the last drop. The first rapid ends in a 3-foot drop, which is difficult to see from above. High water in the center will swamp an open boat. Run either extreme left or extreme right. Left has more room for error. The last two rapids are easier than the first. The usual takeout is at a picnic area on MA 67 (5.25 mi), but quick-water continues to Blanchardville (l0.25 mi).

Blanchardville ➤ Three Rivers		5.25 mi
Description:	Flatwater, Class II	
Date checked:	1999	
Navigable:	Passable whenever ice free	
Scenery:	Forested, towns	
Map:	USGS Palmer	

The final segment of the Quaboag is almost entirely flat. This stretch is not as attractive as the upper river, however, because of obstructions in the river and the towns along the banks.

The dam at Blanchardville was washed out by the 1955 flood, and only three stone bridge supports remain. A center route is recommended here. The cement blocks and protruding reinforcement rods just below can be avoided because the current is minimal. There are more obstacles at an island, with the right channel and its breached earthen dam more easily navigated than the jumble of steel and concrete at the end of the left channel. The earthen dam, constructed by the Palmer Paving Corporation, is usually washed out in the spring and rebuilt in the low water of summer.

One and a half miles of flatwater follow to Palmer (2 mi). The final 3.25 miles to Three Rivers are also smooth. Because of the rough water created by blasting and dredging below the confluence with the Ware River, take out above the first bridge (5.25 mi) in Three Rivers.

Seven Mile and Brookfield Rivers *MA*

Spencer ➤ Quaboag Pond 6.25 mi

Description:	Flatwater, quickwater, Class I
Date checked:	1999
Navigable:	High water: March, April
Scenery:	Forested, settled
Maps:	USGS North Brookfield, East Brookfield

In the early spring, this trip in the headwaters of the Quaboag provides a nice, easy run for two to three hours. At the beginning many houses are visible from the river, but the farther downstream you travel, the less you see of houses, buildings, and roads. Below East Brookfield the Seven Mile River enters a wide, isolated flood plain and empties into the Brookfield River, which in turn flows into Quaboag Pond.

Put in next to the Pine Grove Cemetery where MA 31 crosses the river north of Spencer. The first two miles to the MA 9 bridge are flat and mostly wind through a meadow. Portions of the stream are narrow, but encroaching alders are kept clipped back by canoeists who run it regularly. There may be a few beaver dams, which can be run at high water.

As the river passes a shopping center next to the MA 9 bridge (2 mi) the current picks up, and for the next 2 miles there is a mixture of quickwater and occasional Class I rapids to a high bridge over an old dam site in East Brookfield (4 mi). The river here is typically 10 yards wide, and it is shallow with a gravelly bottom.

The remainder of the trip is on flatwater. The Seven Mile River ends at the Brookfield River (4.5 mi). The latter is almost all flatwater from the dam on Lake Lashaway (0.75 mi upstream). To the left, it flows 1.75 miles to Quaboag Pond (6.25 mi).

Westfield River *MA*

The Westfield River is one of the principal tributaries of the Connecticut River. It has four important branches: the North Branch (which is also considered the main river), the Middle Branch, and the West Branch, which all meet at Huntington to form the main river, and the Westfield Little River, which enters at Westfield. See AMC's *Classic Northeastern Whitewater Guide* for additional information about the Westfield.

Several sections of the Westfield were designated Wild & Scenic by Congress in 1993: the West Branch from a railway bridge 2,000 feet downstream of the Becket town center to the Huntington-Chester town line; the Middle Branch from the Per Worthington town line downstream to the confluence with Kinne Brook in Chester; Glendale Brook; and the East Branch from the Windsor-Cummington town line to the Knightville Reservoir.

Huntington ➤ Connecticut River		21 mi
Description:	Flatwater, quickwater, Class I, II	
Date checked:	1999	
Navigable:	Dam controlled: spring, early summer	
Scenery:	Rural, towns	
Maps:	USGS Woronoco, Mount Tom, West Springfield, Springfield South	
Portages:	1 mi L Texon	
	3 mi R Russell	
	6 mi R Woronoco	

One mile below Huntington the dam at the paper mill can be carried on the left. There are easy rapids in the next 2 miles to the dam at Russell, which should be carried on the right. There are fewer rapids below and several stretches of flatwater in the 3 miles to the dam at Woronoco. This difficult portage is best made on the right bank by taking out at Bull Rock above the pump house, carrying down the highway across the bridge to the left, and dropping down a steep bank through the brush back to the river.

About 2 miles below here the river runs out of the mountains and into a broad valley to meander 4 miles to Westfield. One-quarter mile above the MA 10/202 bridge in Westfield are three river-wide ledges that are excellent for surfing. The river is adjacent to the city ball field, so the put-in and takeout are the same. Below Westfield the river is mainly flatwater. In 1 mile the Little River enters on the right, and in 2 miles more the river cuts through the low hills north of Proven Mountain into the Connecticut Valley, which it crosses for 6 miles to reach the Connecticut River just south of West Springfield.

Westfield River (North Branch) MA

The North Branch of the Westfield River rises in Windsor in the Hoosac Mountains and flows southeast to Cummington, then south to meet the main Westfield River at Huntington. It provides one of the longest whitewater runs in Massachusetts, a fine run in the spring and even later if the season is wet enough. MA 9 follows the valley from Swift River to West Cummington, so one can judge the most suitable starting point for the existing water conditions. If the water is high enough, a good place to start is just below the ski area in West Cummington.

Windsor Forest ➤ Cummington		9 mi
Description:	Class I, II	
Date checked:	1999	
Navigable:	High water: March	
Scenery:	Forested, towns	
Maps:	USGS Windsor, Worthington	

Above West Cummington at Windsor State Forest the river is a rollicking Class II trip in early spring or after a heavy rain. The only problem lies below MA 9. When you see the cemetery on your left, keep to the inside and watch for a small ledge around a left turn. In high water the hydraulic below this ledge is strong enough to keep a boat and paddler. The third MA 9 bridge is Cummington, where the best access is downstream on the right.

Cummington ➤ West Chesterfield		7.5 mi
Description:	Class II, III	
Date checked:	1999	
Navigable:	High water: March, April	
Scenery:	Forested, wild	
Maps:	USGS Worthington, Goshen	

Put in at an old iron bridge on MA 9, south and east of Cummington. There are roadside turnoffs downstream where you can put in. This section is popularly referred to as the Pork Barrel, after a former pothole in the river, since filled in. This section has continuous Class II rapids, with a Class III rapid in every turn. After leaving MA 9, the Swift River enters left and the river runs sharply right. The next 5 miles are isolated. This is a beautiful, wild valley, much of which has been protected by The Nature Conservancy. There are two beautiful waterfalls in this section. About 0.25 mile above West Chesterfield are the remains of an old dam, now totally washed out. This is the first place where a car can reach the river, and it offers a possible takeout. A more popular takeout is below the MA 143 bridge on the right.

West Chesterfield ➤ Knightsville Dam	11 mi
Description:	Class II, III
Date checked:	1999
Navigable:	High water: March, April
Scenery:	Forested, wild
Maps:	USGS Goshen, Westhampton
Portages:	1 mi R Chesterfield Gorge 0.25 mi
	(17.5 mi L Knightsville Dam)

If there is enough water here, there will be enough water for the rest of the trip. One mile below the bridge the river makes a sharp right turn with a heavy rapid. The beach on the right offers a good lunch spot with a swimming hole below. The beach also can be used as a takeout unless the access road to it is too muddy. About 0.5 mile below this spot the river turns left with a sharp rapid and enters the West Chesterfield Gorge, which is runnable by experts at certain water levels. Caution! Take out on the right bank just above the curve. This may be a difficult maneuver, and it is easy to be swept into the gorge. Be sure to plan the landing carefully.

The West Chesterfield Gorge is a spectacular box canyon between sheer granite cliffs topped by tall hemlocks and spruce. At the upper end of the gorge are the remains of a high bridge that carried the old stage road from 1769 to about 1875. Both banks are now owned by the Trustees of Reservations, who have torn down the old houses there to provide a public vista for the gorge. The carry is 0.25 mile along the road, which follows the right bank downstream. A car is handy for this chore. In low water one can line down on the left, carry the largest drop, and run the rest of the gorge.

Put in from the road on the right below the gorge. For the next 8 miles the river continues in a steep, narrow valley with heavy rapids for 4 miles. About 200 yards below the gorge there is a heavy rapid through some ledges, which can be dangerous at high water. This can best be run by keeping well to the left and taking advantage of back eddies between the pitches. After about 1 mile of easier rapids the Border Patch begins. Caution! Land on the right bank when you can see large white boulders ahead. The route is intricate and ends in only one usable chute at the finish. Scouting is necessary, as the route may change with the height of the water. The steepest pitch can be lined or portaged on the right if you prefer not to run it.

Not far below here the river passes under a large telephone cable, beyond which are several very good campsites on the left bank among open pine and hemlock groves. The rapids are easier here and may lull you into a false sense of security. This will be rudely shattered 1 mile below, where there is another steep drop at a right turn. About 2 miles below this rapid the river enters a stillwater gorge that is very spectacular and a fine swimming hole. This is the end of the heavy going, but there are still lively bits for the next 4 miles to the Knightsville Dam. The surroundings are not as attractive here, as flooding by the dam tends to cover the once pretty farmlands with silt. The old roads are still in use in the dam area, and one from MA 12 just above the dam can be used to take out. Be sure to park well above the water; a rapid increase in the water level above the dam has been known to cover cars parked too close to the water. If conditions are unattractive, you may prefer to take out about 2 miles below the stillwater gorge, where the old road borders the river on the right.

Knightsville Dam ➤ Huntington   5 mi

Description:	Class III
Date checked:	1999
Navigable:	Dam controlled
Scenery:	Forested, towns
Maps:	USGS Westhampton, Woronoco

This section often has water when the upper section does not. Water releases from the flood-control dam aid racers and recreational paddlers alike. Release information may be obtained from the U. S. Army Corps of Engineers.

Put in from the picnic area downstream from the dam, reached from a side road off MA 112 north of MA 66. The low, 1–2 foot dam was destroyed in the flood of 1986. The rapids continue for 1 mile, then the river turns left and passes through some vertical strata of rock where a minor gorge is formed. This section contains a 40-foot chute between ledges ending in a deep pool. The next drop is below the pool, a direct drop of 2–3 feet best run on the far right. Next comes this section's most difficult drop, marked by a shallow island in the middle. The right side has a large hydraulic and haystacks, which can flip a boat at high water. In low water, it is the only viable route. The left side of the island presents a shallow, twisting passage in high water. Careful scouting is recommended for those not familiar with the river.

A short distance below the gorge the Middle Branch enters and the water volume increases noticeably. The MA 112 bridge is 1 mile farther, and just below is a beautiful haystack rapid. Approximately 0.25 mile below, as the river nears MA 112, an old washed-out dam signals the start of the Boulder Patch, which is full of eddies. This is a solid Class III rapid at 1,000 cfs.

The West Branch enters at a high railroad bridge. Take out on the right at a picnic area a mile below.

Westfield River (Middle Branch) *MA*

The Middle Branch rises in Peru and flows southeasterly to the North Branch 1 mile above the town of Huntington. It is much smaller than the North or West Branch and is followed by a road. The stream is continuously rapid, but the water is rarely heavy enough to be dangerous.

Smith's Hollow ➤ Dayville		10 mi
Description:	Class II, III	
Date checked:	1999	
Navigable:	High water: March, April	
Scenery:	Forested	
Maps:	USGS Worthington, Chester, Westhampton	

To reach the Middle Branch, go north from US 20 on MA 112, cross the West Branch, and take a left onto Basket Road. Follow the latter along the West Branch and then take a road to the right that leads to Dayville.

Put in anywhere along the road that follows the Middle Branch. The gradient is a constant 30 feet per mile. The 6 miles to North Chester are all rapid (Class II-III), with a short gorge in North Chester. There is a gauge on the right abutment of the bridge in the gorge, with 0.0 considered minimum and 4.0 considered high. The next 2 miles to Dayville are also Class II-III rapids. Most people take out in Dayville because the road to the reservoir is unplowed. If you are lucky enough to run the river when the road is open, another mile of harder, Class III rapids leads to the reservoir.

Littleville Dam ➤ North Branch   1 mi

Below the Littleville Dam, 1 mile of Class III rapids leads to the North Branch. Rapids are dam-release dependent. Access is from a left turn just before the MA 112 bridge crosses the North Branch.

Westfield River (West Branch)

The West Branch of the Westfield is one of the best early-spring Class IV runs in New England. The valley from Becket to Chester is isolated, marked only with beautiful stone-arch railroad bridges and the mill and bridge at Bancroft.

Becket ➤ Bancroft   3.5 mi

Description: Class IV
Date checked: 1999
Navigable: High water: spring
Scenery: Wild, forested
Map: USGS Becket
Portages: 3 mi R double ledge (optional)
                     3.5 mi L dam (recommended)

Put in on the left bank off a side street just below the main bridge in Becket. The run is continuous Class IV. Approximately 2.5 miles into the trip, watch for a steep bank on the right and a sharp left turn. This marks the Stain of Shame rapids, which involve tight maneuvering in heavy waves, with broaching possibilities. After a short pool, there is a long-standing wave rapid that ends in a left turn and a ledge under the railroad bridge. Shortly below comes the double ledge; scout left, portage right. A stream enters on the left between the ledges. The Bancroft Dam follows. Although it is runnable, the spikes and debris there suggest the easy portage on the left. The Bancroft bridge is just below.

Bancroft ➤ Chester   6 mi

Description: Class IV
Date checked: 1999
Navigable: High water: spring
Scenery: Wild, forested
Maps: USGS Becket, Chester

This section is, on average, not as difficult as the upper section, but there are two noteworthy rapids. Watch for an island with the main channel on the right. This should be scouted, as the current is deflected by a large boulder, resulting in difficult crosscurrents at a drop. Class III rapids follow the drop. The next spot to scout is the gorge. A double ledge in the gorge creates large holes at high water. A small difference in the height of the river up above translates to a large difference here. A road runs along the river for the last mile to Chester.

Chester ➤ Huntington   6 mi
Description: Class II, III
Date checked: 1999
Navigable: High water: spring
Scenery: Rural, towns
Maps: USGS Chester, Blanford, Woronoco

At Chester the Westfield is joined by Walker Brook, which adds considerably to its volume. After passing under a railroad bridge about 3 miles below Chester, there is a fine long rapid, steep but easily run at moderate water levels. The two broken dams above Huntington are completely washed out, exposing ledge drops where the dams were constructed. Both are runnable and can be scouted from the road on the north side of the river.

Walker Brook *MA*

Walker Brook is a small tributary of the West Branch that has increased in popularity in recent years. It is an extremely steep and narrow technical whitewater river. In places it is too narrow to make an eddy turn. Eddies are scarce anyway.

US 20 ➤ Chester   3.5 mi
Description: Class IV, V
Date checked: 1998
Navigable: High water: early spring
Map: USGS Chester

Put in anywhere on US 20 as it follows the river. A suggested put-in is 3.5 miles west of Chester. The first mile is Class V. One-half mile below this section is a 200-yard Class V rapid, considered the hardest on the river. A put-in below here will result in steep, narrow, technical Class IV water for the remaining 2 miles to Chester.

Farmington River *MA, CT*

The Farmington River is a gem. It offers something for every canoeist—pleasant flatwater stretches, Class I-II training spots, Class II-III training spots, Class III-IV rapids, and training sites for slalom racers. What makes the Farmington unique is the opportunities for summer paddling. Tarriffville Gorge always has sufficient water to paddle; the rapids below Riverton, Satan's Kingdom, and Collinsville can often be run during the summer. Dam releases provide Class III-IV rapids for experts and a Class II section in the upper area of the river. The river's water is clear but not potable.

The segment of the West Branch and main stem extending from immediately below the Goodwin Dam and Hydroelectric Project in Hartland to the downstream end of the New Hartford-Canton town line were designated Wild & Scenic by an act of Congress in 1994.

The Farmington River Watershed Association, 749 Hopmeadow Street, Simsbury, CT 06070, is an excellent source of river information. Its book, *The Farmington River Guide* ($5 postpaid), is an excellent source of river descriptions and information on the wildlife and geology of the valley, the trails, the parks, and the forests. The FRWA (860-658-4442) can be contacted after business hours on Thursdays for river level information.

MA 8 ➤ Below New Boston		7 mi
Description:	Class II, III-IV	
Date checked:	1998	
Navigable:	High to medium water: March, April, annual drawdown of Otis Reservoir	
Scenery:	Forested, town	
Maps:	USGS Otis, Tolland Center	

The 2 miles from the bridge adjacent to MA 8 to the green bridge leading to Tolland State Forest are Class II and provide a good warm-up for the more difficult rapids below. The 3 miles from the bridge to the MA 8/57 bridge in New Boston are Class III-IV and the 2 miles to the impoundment area for Colebrook dam are Class II, ending in a series of Class III rapids. The run can be made in the early spring or in October, with the aid of water releases from Otis Reservoir. The rapids are continuous Class III-IV below the Tolland State Park bridge. The entire run is paralleled by MA 8, which facilitates scouting or impromptu takeouts.

There is a gauge on a side-road bridge between the two MA 8 bridges south of New Boston. The minimum acceptable level is 3.6, with 4.0 required for a fluid run. The fall releases from Otis

Reservoir result in a gauge level in this range, although the addition of natural runoff provides the potential for a higher level. The middle 3 miles are Class IV at levels above 5 feet, with no rests.

Put in at a side-road bridge 2 miles above the Tolland State Park bridge. Flatwater leads to an easy Class II rapid, then a harder, longer Class II stretch. Eddies and surfing opportunities abound. A pool by a campground ends at a rock dam, which is easily run. There are often beaver dams in the next section. More Class II rapids lead to the Tolland State Park bridge (2 mi), the site of an annual slalom race.

Otis Bridge ➤ Race Course   2.5 mi

Description:	Class II
Date checked:	1997
Navigable:	Medium water: early spring, fall
Scenery:	Rural
Map:	USGS Otis, Tolland Center

This is the Class II section of the New Boston run. It contains some easy Class II rapids at the start and end of the trip, with some easy water in the middle. Like the lower part of the New Boston section, water level is critical for an enjoyable trip. At lower levels many rocks will acquire a fresh coat of paint. The put-in is located 5 miles north of New Boston along CT 8. The river is smooth but fast at the put-in, leading to some easy Class II rapids. There are several surfing opportunities as the river runs along CT 8 for 0.5 mile. Next the river turns left away from the road and loops around a campground and a picnic area. The river here is an easy Class I-II. When the river returns to the road, more rocky rapids start and continue to the takeout at the Tolland State Park bridge. This is the start of the harder Class III-IV section.

The Race Course rapid marks the beginning of the more difficult section. A 3-foot drop follows in a straight section. The next rapid is long and technical and involves moving from right to left and back right. The end of this rapid is marked by an undercut eddy on the right. Ferry left and scout Decoration Rock rapid (Class IV). Decoration Rock (2.5 mi) changes from year to year. Recent highway construction on the right bank has resulted in the potential for double-broaching. Carry on the left if you're unsure of your abilities. This is the most dangerous spot on the river.

Continuous Class III-IV rapids continue for the next 2 miles. A small bridge (4.5 mi) followed by a rapid and a right turn indicates the approach to the Washing Machine (a.k.a. Corkscrew). Take out on the right following the right turn and walk down MA 8 to scout.

Below New Boston (5 mi) the Farmington is generally Class II. Access at the New Boston bridge is a problem. We suggest paddlers complete the run to the Bear's Den.

From the MA 8 bridge there are 2 miles of rapids mixed with flatwater that extend to the next MA 8 bridge. The gauge is along the way, downstream on the left abutment at a small bridge. One-quarter mile below the lower MA 8 bridge lies a Class III rapid called the Bear's Den; scout from the right bank. If you can't make an eddy turn, don't try this rapid. The best takeout is below this rapid (7 mi).

Below New Boston ➤ Hogback Dam   6 mi
Map: USGS Winsted

This description is for information only. It is not anticipated that anyone will wish to make the necessary portages. The river below the Bear's Den is mildly riffled until it enters the backwater of Colebrook Dam (0.75 mi). The carries around Colebrook Dam and Hogback Dam are on the right, and posted signs must be followed.

Hogback Dam ➤ Satan's Kingdom   11 mi
Description: Flatwater, quickwater, Class II
Date checked: 1998
Navigable: High to medium water: March, April, October
                          drawdown of Otis Reservoir
Scenery: Forested, rural, settled
Maps: USGS Winsted, New Hartford

This section from Hogback Dam to Satan's Kingdom is a beautiful run of mixed quickwater and Class I-II rapids between hills and woods. The upper section is largely bordered by state land.

The nature of this section is dependent upon rainfall and the discharge from Hogback Dam, with 150 cfs the minimum level; 250 cfs is preferred. In summer and fall the river provides many miles of easy rapids mixed with flatwater. The river can be dangerous in high water, as it flows around shoreside vegetation.

Put in just below Hogback Dam at a little turnout on Hogback Road, which leaves CT 20 about 0.5 mile north of Riverton. The run to Riverton consists of 1.75 miles of Class II rapids. A state picnic area opposite the Hitchcock furniture factory in Riverton provides another convenient access to the river. There is a gauge at the CT 20 bridge in Riverton, downstream on the river-right side of the bridge.

The Still River enters on the right in 0.25 mile. Class II rapids alternate with flatwater until you reach a stand of tall pines on a high bank with a fence on the left. High Bank rapid is the most difficult in this stretch, with big rocks in its midst. After the CT 181 bridge (6 mi), the river broadens out with occasional narrow areas that produce riffles. The CT 29 bridge is next. The high US 44 bridge marks the entrance to Satan's Kingdom. There is a good takeout on the right 75 yards above the bridge.

Satan's Kingdom ➤ Collinsville		5 mi
Description:	Flatwater, quickwater, Class II	
Date checked:	1998	
Navigable:	High to medium water: March, April, October drawdown of Otis Reservoir	
Scenery:	Forested, rural, settled	
Maps:	USGS New Hanford, Collinsville	

A small set of rapids under US 44 is followed by a short section of flatwater and then the Class III drop in Satan's Kingdom. It should be scouted on river left. The normal course is left of center to avoid boulders located in midstream halfway down the drop. Depending on the water level, these boulders may be difficult to see. The right side is shallow and should therefore be avoided in low and medium water.

You can park and play for this drop. Follow a dirt road on river right off US 202. A short 400-yard paddle on flatwater will bring you to the bottom of this rapid.

Mosly flatwater interspersed with a few Class I rapids follows for a mile to the next drop, where a large boulder can be seen in midstream. Here the river turns left. The right side contains ledges. The preferred route passes left of the boulder through some haystacks. Avoid the temptation to surf here as the water is very shallow.

The remainder of the route is again quickwater with an occasional Class I rapid until a boulder field is reached as the river approaches US 44. This section is Class I at most levels. There is a convenient takeout along Rte 44 just past the boulder field. The rest of the run to Collinsville Dam is intermittent, easy rapids up to a high silver bridge, where the river becomes flat for the remaining mile to the dam. Keep right in this area when water-skiers are present. Land on the left for the takeout, next to the Collinsville Canoe store.

CT 179 ➤ River Road (Collinsville section)		3.5 mi
Description:	Class II	
Date checked:	1998	
Navigable:	Sufficient flow for most of year; too low during drought	
Recommended:	Gauge readings of 6.0-7.0 (Unionville)	
Scenery:	Rural	
Map:	USGS Collinsville	

The Collinsville section of the Farmington River provides one of the best Class II training grounds in New England. The river has a very dependable flow and can be run for much of the year. The river is fairly wide, allowing for different choices of routes and minimizing the danger of complete blockage by fallen trees. There are many rocks and waves here to practice eddy turns and surfing. Although the run is paralleled by CT 179, the scenery is quite good. Wildlife is abundant in this section. Osprey and bald eagles are sometimes seen here.

The put-in is located at a parking area on the side of CT 179, 1 mile south of Collinsville. The river is slow here, giving one time to stretch out and enjoy the scenery. After several easy rapids to warm up on, the Farmington enters Punch Brook rapid (just below the CT 179-CT 4 intersection), where the main channel flows to the right of a small island (the left side is usually blocked) through some rocks and waves. Larger waves are found at the bottom left of the rapid, providing a challenging surf. Several more easy rapids follow this one, each separated by a long pool. The Farmington then enters Crystal rapid, which starts out easy but contains several strong waves at the bottom, The next rapid is a short drop funneling the water toward a stone wall high on the left bank with a large eddy on the right. This is followed closely by another rapid as the river curves slightly to the right and flows into another long pool. The last two rapids are the hardest of the trip, containing an assortment of rocks and waves in a fast current.

There are many opportunities for eddy turns and playing in the waves here, as well as many different routes to take. The first drop is best run in the right center, since a group of rocks are exposed on the left side near the center of this rapid. The second can be run anywhere, though the bottom of this drop should be run on the right, since a line of rocks extends from the left bank. Fast current continues past the CT 4 bridge, where you can take out 0.25 mile downriver on the right. For a longer trip, you can run 1 mile of quickwater to Boateater rapid (Class II+), where the river water flows against the right bank and through some ledges. The river then settles down for the remaining distance to the next takeout in Unionville.

The gauge for this section is in Unionville on river right just upstream of the CT 179 bridge.

Boateater Rapid ➤ Tarriffville Park   18 mi

Description:	Flatwater
Date checked:	1998
Navigable:	Navigable at all water levels
Scenery:	Rural, towns
Maps:	USGS Avon, New Britain, Tarriffville
Portage:	2.5 mi L dam at Farmington

Run the railroad bridge at the put-in to the left of the left abutment. The river then flattens out and flows through a large gravel pit. The Pequabuck River (2 mi) enters from the right where the river turns left. Portage the dam (2.5 mi) on the left. There is a takeout on the left at the CT 4 bridge in Farmington.

The river below Farmington is very pleasant, providing good views of Talcott Mountain. It is 6 miles from the CT 4 bridge to the US 44/CT 10 bridge and an additional 7.5 miles to the CT 315 bridge (16.5 mi) north of Simsbury. The latter is the seventh bridge, counting the CT 4 bridge at Farmington and both bridges at Drakes Hill Road at Simsbury, and is the recommended takeout for flatwater paddlers. One and a half miles below (18 mi), after a bend in the river, are high bridge abutments. All flatwater paddlers should take out on the right here, just below lies Tarriffville Gorge. This takeout can be reached by following the main street in Tarriffville to the end and turning right down a gravel road to Tarriffville Park.

Tarriffville Park ➤ CT 187		1.5 mi
Description:	Class II-III, IV	
Date checked:	1998	
Navigable:	High water: spring, after heavy rains; over 3.5 on gauge	
	Medium water: late spring. 2.3-3.5 on gauge	
	Low-medium water: normal summer level; 1.4-2.2 on gauge	
	Low water: during Stanley Works shutdown, two weeks in summer	
Scenery:	Forested, settled	
Map:	USGS Tarriffville	
Portage:	1 mi L Spoonville Dam (optional)	

The gauge is behind a house on Tunxis Street, and there is a trail to it. High water results in Class IV conditions, with large waves and holes. Playing is largely confined to Cathy's Wave. Medium levels find the classic play hole largely washed out, but there are other surfing opportunities. The run is Class III at these levels, with the dam considered Class III-IV. At low to medium water you find the most surfing opportunities. Low water occurs when the Stanley Works, which owns the water rights to Rainbow Dam downstream, shuts down. The river is Class II at this level, and the holes are difficult to escape. This section is rarely too low to paddle, although the run above the Bridge Abutments rapids is scratchy at low water. Watch for sharp rocks.

To reach the put-in, follow the main street off CT 189 to the end and turn right down a gravel road. Small ledges greet you shortly below. These ledges can be run almost anywhere and provide an introduction to surfing. A small island is passed following the CT 189 bridge (0.25 mi), followed by a surfing wave above a factory on the right; this wave is best at normal summer levels. Cathy's Wave, which is best at high water, is formed by the concrete retaining wall at the factory. The gauge is below this area, on the right bank. Lower Brown Ledge follows, with good surfing waves.

Bridge Abutment rapids are next. It is possible to carry up from the dead end on river left to a point above this rapid. Two sets of abutments are present. At normal summer levels the best route is to the right of the abutments, enjoying many right eddies. A safer route at high water leads between the sets of abutments.

The next drop should be scouted from the left bank by novices. This drop, known as Sandy Beach rapid, is riddled with holes. The clearest route is left; the most fun, down the middle. The beach follows on the left. This area is at its prime in low to medium water, when the run is Class II-III, and is a great place for paddlers to advance their skills. The Lower Hole, which is the most benign, is followed by a good pool; the Top and Upper Holes are also interesting. Try to avoid surfing the Pencil Sharpener on the right—the river is too shallow in this area. Access to this area is gained by crossing the river on CT 187 north, turning right on Spoonville Road, and bearing right twice to a dead end.

The rapid following the beach is best run as a series of left eddy turns at normal summer levels. High water opens up other possibilities.

Spoonville Dam (1 mi) follows a flatwater stretch; scout or portage left. The hazard is a piece of the dam (Car Rock) that has been deposited downstream. Avoid the left side of the chute because of debris on the bottom; the right side has a nasty hole. The best run at normal summer levels is right center, through the largest wave, heading right. At levels around 3.0 on the gauge this wave forms a hole, so the chute left center should be run. Then execute a mandatory left eddy above Car Rock, followed by a ferry move across the current to the large right eddy below the dam. Scout first and make your own decision.

The Farmington then goes sharply left around an island, then sharply right. The best move is to make this left eddy and surf across Typewriter Wave to below the island. The river then enters a slalom training area. A low dam on the right forms dangerous hydraulics and should be avoided. The rest of the run to CT 187 (0.5 mi) is through shallow water.

CT 187 ➤ Connecticut River		11.5 mi
Description:	Flatwater, Class II	
Date checked:	1998	
Navigable:	Navigable at all water levels	
Scenery:	Rural, towns	
Maps:	USGS Tarriffville, Windsor Locks, Hartford North	
Portage:	3.5 mi R Rainbow Dam	

River access here is under the CT 187 bridge. Go south on CT 187/189 to the Tarriffville Road exit, turn left at the exit, and take the next left to the end, going down a rough road. Below CT 187 the river continues shallow and broad until reaching the backwater from Rainbow Dam (3.5 mi). The state access is on the left bank about 0.5 mile upstream of the dam, and the portage is on the right about 30 yards upstream of the dam. On the left side of the dam is a fish ladder that is providing for re-entry of salmon into the river.

The water level for the rest of the river is dependent on the Rainbow Dam. It is 1.5 miles to the CT 75 bridge (5.25 mi) in Poquonock, below which are 0.25 mile of Class II rapids. The river becomes flat and flows under I-91 and the CT 159 bridge, where there is a good takeout (10.25 mi). There remains then 1.25 miles of flatwater to the Connecticut River (1.5 mi).

Sandy Brook *CT*

Sandy Brook rises near South Sandisfield, Massachusetts, and flows southeastward into Connecticut. Above the CT 8 bridge the Sandy provides one of the best whitewater runs in Connecticut. The rapids moderate below CT 8. There are no major lakes or reservoirs in its headwaters, so it is rarely runnable.

Campbell Road Bridge ➤ CT 8		4 mi
Description:	Class IV	
Date checked:	1998	
Navigable:	High water: March, early April, after heavy rain	
Scenery:	Forested	
Maps:	USGS Tolland Center, Winsted	

There is no gauge at CT 8. The gauge is on the second bridge going up Sandy Brook Road, on river left on the upstream side of the bridge. The river is runnable at a reading of 0.5 and high at 2.0 and above.

To reach the put-in, turn west off CT 8 onto Sandy Brook Road. The road follows the river closely and crosses it several times, facilitating scouting, putting in, and taking out. A start can be made wherever desired, with one possibility being the Campbell Road bridge about 4 miles upstream from CT 8.

Rapids begin immediately, and a couple of small ledge drops are followed by a 4-foot ledge best run in the center; this drop should be scouted. Shortly below is the Block rapid, where a series of ledges and large holes finish with an extremely tight drop around either side of a rock outcropping. Scout this drop also.

A bridge 0.75 mile downstream offers a put-in for those who do not want the difficulties above. What follows is extremely steep and narrow, with continuous Class IV rapids. The water is rarely heavy enough to be intimidating, but fallen trees present a frequent and formidable hazard throughout this run. Many rapids may require scouting, if only because the large rocks, tight turns, and steep gradient make it difficult to boat-scout. This entire run approaches Class V in high water.

CT 8 ➤ Riverton   2 mi

Description:	Class II-III
Date checked:	1998
Navigable:	High water: March, April, after heavy rain
Scenery:	Forested, pasture
Map:	USGS Winsted

This section of Sandy Brook is still rapid but not nearly as difficult as the upper stretch. The river is wider, with fallen trees less a hazard. This section can be run when the upper section is too low.

Put in from the CT 8 bridge. Rapids follow for 1 mile and are generally Class II-III. Once the river empties into the Still River, the rapids are easier Class II to the town of Riverton.

Nepaug River _CT_

The Nepaug rises in New Hartford and flows east through Tunxis State Forest into the Nepaug Reservoir. Above CT 219 this crystal-clear, sandy-bottom stream is shallow, steep, and full of blowdowns. The river is runnable from Dings Road to the last US 202 bridge above the reservoir.

Ding Road ➤ US 202   4 mi

Description:	Class I-II
Date checked:	1998
Navigable:	High water: March, early April, after heavy rain
Scenery:	Forested, pasture

There is a gauge 0.3 mile east of the US 202 takeout. The Nepaug is barely runnable at a reading of 1.0. For a fluid run, 1.75 is suggested. To reach the put-in take Carpenter Road to Dings Road off US 202 in New Hartford. The river crosses Carpenter Road and US 202 several times.

The river meanders through an old pasture and then crosses US 202 at an easy rapid (0.25 mi). Below this crossing is another Class II pitch, ending just before the second US 202 bridge. The remainder is Class I through deep woods, with occasional blowdowns. Do not proceed below the last US 202 bridge, for this is owned by the MDC and is posted.

Hubbard Brook *MA*

Hubbard Brook rises in West Granville, Massachusetts, east of the Upper Farmington, and flows south into the Barkhamsted Reservoir in Connecticut. The river is crystal clear, ledgy, technical, and steep. With a gradient of 60 to 300 feet per mile, it is by far the steepest river described in this guide. All rapids are runnable by experts under certain conditions, but everyone should decide for him- or herself. See AMC's *Classic Northeastern Whitewater Guide* for additional information. The Barkhamsted Reservoir provides drinking water for the Hartford area.

MA 57 ➤ CT 20	2.75 mi
Description:	Class IV-V
Date checked:	1998
Navigable:	High water: March, April, after heavy rain
Scenery:	Forested
Portages:	Nosepin, the Big One, Outer Limits, others

To put in, turn south from MA 57 onto West Hartland Road, between Tolland and West Granby. Park where it crosses Hubbard Brook. The river to Granville State Park is generally Class III-IV, with a difficult pitch just before the park bridge. Below the bridge, an 8-foot boulder on the left marks Seven-Foot Falls. If you're having trouble so far, take out on the right. The rapids get significantly harder.

The next drop after leaving the camping area is Nosepin. Even though it runnable, scout it and be prepared to portage. Class IV rapids continue to a river-wide horizon line. Bump and Grind Slide should be scouted. Following are a series of 5- and 6-foot ledges leading to the Big One. Most will portage this rapid. The river gets even steeper below here, culminating in Outer Limits, a 0.5-mile rapid with a gradient of 300 feet per mile. The take-out is at the gauge pool approximately 0.5 mile from CT 20 on a dirt road on the east side. The suggested gauge readings for this river are 3.5 to 4.3.

Hockanum River CT

The Hockanum River rises from Shempsit Lake on the borders of Ellington, Tolland, and Vernon and flows westward to the Connecticut River in East Hartford. The watershed is heavily developed and it is a notorious flash river, rising and falling quickly. Once regarded as one of Connecticut's most polluted rivers, the "Hock" has made remarkable progress, although there is still ample opportunity for improvement. Local river advocates started to establish a linear park along the river, and a popular annual canoe race was established in 1977 to draw attention to the river. Despite passing through the heart of Manchester, many stretches remain very scenic. Remnants of historic mill sites are still visible.

Rockville Section of Vernon ➤ Talcottville Section of Vernon	7 mi
Description:	Quickwater
Date checked:	1998
Navigable:	High water: March, April, after heavy rain
Scenery:	Rural, suburban
Maps:	USGS Rockville, Manchester

The stream in Vernon is very small, often flowing through backyards, and can be run only during very high water. There are three dams in the Rockville section. The first practical put-in is at West Street, but a better bet may be Windsorville Road, easily reached west off of CT 83 (1 mile downstream from Dart Hill Road). The 2 miles to I-84 are winding, flat, and quickwater, with a lot of brush and some shopping carts. Shortly below I-84, the Tankerhoosen River enters in the middle of a mini-golf course, quickly followed by a footbridge, which is the starting point for the annual Hockanum River Canoe Race. There is good access here.

Talcottville ➤ Powder Mill Plaza, East Hartford   6.5 mi

Description:	Quickwater, Class I-II
Date checked:	1998
Navigable:	High water: March, April, after heavy rain
Scenery:	Urban, suburban, densely forested
Map:	USGS Manchester
Portages:	1.25 mi L Union Pond dam 50 yd
	(6.5 mi R Powder Mill dam 20 yd)

The stretch in Manchester is the racecourse and is generally free of obstacles. It is a bigger stream than above, but still runnable only after rains (except below CT 44). The first mile is a pleasant meadow stream with quick current, running between I-84 and CT 83. After a high exit-ramp bridge, the river drops over a series of ledges that can be Class II or III (in high water). Scout via the Beacon Light parking lot (across from an old brick mill) off CT 83, Oakland Street. Portage if necessary on the left.

After the rapids is the large, shallow Union Pond. Portage the dam on the left. The river is accessible down steps between the dam and Union Street bridge. The next 2 miles are winding quickwater with some tight turns, They can be negotiated by novices but are challenging enough to hold the interest of veterans. The river passes under several bridges and the scenery slowly changes to residential. Shortly after the Hilliard Street bridge (the fourth bridge), the river enters a low, flat stretch with many bends that give way to the CT 44 bridge and an expansive marsh known as Laurel Marsh. There is good access just below one CT 44 bridge. Note the high-rise landfill to the left. The USGS map still shows a lake, but the dam is breached and the stream winds around cattails. The old Powder Mill Dam is about 10 minutes' paddle below the triple I-84 bridges. Portage on the right behind McDonald's and a tall concrete wall. This is the usual takeout point. You might have to arrange to use the fences behind the Powder Mill shopping plaza for access, but hiking trails closely follow the riverbanks through most of Manchester.

Powder Mill Plaza ➤ Connecticut River · 5.5 mi

Description:	Flatwater, tidal
Date checked:	1998
Navigable:	Medium water: may be scratchy in riffles and shallow in muddy areas
Scenery:	Urban, suburban, mostly forested
Maps:	USGS Manchester, Hartford North
Portages:	1 mi R Scotland Road dam 10 yd
	1.25 mi L Church Street dam 10 yd
	1.5 mi L dam below Church Street 10 yd

This stretch is mostly dam impoundment or tidewater from the Connecticut River and can be canoed during most seasons. This stretch has gentle current and is scenic in the densely forested middle segment. Occasional fallen trees are obstacles.

Portage or put in on the right bank. Within 1 mile you reach a shallow millpond behind the high school. The new Scotland Road bridge is around the corner; approach to the right. A 15-foot dam shortly after the bridge requires a portage on the right very close to the spillway. Exercise caution in very high water. A suitable parking place is adjacent. Two more dams follow in close succession. They can be carried in one portage (about 1,000 ft) behind the brick mill and down Church Street, or paddled and portaged individually (scout first). The first portage is to the right (easy) and the second is to the left (moderate), followed by a series of ledges runnable in high water. The third is to the left (difficult). A short riffle follows the lower dam. It is scratchy in low water. There is good access at Hillsideston, river left, before the bridge. After 3 miles of flatwater, the stream opens into a large pond. In another 1.5 miles, the river passes a sewage-treatment plant, flows through a dike, and joins the Connecticut River adjacent to the (new) Charter Oak Bridge. The best takeout spots are on the Connecticut River: a boat launch upstream on the East Hartford side and one slightly upstream across the river at Charter Oak Landing in Hartford.

Coginchaug River *CT*

The Coginchaug River begins in northern Guilford and flows north through Durham, Middlefield, and Middletown before flowing into the Mattabessett River about 0.5 mile upstream of that stream's confluence with the Connecticut. The river from Myer Huber Pond to Meetinghouse Hill Road is very small. From Meetinghouse Hill Road to Durham Road (CT 157) it is swampy and probably runnable at highwater, but possibly littered with a lot of deadfalls. Durham Road is a good put-in, as is the Strickland Road bridge, about 1 mile farther down the river. Even with numerous portages and the landfill, it is a worthwhile trip.

CT 157 ➤ CT 66	5.75 mi
Description:	Flatwater, quickwater, Class I-II
Date checked:	1998
Navigable:	High water: March, April, after heavy rain
Scenery:	Forested, rural, urban
Maps:	USGS Durham, Middletown
Portages:	2.75 mi L dam/falls at Rockfall 135 yd
	2.75 mi R dam at Rockfall 20 yd
	2.75 mi R dam at Rockfall 10 yd
	3 mi L dam at Rogers Manufacturing Company 7 yd
	4.25 mi R dam at Spring Street 125 yd
	4.75 mi R dam at Starr Mill 20 yd

The first 1.5 miles flow through scenic, undisturbed swampland, passing the Strickland Road bridge at 1 mile. At 2.5 miles you come to a small stone dam in front of a bridge. Pull out on the left and scout across the road, which is part of Wadsworth Falls State Park. Shortly below the dam are the Wadsworth Falls, one of the state's most impressive waterfalls. There is no good portage for the falls, so the dam and falls are best carried as one. Follow the stairs to left of the falls. Around the corner below the falls is a second dam with an easy portage via a right-bank trail. Under the railroad bridge and around another bend is a third dam, which can be portaged easily on either side, but we recommend the right (state park) side to avoid private property. A fourth dam, at Rogers Manufacturing Company (easily missed on a topographical map), is a short distance below; there is no good portage. At moderate water levels, you can line the eight-foot concrete spillway to the right, which tends to be dry. At high levels, take out at the forebay to the left and lower your canoe(s) to your partner by crawling down broken concrete alongside the factory building (moderately difficult). It is best to scout on the left.

Below the dam enter the main portion of the state park and ride quickwater under a new wooden bridge (CT 157) and soon reach another millpond. A thick growth of thorns obstructs a portage on the left. Carry on the right, close to the spillway, to the street. Turn left and put in upstream of the bridge in front of the factory. After 0.5 mile of residential area you will reach the Starr Millpond and the fifth and last dam. The dam is best portaged via a fishing trail to the right about 25 feet above the dam. The path leads directly below the 13-foot dam, but if the downed elm tree still blocks the river below the nearby abandoned bridge, it may be best to carry beyond it. The next 0.5 mile to Washington Street is mostly quickwater with a series of standing waves in the last straightaway. Behind an apartment building is a breached dam you will easily see in advance. Although the breach is no problem, the downstream portion is braided and the best route requires a 180-degree turn to the left at the breach. Whitewater novices should scout.

CT 66 ➤ Mouth		2.5 mi
Description:	Quickwater, mostly tidal	
Navigable:	High flows: recommended for nontidal portion	
Scenery:	Urban, extensive flood-plain swamp/marsh complex	

In the first 0.75 mile you will paddle behind Palmer Field and then pass under an abandoned steel bridge, the new CT 72 bridge, and the old stone CT 72 bridge in rapid succession. During normal flows, the head-of-tide will be encountered below the riffle under the last bridge. When this river is runnable, however, the Connecticut River may be in freshet and backed up to Palmer Field. If you can tolerate trash, power lines, and a few houses, the swamp below is scenic and full of wildlife. You reach the Mattabessett in the middle of an expansive tidal marsh under a railroad bridge. Hook to the right around the insulting landfill and paddle another 0.75 mile toward the Connecticut River. Take out at the end of a dirt road between the last railroad bridge and the CT 9 bridge. Another takeout option is Harborpark (Middletown's riverfront park), 1 mile downstream on the Connecticut.

Salmon River *CT*

For many paddlers, the whitewater season begins on the Salmon River, which flows into the Connecticut River near East Haddam. Runs on the upper part of the river usually begin on the Blackledge or Jeremy River, the two small streams that combine to form the Salmon. A large portion of the routes described here pass through the Salmon River State Forest. This is a heavily fished trout stream, and canoeing is not advised on weekends from opening day (third Saturday in April) to early May.

Just upstream from the CT 16 bridge is the covered Comstock Bridge. On the downstream side of the right abutment is an iron ring. The river is passable when it is within 2 feet of the iron ring.

Old Route 2 ➤ CT 16		6 mi
Description:	Class II	
Date checked:	1998	
Navigable:	Medium-low water (above 3.5 on gauge)	
Recommended:	Gauge readings of 3.8-4.4	
Scenery:	Forested, rural	

The Salmon River, along with the Blackledge and Jeremy, provides an excellent opportunity to train beginners or to warm up after a long layoff. The current is usually not too overpowering, and the many rocks provide endless opportunities for practicing eddy turns, surfing, and ferries. Another plus for this river is that the rocks are well rounded and as boat friendly as rocks can get. The river is very heavily fished, so paddling should be done in the early spring before the middle of April.

The Salmon River, which is the product of the merged Jeremy and Blackledge Rivers, meanders for several hundred yards before coming to the first rapid. If the water is low or a shorter trip is desired, a good put-in can be found at the head of this rapid, providing the road paralleling the river is open. This rapid should be entered from the left center, maneuvering around several boulders; it ends with a large eddy on the right. Continuous rocky rapids continue for several miles to a long, shallow pool. The river here flows through a beautiful valley, with several small streams tumbling into the river. There are many opportunities for beginners to practice eddy turns and surfing.

At the end of the pool Dickinson's Brook enters from the right and the current quickens to the hardest rapid of the trip (Class II+ to III). This rapid is the remains of an old dam and consists of three ledges which vary in height from 1 to 2 feet. The dam is best run through a chute on the far right. If the water is high enough, other routes open on the left. At levels above 5 feet, the left three-quarters of this dam form a dangerous keeper. The dam washes out at levels above 8 feet. Just below the dam are several large waves to play in.

The river then enters an easy rapid as it turns right and flows into another long, shallow pool. There are several nice waves on the far left side, and a very nice one in the center 10 yards above the bottom of the drop. At the head of this pool a ledge extending from the left forms a smooth surfing wave. The rapid before the covered bridge may be scratchy unless the water is high. An easy takeout can be made on the right just above the CT 16 bridge or past the bridge at a large picnic area on the left. Just above the CT 16 bridge there is a nice hole in the center which can be quite playful if the water is at medium levels. An old external gauge just downstream from the bridge on the left has roughly the same correlation as the automatic gauge. If you care to extend the trip even farther, nice waves continue for another mile before flattening out to Class I. The next takeout is on the left just above the Leesville Dam, located just above CT 151.

CT 16 ➤ Leesville Dam   3.5 mi

Started at the covered bridge above CT 16 or below the bridge at a large picnic area. Once the river leaves the picnic area it enters a secluded valley with good scenery. The river is still rapid for a mile before flattening to quickwater and Class I. This section contains large waves at high water levels. The last 2.5 miles of this trip are mostly quickwater with several shallow spots. The current slows as you approach the Leesville Dam. Approach to the left here and tuck into a marshy inlet about 50 feet above the fish ladder. It is then a short carry to a small parking area below the dam.

CT 16 ➤ Connecticut River   8.25 mi

Description: Flatwater, quickwater, Class I; tidal
Date checked: 1998
Navigable: High or medium water: February, March, after heavy rain
Scenery: Forested, towns
Maps: USGS Moodus, Deep River
Portage: 3.5 mi L Leesville Dam

Below the covered bridge next to CT 16, the Salmon River is less steep than above but still contains rapids and requires a good runoff. Put in either below the covered bridge on the right or at the picnic area on the left, downstream of the CT 16 bridge on Gulf Road. To the left are two imprinting ponds, where salmon smolts are acclimated to the stream prior to being released into the river to swim to the sea. This is part of the effort to restore the salmon run. Downstream, below Leesville Dam, the first salmon caught on rod and reel within Connecticut during this century was taken in 1977. The dam (3.5 mi) comes after an S-turn and an overhead cable designating the upper limit to a no-fishing area in the pond. The 12-foot dam is 600 feet below. Approach to the left and tuck into a marshy inlet along the riprap about 50 feet upstream of the fish ladder. There is a small parking lot about 300 feet south. Continuing downstream, you can put in behind the fish ladder. The fish ladder is used to trap returning adult salmon. Information about the salmon restoration program is posted on a bulletin board from April to November.

One and three-quarters miles below CT 151 (3.75 mi), the river enters Salmon Cove (5.5 mi), a tidal inlet on the Connecticut River. You can take out on the main river at the Salmon River boat-launching area on the left (7.5 mi) or 0.75 mile farther at the parking area by the Goodspeed Opera House on the left, just past the CT 82 bridge (8.25 mi) over the Connecticut River.

Blackledge River *ct*

The Blackledge River flows out of Gay City State Park in Hebron, flowing south before joining the Jeremy River to form the Salmon River. The Blackledge consists mostly of quickwater with several easy rapids. At high levels the river can be run from West Road in Hebron. Several bridges downstream provide alternate put-ins or takeouts depending on the water level. When the water is at medium levels (gauge readings of 4.4–4.8), it's a long, scenic Class II run from CT 66 all the way down to the Leesville Dam (12 mi).

The Blackledge is the more frequently used approach to the Salmon River. The rapids are easier than those on the Jeremy. See the description of the Jeremy River for information about the Salmon below the confluence.

West Road ➤ CT 66		2.75 mi
Description:	Quickwater, Class I-II	
Date checked:	1998	
Navigable:	High water: February, early March	
Scenery:	Forested	
Map:	USGS Marlborough	
Portage:	1.5 mi L dam 20 yd	

Begin north of the center of Marlborough at the bridge on West Road, just east of the intersection with Jones Hollow Road. The river here is small as it flows through a marsh. The stretch down to Parker Road is advised only for the adventurous who are prepared to tangle with swamp and beaver dams.

After 50 yards of bushes, the stream is channeled through a gravel pit for 0.25 mile. Quickwater continues as the valley narrows beyond the gravel pit and the stream enters the woods, where bushes occasionally crowd the channel. There are some Class II rapids at an S-turn above a small pond where a dam must be portaged. The dam is in a private backyard, so be courteous. Immediately below the dam is the Parker Road bridge, reached through Hebron from the east; this is an alternate put-in. Below the dam (1.5 mi) the river flows through a very attractive wooded valley with few obstructions. There are intermittent Class I and II rapids for 1.25 miles to the CT 66 bridge (2.75 mi).

CT 66 ➤ Salmon River   6 mi

Description:	Quickwater, Class I-II
Date checked:	1998
Navigable:	Medium to high water
Scenery:	Rural, forested

Below CT 66 the Blackledge flows through intermittent Class I-II rapids that extend for 3 miles to Old Hartford Road (the most common put-in for the Blackledge/Salmon River run). The river is very small here, requiring high water levels. Many rocks require maneuvering at medium levels, while high levels bring the danger of fallen trees and several low footbridges,

The put-in can be reached by taking Exit 13 off of CT 2. After several miles a bridge is reached with parking on the left. The put-in for this run must be made on the upstream side of the bridge, since the downstream side is heavily posted. Class II rapids start under the bridge and continue for 1 mile as the river flows through a beautiful forested area. The next mile is calmer as the valley broadens out. Watch for several low footbridges in this area. Class I-II rapids pick up again for the next mile to the Old Route 2 bridge. Just before the bridge Lyman Brook tumbles into the river and the current picks up. Beneath the bridge the river turns left and flows through a series of small drops. Several closely spaced meanders with easy rapids begin next. Approach each turn with care, being alert for fallen trees. Soon the river straightens out and is joined by Fawn Brook. There is a large parking lot on the left here, which is a better starting point if the river is low or a shorter trip is desired.

The river is much wider after Fawn Brook. After several hundred yards the river runs under the highway and away from civilization for several miles. The river is mostly quickwater in this section. The next bridge on River Road provides another opportunity for a takeout. Below this bridge the river flows easily for another 0.5 mile before meeting the Jeremy River to form the Salmon River.

Jeremy River *CT*

Description:	Class II-II+
Date checked:	1998
Navigable:	High water
Scenery:	Rural, forested
Portage:	1.3 mi e dam

The Jeremy River is more challenging than the Blackledge and contains continuous Class II-II+ rapids. Most rapids consist of standing waves and an abundance of rocks. Because of its steepness and abundant rocks, the Jeremy requires higher water levels, becoming runnable when the gauge reads over 4 feet. The put-in for the Jeremy is off Old Route 2, located 0.5 mile east of Exit 16. Here the Jeremy meanders beneath overhanging trees for 0.3 mile until the CT 2 bridge is passed. Then the river turns sharply right and Meadow Brook enters from the left. The Jeremy then flows along the highway then turns left, and rapids start. Rapids are continuous Class II-II+ for the next mile to the dam at North Westchester. Portage on the right near a small iron bridge (above the CT 149 bridge), carrying across the road and putting in below the CT 149 bridge, or up a steep slope on the left bank above the dam. Rapids start immediately and continue past a right turn where there is a small ledge on the left. The current then gradually slows to the confluence of the Blackledge River.

Eight Mile River *CT*

The Eight Mile, along with the East Branch, provides an enjoyable trip in the early spring. They make a good alternate trip if the Salmon River is too high. Both branches flow through lightly settled valleys with good scenery. The trips vary in difficulty between Class I and Class III. Because these rivers are small, a fallen tree can easily block the whole river.

Chapman Falls ➤ Route 82		3 mi
Description:	Class II	
Date checked:	1998	
Navigable:	High water	
Scenery:	Forested	
Map:	USGS Hamburg	
Portage:	1.5 mi L dam	

The Eight Mile river is a very small river flowing through Devil's Hopyard State Park. It is rarely high enough for an enjoyable run. The put-in is below scenic Chapman Falls, where there is a large picnic area. To reach the put-in, take Exit 19 off CT 2 onto CT 11. Follow this to the end and take a right onto CT 82 west. Follow this for 3.6 miles and look for a sign for the entrance to Devil's Hopyard. Take a right and follow this road for 3.3 miles to a large picnic area on the right. If the picnic area is closed, carry down from the parking area above the falls. This is quite a spectacular place to start a trip: looking upstream from the put-in, Chapman Falls is on the left and another smaller waterfall is visible on the right.

Class II rapids start immediately and continue most of the way. After leaving the picnic area, the river turns left and drops over a small ledge with a nice wave. After 0.75 mile the river returns to the road and there is a large pool followed by a short drop over a shallow rock dam. Just before this pool is a tricky Class III drop around large rocks followed by some small ledges. This drop is best run by starting from an eddy on the right and head left of center. The river is calmer for the next 0.25 mile as several side streams enter, adding to the flow. Easy rapids pick up again as the river runs along the road. The river then turns left away from the road.

When it turns sharply right, stop and scout the next rapid, which is rated Class III+. It drops 8 feet over 50 yards and consists of three ledges. The first is best entered on the left and drops about

3 feet into a short pool. Be wary of rocks hiding at the bottom of the drop. The second ledge can be run on the left or right, turning sharply to the center. The third drop consists of a 5-foot-wide chute on the extreme left dropping 2 feet, with another sharp turn to the right. The run-out to this last drop can be shallow and rocky.

Class II rapids continue as the river returns to the road. A good takeout can be made just as the river turns left (2 mi). Beyond this point the river flows through private lands where fallen trees and barbed wire may be encountered, and rapids diminish to quickwater as the CT 82 bridge is reached. **Caution!** Take out above the CT 82 bridge, since there is not enough room for passage when the river is high enough to run.

Route 82 ➤ North Lyme   4.25 mi

Description:	Quickwater, flatwater, Class I
Date checked:	1998
Navigable:	Medium water
Scenery:	Rural
Map:	USGS Hamburg
Portage:	3.25 mi L dam at North Lyme 20 yd.

This section can be run as a continuation of the main stem or the East Branch, providing 3 miles of quickwater and easy rapids. Put in at the CT 82 bridge in East Haddam, or along CT 156 in Lyme. From the CT 82 bridge it is quickwater to the portage around a small dam, best done on the right. At 0.75 mile the river flows under the CT 156 bridge and is joined by the East Branch, which doubles its size.

The river then flows in a loop away from the road and through some farmlands. When it returns to the road some rapids start, consisting of easy rock-picking and several small drops and turns. These rapids continue to the first takeout, located at the Macintosh Road bridge (3 mi). If you care to venture farther, quickwater continues to the ponding behind a small dam, which should be carried on the left. It is then 1 mile to the Joshuatown bridge and tidewater. There is a convenient takeout on the upstream left side of this bridge.

CHAPTER 5

Thames
Watershed

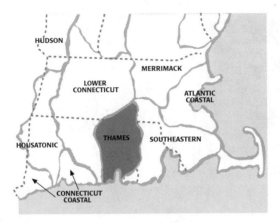

THAMES WATERSHED

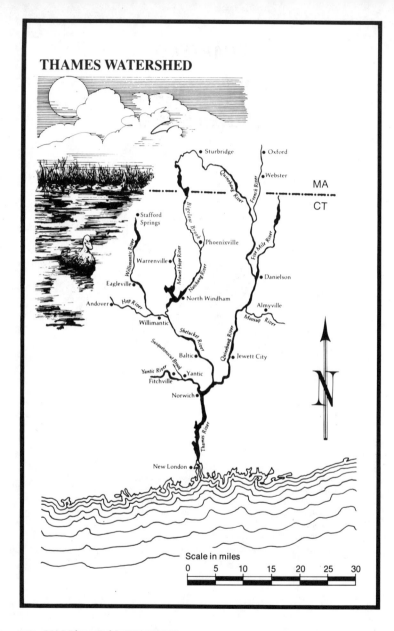

Sturbridge
Oxford
Webster

MA
CT

Stafford Springs
Phoenixville
Danielson
Warrenville
Eagleville
Andover
Almyville
Willimantic
North Windham
Baltic
Jewett City
Yantic
Fitchville
Norwich
New London

Quinebaug River
French River
Bigelow Brook
Five Mile River
Willimantic River
Mount Hope River
Natchaug River
Hop River
Moosup River
Shetucket River
Quinebaug River
Susquetenscut Brook
Yantic River
Thames River

N

Scale in miles

0   5   10   15   20   25   30

The rivers of the Thames watershed are underappreciated alternatives to some of the other rivers in this guide. Whitewater is not the main attraction, but for spring and fall canoeing, these rivers offer several fine trips. If you want a gentle stream with a good current, try the Willimantic. The Hop River is more difficult—narrower and faster with sharper turns. The Five Mile between the Quaddick Reservoir and Dayville has some fine, country stretches. And the Natchaug River has many scenic miles of intermittent quickwater and Class I-II rapids.

The Thames River is a wide tidal river and offers interesting canoeing among some side coves. Access points are at Brown Park in Norwich, off CT 2; at Stoddard Hill State Park, off CT 12; and under the I-95 bridges and a state-maintained ramp. The main problem for canoeists is the wind. It always seems to blow in your face no matter which way you're going. The river becomes intensively industrial in New London and Groton, where Electric Boat's submarine shipyard and the U.S. Navy's sub base are located.

Yantic River CT

The Yantic flows eastward from Lebanon, emptying into the Thames River in Norwich. The two sections described differ greatly. The first is a small, rocky whitewater run which is runnable in the early spring. The rapids are somewhat harder than the nearby Salmon River, but the scenery is not as nice. The lower section is much larger and provides an easy paddle for most of the distance. This section can be run later in the season and usually has fewer portages. The scenery is best at the headwaters, deteriorating as it reaches Norwich.

Camp Moween Road ➤ Randall Road   3.25 mi

Description:	Lake, quickwater, Class II-III
Date checked:	1998
Navigable:	Medium water: Fitchville Pond gauge readings of 0.75-3.0
Recommended:	Gauge readings of 1.0-2.25
Scenery:	Forested, rural, towns
Map:	USGS Fitchville
Portage:	2 mi L dam
	2.5 mi e dam at Gilman 70-300 yd

This section of the Yantic is small and rocky, with two dams to portage. There is a painted gauge on the top of the Fitchville Pond Dam (about 0.75 mi east of Exit 21 off CT 2), with readings of 1 foot or more providing a good run. The trip can be started on Camp Moween Road, which is 1.3 miles upstream of Exit 22 off CT 2.

Below Camp Moween Road are quickwater and a few trees down over the river. After a mile, a right turn marks the beginning of a 0.3-mile-long rapid. It starts as an easy Class II rock garden for 300 yards. The river then turns left and enters a fast, narrow rapid where the current heads straight for two lines of rocks across the river. If the Fitchville Pond gauge is below 1.25, passage between these rocks will be very tight and some quick maneuvering is required. If the water is high, you can go right over these. The current soon slows and a short portage on the left must be made.

Below the dam a short, intense Class III+ rapid starts, which should be run on the right. There is a small eddy on the right after this rapid. The river then runs quickly under two closely spaced bridges. When the river turns to the right, a small drop produces a nice surfing wave, best entered from an eddy on the right. After several easy rapids where the river splits around two islands, the current slows to the portage around the next dam.

Take out on either side and put in as close to the dam as you would like, but be sure to scout the Class III rapid that runs for 200 yards below the dam. This rapid has a very fast current and ends in a ledge beside a factory that must be run on the right to avoid sharp rocks below the ledge. The run-out from the ledge contains many barely submerged rocks on the right, so head left after the drop. Shallow rocks above the ledge complicate the approach. If the water level is medium (above 1.25 feet on the Fitchville Pond dam), several play spots form just above this drop, but be careful not to be swept down the left side of the ledge. The first play spot occurs just below the dam as the river runs through a narrow channel. The river then widens and splits into two channels. The right side contains many boulders and requires lots of maneuvering. The left channel is small, and drops 2 feet into a small pool. The next 100 feet contain several nice waves depending on the water level. Following the ledge is 0.5 mile of continuous rocky Class II rapids, which, as in other parts of the run, has many rocks hidden in seemingly clear channels. Depending on the water level, there are several nice waves and a large assortment of rocks waiting for eddy turns. The easiest takeout is just beneath the bridge on the left. If one wishes to continue farther, rapids continue for 0.25 mile to the confluence with Pease Brook. The current then diminishes to quickwater and Class I. This section is pretty and contains abundant wildlife. The next takeout is located 1 mile downstream at the Old Route 2 bridge, where there is parking on the left next to a cemetery.

Fitchville Pond ➤ Norwich   5 mi

Description:	Flatwater, quickwater, Class I
Date checked:	1998
Recommended:	Gauge readings of 0.75-2.0
Navigable:	Medium water: spring
Scenery:	Rural, settled

This section is much larger than the previous one, having received the water of several tributaries. The river is mostly quickwater with several easy Class I rapids and one Class II rapid at an old dam site in Norwich. The scenery starts out fair but deteriorates closer to Norwich. The gauge is located at the top of the dam (Fitchville Pond) just above the first put-in. The river is runnable with gauge readings of 0.5 foot or more. At 3 feet, the Yantic is in flood. This level is not recommended, since many trees are in the water, creating dangerous strainers.

The starting points on the Yantic are below the Fitchville Pond dam and farther down on Stockhouse Road. The first put-in is reached by a carry below the Old Route 2 bridge 100 feet below the dam. From here the river flows through Class I rapids with Stockhouse Road coming close on the left bank. It is much easier to put in from Stockhouse Road 0.5 mile below the dam since the carry is much shorter and there is a nice pool to enter. The river then flows through more easy rapids before turning away from the road into farmland. After several turns there is a low, sloping dam that can be run almost anywhere. In low water it is scratchy and may have to be carried, best done on the left. In high water the dam washes out. The river continues with flatwater and quickwater for another mile and passes under the CT 32 bridge. The only hazard in this section is the possibility of fallen trees. A fast rapid starts below the bridge, ending in a sharp right turn. The river is then mostly quickwater and flatwater for the next mile to the Norwich Industrial Park. The current speeds up as the river passes under a bridge, soon entering a long pool in a sweeping left turn.

When the river turns back to the right, the hardest rapid of the trip begins. This rapid can be scouted easily from the left. It starts as a very fast current with a 1–2 foot drop at the end. This drop can produce a strong wave in the center at medium levels. High levels wash this drop out. As the next bridge is passed, the river turns right, then left in a fast channel with the water funneling against the bank. The last easy rapid is found past the next bridge (I-395). This rapid can be scratchy at low levels, requiring careful route selection. The best takeout is below the next bridge on the left, where there is a large parking lot. Travel beyond here is not recommended due to the amount of trash along the banks.

Shetucket River _CT_

This river begins at the confluence of the Natchaug and Willimantic Rivers and flows into the Quinebaug near Norwich. It makes a pleasant, easy run with no rapids. The wooded banks over much of the way make this an attractive trip, although there is no outstanding scenery.

Willimantic ➤ Baltic   12 mi

Description:	Flatwater, quickwater
Date checked:	1998
Navigable:	Passable at most water levels
Scenery:	Forested, settled
Maps:	USGS Willimantic, Scotland, Baltic
Portage:	8 mi R dam
	(12 mi R dam)

Begin on the Natchaug River at Lauter Park off CT 195 in Willimantic. The Shetucket starts at the confluence of the Willimantic in 1.5 miles. The CT 203 bridge in South Windham offers a possible takeout at 4.75 miles. Portage the Scotland Dam on the right (8 mi). **Caution!** Stay away from the dam.

The water level below the dam is controlled by the dam. Expect a scratchy trip to Baltic with some canoe-dragging if the dam is closed. It is possible to take out 100 yards below the dam on the left by carrying across the railroad track to Jerusalem Road. There are two takeouts in Baltic—just above the CT 97 bridge on the left, or at the baseball field on the right.

Baltic ➤ Quinebaug River   5.25 mi

This section is not recommended due to the frequent portages. In addition to the dam at Baltic, which should be portaged on the right, there are two more dams: the one at Occum (2.25 mi) and the one at Taftville (4.5 mi). Take out at CT 12 just above the confluence with the Quinebaug (5.25 mi).

Willimantic River *CT*

The Willimantic River begins at Stafford Springs and flows south to join the Natchaug River in the city of Willimantic. Together they form the Shetucket River.

This stream has a good current with alternate riffles and quickwater. It provides a good introduction for canoeists wishing to try river paddling for the first time. There are no tricky drops, and a road is always nearby.

The scenery is attractive for most of the way, but there are occasional sand and gravel operations and at least one sewage-treatment plant, although it is not obtrusive. The stream is stocked with trout by the state and the water is relatively clean.

Stafford Spring ➤ Eagleville	14.75 mi
Description:	Lake, flatwater, quickwater
Date checked:	1998
Navigable:	High or medium water: spring and fall
Scenery:	Forested, towns, settled
Maps:	USGS Stafford Springs, South Coventry

Put in just below the center of Stafford Springs where CT 32 comes close to the river. After a short distance there is a broken dam with large concrete abutments on each side. It can be run on the left. The river then runs for several miles in a narrow valley which widens somewhat as you approach the I-84/CT 15 bridge (4.75 mi). The current remains steady for the length of the trip. In West Willington, US 44 (6 mi) crosses the river, as do several other roads before Mansfield Depot (12.5 mi), where US 44A crosses. After another 1.5 miles you reach Eagleville Lake, which is the impoundment above the Eagleville Dam. Take out next to the dam (14.75 mi), where there is a large parking area.

Eagleville ➤ Willimantic	9 mi
Maps:	USGS Columbia, Willimantic

Below the Eagleville Dam, the current lessens. The river winds past the mouth of the Hop River (5.75 mi), which enters on the right just below the US 6 bypass bridges to join the Shetucket River. You could take out with difficulty at the CT 66 overpass, on the right.

Hop River CT

This clear, narrow river flows east to the Willimantic River. US 6 follows it closely but is not generally noticeable from the water.

Andover ➤ Willimantic   12 mi

Description:	Flatwater, quickwater, Class I
Date checked:	1998
Navigable:	High or medium water: early spring, late fall
Scenery:	Forested, rural
Maps:	USGS Rockville, Marlborough, Columbia, Willimantic
Portage:	7 mi L dam at Hop River Road 10 yd

Put in on Hendee Road off US 6 in Andover, near a restaurant, 2 miles east of Bolton Notch. There is a short Class I rapid (1 mi) below a broken dam and slight drops at each bridge. The dam at the Hop River Road bridge (7 mi) is partially washed out and must be portaged on the left; this is a possible takeout. After the dam, pass under another bridge, then US 6, then a power line. The next railroad bridge (10.25 mi) has a sharp Class II drop, passable only on the extreme left. It may have a log and brush pile across it. It can be portaged with difficulty on the right. The next bridge is Flanders bridge, with a possible takeout (10.5 mi). Below this bridge, the Hop passes beneath the US 6 bypass highway ramps and joins the Willimantic. The old picnic area takeout on the right, on the Willimantic just below the end of the Hop, is fully overgrown and not accessible.

Natchaug River *CT*

The Natchaug River starts at the junction of the Still River and Bigelow Brook in Eastford, flowing south to Willimantic. The upper parts of this river are quickwater alternating with easy rapids. The river here flows around campgrounds and through the Natchaug State Forest. The middle section has continuous Class II rapids to challenge expert boaters. The lower section has nice some Class II rapids and a long section of quickwater. The middle and lower sections flow away from the road, providing for nice scenery.

Phoenixville ➤ England Road 7.25 mi

Description:	Quickwater, Class I-II
Date checked:	1998
Navigable:	Medium water: spring
Scenery:	Forested, rural
Map:	USGS Spring Hill

This section can be run as a continuation of trips on the Still River or Bigelow Brook, or as a separate trip. This trip is usually started from the bridge on General Lyons Road or 2 miles downstream at the state forest picnic area. From General Lyons Road there is 0.25 mile of Class II rapids, that wind down to a 2-mile mix of quickwater and flatwater. At the state picnic area Class I and II rapids start and continue for 0.75 mile. Past a campground there are several rock dams that may require scouting. Another rock dam is located 0.5 mi below the Morey Road bridge. Intermittent Class I and II rapids continue past the third bridge (4.75 mi) and ease up as you approach the bridge on Bear Hill Road (6.25 mi). The next mile to the England Road bridge is flatwater. Take out on the left, where parking is available.

England Road ➤ CT 198 (Diana's Pool), Chaplin, CT 1 mi

Description:	Class II, III-IV
Date checked:	1998
Navigable:	Medium water: spring
Scenery:	Forested
Maps:	USGS Hampton, Spring Hill

This is the Diana's Pool section, which contains several Class IV rapids, including an undercut ledge. To reach the put-in, follow US 6 to CT 198. Take CT 198 north and travel about 2.25 miles and take a right onto England Road. There is an area for parking just past the bridge on the left. The river below England Road has intermittent Class II rapids followed by several large pools. After the short rapids leading out of the last pool, stop on the right to scout Mousetrap. A large boulder forms an island with a ledge on the right and a sneak route on the left which is often blocked with debris. There is a large eddy behind this boulder in which to scout the best path through the many rocks below. One hundred yards of rocky rapids requiring careful route selection leads to the next good drop where the river funnels towards the right and has several angled hydraulics. Below this drop is an eddy on river left and a nice play hole in the center. The next rapid leads to the Cow Sluice rapid, where the river drops 5 to 6 feet through a narrow slot into Diana's Pool. The rapid below is full of ledges, with a few small eddies on the right side. The last drop is a 2-foot ledge which should be run on the right since there is an undercut ledge on the left side, with most of the current flowing toward the ledge. Below this last ledge there is a large rock on the left (Michaud's rock). The river is runnable when the water is flowing over this rock. The takeout is just above the CT 198 bridge.

CT 198 ➤ Old Boston Post Road		3 mi
Description:	Quickwater, Class II	
Date checked:	1998	
Navigable:	Medium water: spring	
Scenery:	Forested	
Maps:	USGS Hampton, Spring Hill	

This section of the Natchaug contains Class II rapids and quite a bit of quickwater. There are several play spots, but rocks and a strong current make getting and staying in them difficult. The put-in for this section is right above the CT 198 bridge, just below an undercut ledge. There is a small drop under the bridge with a nice surfing wave that may get sticky at higher levels. Following this is 0.75 mile of continuous rapids with many rocks and waves. The first drop comes as the river turns right, away from the road. There are only a few small eddies on river left. Avoid the right side of this rapid as it may be scratchy. The next drop is easier and ends in a long pool. At the end of this pool look for a large ledge extending from the left shore. Behind this is a large eddy from which you can scout the rapid below, which contains a good play hole in the middle of the river. This hole may take some effort to enter, as the side eddies are small and the current is very fast. The best approach is from a small eddy on the right just above the hole. The following rapid should be run on the left, as there are several shallow rocks blocking the right side. The next rapid has a nice drop to the left of the center rock. It requires quite a bit of effort to get into this hole. Soon the rapids end, with the remaining 2 miles to Station Road consisting mainly of quickwater.

Take out on the left above the Station Road bridge, or run another 400 yards farther and take out on the left just before the current slows to the ponding behind Mansfield Hollow Reservoir. This last 400 yards can be the nicest part of the run, with several nice play spots that are easier to enter than many of the holes farther upstream. The first is just above the bridge where a ledge forms a nice hydraulic on the right. The next is at the bottom of a small drop in a slight left turn, where there is a nice eddy on the left. The last drop is in another left turn at the takeout, where a cove on the left forms a nice eddy. From there it is a short carry to the takeout at the end of Old Boston Post Road. During periods of heavy runoff this last section, as well as much of the quickwater section, may be flooded out.

Mount Hope River CT

The Mount Hope is a small tributary of the Natchaug River in eastern Connecticut. This is a fun run when the water is up, though levels are high enough only a few weeks a year. The rapids are continuous and progress from easy Class II to harder Class II-III. The river can be paddled after heavy rain in the early spring, providing the ice is out on Mansfield Hollow Reservoir. The river can be paddled for another 5.5 miles above Juniper Road, a mixture of flatwater and several easy rapids. There is also a high probability of tree obstructions in this section.

Warrenville ➤ Juniper Road		5.5 mi
Description:	Lake, flatwater, quickwater, Class I-II	
Date checked:	1998	
Navigable:	High water: March	
Scenery:	Forested, rural, settled	
Map:	USGS Spring Hill	

The Mount Hope River can be run from the CT 89 bridge 0.5 mile above US 44 in Warrenville. Above this point the river is very small and access is restricted. A mixture of flatwater and quickwater extends for 3.25 miles past the US 44 bridge (0.5 mi) and the next bridge on CT 89 (2.25 mi). The river then narrows and enters a 100-yard Class II rapid in a left turn. Intermittent rapids continue for 0.25 mile to Mount Hope Bridge (3.25 mi), which is next to a traffic light. These rapids become more difficult in very high water, containing several strong waves. There is good access below this bridge on the right.

Flatwater and quickwater extend for 2.25 miles, past the next small bridge, and continue to the Juniper Road bridge (5.5 mi). This section is on a fairly wide flood plain, providing some interesting exploring in very high water. Be wary of fallen trees and the possibility of beaver dams here. Take out above the bridge on the right, or continue down the Class II+ section to the Mansfield Hollow Reservoir.

Juniper Road ➤ Mansfield Hollow Res. Boat Launch	2.5 mi
Description:	Class II+
Date checked:	1998
Navigable:	Medium water (above 2.5 on Warren gauge)
Recommended:	Gauge readings of 2.8-3.5
Scenery:	Forested
Map:	USGS Spring Hill
Portage:	1.25 mi e Class 3+ double ledge in Atwoodville (optional)

The put-in for this run is above the Juniper Road bridge, which is reached by taking a right onto CT 89 from Route I-84 and traveling 2.8 miles to Juniper Road. The rapid below the bridge may be scratchy if the water is low. Rapids continue for several hundred yards to a good drop with several large boulders in a left turn. Next you pass a low rock dam that is a great place to practice side-surfing if the gauge is between 3.0 and 3.5. Downstream several islands split the river, with the best route on the right. Keep an eye out for fallen trees in this section. The river gets steeper as it approaches Atwoodville, with several play spots. In a sharp right turn above the Atwoodville bridge, there is a Class III+ double ledge that can get sticky at higher levels. This drop should be scouted from either side. The ledges drop about 2 feet, then 1.6 feet. The top ledge can be run on the left (most exciting) or on the right through a narrow, turning channel. Several rocks on the left complicate the approach. The second drop should be run in the center to avoid rocks on the sides. Below the bridge is 0.25 mile of continuous Class II+ rapids. It starts as a 50-yard chute of fast water. When the river turns right, several large rocks force some maneuvering, with the clearest passage on the left. The next section contains an assortment of rocks and several sharp drops. If the water is up, several nice eddies form on the sides. The rapids end in a steep Class III drop which must be run on the left due to sharp rocks blocking the right side. During periods of extended heavy runoff, this drop may be flooded out. From here it is 0.5 mile of lake paddling to the takeout, which may still be frozen early in the season.

Bigelow Brook *CT*

Westford Road ➤ US 44		3 mi
Description:	Class I-II	
Date checked:	1998	
Navigable:	Medium to high water	
Scenery:	Forested, rural	

Bigelow Brook is a small tributary of the Natchaug River that can be run early in the season. The difficulty is mostly Class II, but you should be alert for the downed trees. This trip can be started from Westford Road, which runs alongside the brook. For 3 miles the brook flows through easy rapids in an attractive forested setting. Most of the rapids consist of a sprinkling of large rocks and small drops flowing into deep pools. None of the rapids should be too difficult unless a tree is trying to get into the act. A takeout is at the US 44 bridge (difficult) or continue for 1 mile down diminishing rapids to the Natchaug River, where you can take out where the river comes near CT 198 (1.25 miles below US 44) at a campground.

Quinebaug River *MA, CT*

Maps: USGS Wales, Southbridge, Webster, Putnam,
                 Danielson, Plainfield, Jewett City, Norwich

The Quinebaug River rises in Holland on the Massachusetts-Connecticut line, flows in a big loop to the north and east through Brimfield, Sturbridge, and Southbridge, and crosses the state line flowing southeast at Dudley. It then flows south through Putnam, Danielson, and Jewett City until it turns west to join the Shetucket River near Taftville and the Thames River at Norwich. There are a number of dams, some of which are no problem and others, particularly in urban areas, that must be approached with considerable caution. The water is dark and in places somewhat polluted, but there is much pleasant canoeing available on this stream.

Hamilton Reservoir ➤ East Brimfield   5 mi

If water is high enough, the 0.5 mile stream below Hamilton Reservoir is a pretty run, but be prepared to lift across a few shallow, rocky places and ledges. If water is low (judge by the flow over the dam), you may want to portage on foot or by car about 1 mile via Dug Hill Road to Holland Pond Recreation Area, which is a good put-in at any water level. From the outlet of Holland Pond, the river flows as a broad, placid stream. Holland Pond is also the start of the East Brimfield Lake & Quinebaug River Canoe Trail. In 0.5 mile there are a road bridge and a camping spot on the left. Mill Brook enters from the left here and can be used as an alternate starting point from Brimfield. The Quinebaug continues as a broad stream for 3 miles through open marshes bordered by pretty hills, and soon it widens into the permanent pool behind the East Brimfield flood-control dam. An extension of the lake stretches north of US 20, forming what was previously Long Pond. There is a good takeout place at its north tip, at Champeaux Road.

East Brimfield Dam ➤ Sturbridge   2.75 mi

Below the East Brimfield flood-control dam is 0.75 mile of riffles, easily run if the release from the dam is around 120 cfs (2.7 feet on the tailrace marker). Scout the broken dam just around the bend below the Holland Road bridge before running it. The dams in Fiskdale can be portaged on the left and over the dam. The river is then fast flowing for one mile to the Leadmine Road bridge and the pond at Old Sturbridge Village.

Sturbridge ➤ Westville Dam   5.75 mi

At Old Sturbridge Village, is a dam that is portaged easily on the left. For the next 4 miles the Quinebaug is a pretty, placid stream with few rapids, running through woods and marshy meadows. There is then a low dam to portage left or to take out on the right. The river descends 20 feet in the next 0.75 mile to the head of the permanent lake, 1 mile long, at the Westville Flood Control Dam. This 20-foot descent has both heavy and thin spots, depending on the amount of water being released from the East Brimfield dam. Scout this section before running it.

Westville Dam ➤ West Dudley   5.5 mi

This section is not pleasant. It is best to take out either at the head of the lake at the Westville dam, where there is a boat ramp and parking area on the left, or at the low dam 0.75 mile upriver, and then to portage by car around the entire city of Southbridge. For those who are willing to labor up and over the Westville dam, there is 0.5 mile of rapids, easy if the water release is adequate, to a small millpond below the Mill Street bridge in Southbridge, where there is another dam to portage; then another 0.5 mile of easy rapids. Canoes must be taken out at the Mechanic Street bridge at the head of this pond and portaged 1 mile via Mechanic Street and MA 131. This route bypasses one dam on the American Optical grounds and another about 0.5 mile below. Return canoes to the river below the second dam. It is then 2.5 miles of mostly foul slack water to the dam at West Dudley.

West Dudley ➤ West Thompson   10 mi

Below Southbridge the river runs through a broad valley with bushes on the banks and cultivated fields or meadows on the flood plain. The bridge at Dudley Hill Road is a possible put-in, or drive 2 miles farther and put in below the dam at West Dudley, avoiding some of the foul water below Southbridge.

From West Dudley the river runs with fair current to the broken dam at Fabyan, which can be run through the open sluice. It is then six miles to the flood-control dam at West Thompson. The French River enters just below this dam.

West Thompson ➤ Jewett City   33 mi

You can put in below the dam at West Thompson and run 2 miles to Putnam. But with three dams in quick succession in Putnam, you may prefer to put in below there. Be cautious approaching the upper dam at Putnam, and make a landing on the left, well upstream from the dam. A single carry of 0.75 mile via city streets bypasses all three dams. An attractive new park, the Putnam River Walk, which opened in 1998, borders the river between the three dams. Below the third dam, at Cargill Falls, the river meanders somewhat for the next 2 miles to Danielson, flowing through broad flood plains for much of the distance. The only interruptions come about midway, where there are two road bridges 0.5 mile apart, the second being CT 101, where there is access. Half a mile farther is the dam at Rogers, which can be portaged with care on either side. Then it's slack water to Danielson. A car portage from Danielson to Wauregan is recommended to avoid hazards in the next 6 river miles. The preferred takeout point is on the left upstream of the US 6 bridge.

For those electing to run the river, Class II skill is needed. Take care at Danielson. Only if the powerhouse is taking the full flow of the river and the lip of the dam is dry can the first dam be portaged on the left. Be cautious about currents. The right bank pullout point is no longer safe. The Five Mile River enters here on the left through culverts under the new divided highway. The next 0.25 mile involves broken dams and heavy rapids that should not be attempted without a careful scouting of the entire length. Portage around them on the left if you are not thoroughly expert in such water, as this is a potential people-eater. Land upstream of the US 6 bridge and scramble up a steep bank, then portage through the River Walk. Below Danielson 1.5 miles are the broken remains of Dyer Dam. Scout the dam before running from right bank, but portage on left bank. One-third of a mile below Dyer Dam are the remains of an old rock dam, sometimes runnable on left; scout first. Another 2.5 miles brings you to Wauregan, where you have to avoid the potentially dangerous situation at the jagged remains of a broken dam. Portage left, near the sluice gates, to avoid the fast current sweeping into the jaws of the break. The drop through the dam is a staircase with numerous hidden iron rods and is too dangerous to be run, despite how it may look.

The section from Wauregan to Jewett City offers pleasant canoeing. It is 6 miles without interruption through wooded country to the CT 14 bridge near Canterbury, with the Moosup River entering from the left early in this stretch. From CT 14, the river meanders 5 miles through broad flood plain to the next road bridge and railroad crossing near the head of Aspinoak Pond. Another 3 miles of lake paddling brings you to the dam at Jewett City, where the vertical drop is 20 feet. Portage here on the right, starting well upstream from the strong current at the masonry wing wall at the approach to the crest of the dam.

Jewett City ➤ Norwich   11 mi

Caution! This stretch is not recommended. The power plant in Jewett City causes rapid and unexpected changes in water level.

The first 5 or 6 miles are flat water, but when the Jewett City dam is running, swift current makes it more challenging. There are problem rocks and currents, and no takeouts along the way. About 3 miles below Jewett City, the river makes a sharp right to flow west for 1 mile, then south 1 mile, and then west again for 1 mile, entering a narrow gorge at the far end of which is the tall and dangerous power dam at Connecticut Light and Power Company's Tunnel plant. There is a landing point at the left (upstream) end of the log boom. Follow the elevated boardwalk for some 500 feet above ledges to the service yard. Then find a convenient way down to the pool below.

One-quarter mile below the power dam, the Shetucket River enters from the right. Put in at state-owned (but closed) launching area at the confluence. It is very pretty canoeing here. Paddle upstream to the power plant to see the dam. One mile downstream is the dam at Greenville in Norwich. Portage on the left. It's another 1.5 miles through Norwich via the Shetucket River on tidewater to the junction with the Yantic River on the right, forming the Thames River estuary.

French River MA

Maps: USGS Leicester, Webster, Oxford

The French River rises in a cluster of ponds on the border between Leicester and Spencer, where there is some pleasant lake paddling. From there it flows south through a rapid succession of shallow brooks, millponds, and dams to Hodges Village Flood Control Dam in Oxford. The run from there to Webster is quite pretty and without dams. Below Webster the dams are frequent until the river joins the Quinebaug just below the West Thompson Dam. Water-quality problems exist due to industrial discharges and low flows and sedimentation in the impoundments.

Oxford ➤ Webster   8 mi

When there is a good flow of water, start in North Oxford west of MA 12 opposite Old Worcester Road, about 2.75 miles above Hodges Village Flood Control Dam. Another good starting point is in the pond just below the dam. The river is placid and pretty, with some mild quickwater under bridges, where the river narrows, for the next 5.5 miles to the dam at North Village in Webster. The river is wide, with quite a few islands. You can pick different routes among the islands to give yourself different outbound and return scenery. Mill Brook, the outlet of Webster Lake, enters on the left 200 yards upstream from the high abandoned railroad bridge at North Village. At this point, the water quality declines; takeout is recommended. There is parking next to the railroad tracks in North Village.

Five Mile River CT

The Five Mile River rises in Thompson near the south end of Webster Lake. It flows south into Quaddick Reservoir, continues south through Putnam into Killingly, and then swings southwest and then south again to meet the Quinebaug River at Danielson.

Much of it flows through wild, unspoiled country, mostly woods but some of it through open farmland. It appears to hold its water well, and parts of it can probably be run even in the summer.

Quaddick Reservoir Outlet ➤ Pineville   7 mi

Description:	Flatwater, quickwater, Class II
Date checked:	1998
Navigable:	Passable at most water levels
Scenery:	Rural, forested, farms
Map:	USGS Thompson
Portage:	1 mi e 20 yd (optional)

There is an easy put-in below the Quaddick Road bridge, just south of the Quaddick Reservoir, from a small dirt parking lot adjacent to a small hydropower plant. You'll find riffles and Class I water for 300 yards below this point, the only obstruction being a large metal mill remnant in the center of the stream. The river emerges into a placid 20-acre pond, then continues to the south through an Atlantic white cedar swamp.

A small set of Class II rapids just upstream of Munyan Road (1 mi) can be run by experienced paddlers in medium to high water or portaged left or right 20 yards through the shrubby undergrowth. Below Munyan Road there are no portages or rapids (other than those created by the occasional beaver dam) until the takeout in Pineville. The next 5 miles of stream will have some shallow, scratchy spots if the water is not high until reaching the slack water below the Stone Road bridge (6 mi). The run is narrow and winding, through farmland and well-wooded areas.

There's another good put-in/takeout point at a roadside park along US 44 (2 mi). This is a good place to check the water level—if the surface of the water is 25 inches or less below where the curved sides of the bridge become straight, then there is more than adequate flow in this section.

Below US 44 the river meanders through sparsely settled farmland and woodland. There are informal access points at the River Road (2.5 mi) and Chase Road (4.5 mi) bridges. Below the Stone Road bridge (6 mi) the current slows for the last mile to the dam in Pineville. There's an easy takeout left or right above the dam, but scout beforehand to avoid trespassing on posted land. A small beach on the right along Stone Road should be good for swimming (if, once again, the area is not posted).

Pineville ➤ Ballouville   1 mi

If the water is too low to negotiate the riffles and Class II white-water below the Pineville Dam, carry 700 yards along the paved road to the next bridge, where the slack water above Ballouville Dam begins.

Ballouville ➤ Danielson   7 mi

At Ballouville, put ashore between the dam spillway and the gate-house on the left. If the water is too low to run the riffles below the dam, portage 600 yards left around the mill via streets and put in at the canal below the mill. About a mile beyond Ballouville is a drop that should be looked at before running. There are a number of little drops over ledges throughout this 1.5-mile run to Attawaugan, which can be impassable during low water. There is a low dam to be portaged just above CT 12, and a good flow of water is needed to navigate the next mile to the slack water above Killingly. There are probably two short portages around obstructions in this stretch. At Killingly, carry 600 yards via streets, starting from the first spillway and sluice gates and going around the right side of the factory. Or portage 300 yards along the embankment, left of the mill pool to the second spill-way, scrambling down through the poison ivy to enter the river at the foot of the spillway. The river below is shallow and scratchy during low water until the slack water above the Rock Avenue bridge 1.5 miles below Killingly. Another 2.5 miles of slack water leads to the center of Danielson, where there is a dam.

Moosup River _RI, CT_

Maps: USGS Oneco, Plainfield

The Moosup River rises in Rhode Island, flowing south at first and then swinging westward through the towns of Moosup and Central Village to join the Quinebaug below Wauregan. Its upper portion offers remote wilderness canoeing. Above Almyville, however, there are many fallen trees, and it should be run only in the spring. Its central part has frequent dams, and its final stretch is wooded and remote.

Moosup Valley ➤ Quinebaug River   23 mi

Start at the CT 14 bridge near Fairbanks Corner. From there the river runs a good 6 miles to Oneco, meandering through isolated, wild, wooded country most of the way. Portage the dam at Oneco by starting at the landing on the left side above the highway bridge, crossing the bridge, and putting in behind the mill on the right. It is then 2 miles with riffles to the dam at Sterling, where the portage is on the far right near the mill and runs 100 yards along CT 14 to the Main Street bridge. In another 3 miles you come to the high upper dam at Almyville. Portage on either side, carrying around the mill buildings. The topographic (1953) map shows five dams in the next 3.5 miles, but two of these have broken, making a reasonably fast river with some boulder-dodging. The dam below Almyville is easily portaged on the right if you're not concerned about poison ivy. The river runs fast for the next mile to the broken upper dam at Moosup, which experienced whitewater canoeists likely will find runnable; others can easily lift over on the left. The second dam at Moosup is broken and has been replaced by a low dam, easily portaged, located at the head of the old pond.

The river continues through the dry bed of the old pond to a 1-foot drop located at the site of the old dam. This and the short rubble pile below are easily portaged. Just beyond I-395 there is a brief portage over the left end of a low dam. The map does not show the next low dam just ahead, located 150 yards above the CT 12 bridge. At Central Village there is a 1-foot drop at the railroad bridge to run or lift over. Fifty yards ahead are the remains of the old dam shown on the map, which can be run. One-half mile farther are two road bridges, which are the last takeout points on the Moosup River. The next takeout beyond these bridges is at CT 14, 6 miles downstream: 2 miles of the Moosup River to its junction with the Quinebaug, then 4 miles on the Quinebaug.

CHAPTER 6

Southeastern
Watersheds

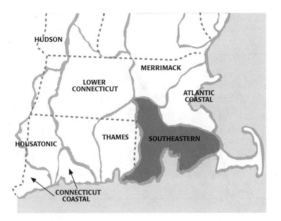

SOUTHEASTERN WATERSHEDS

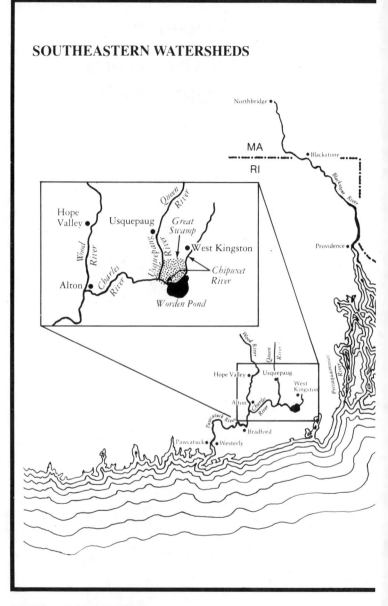

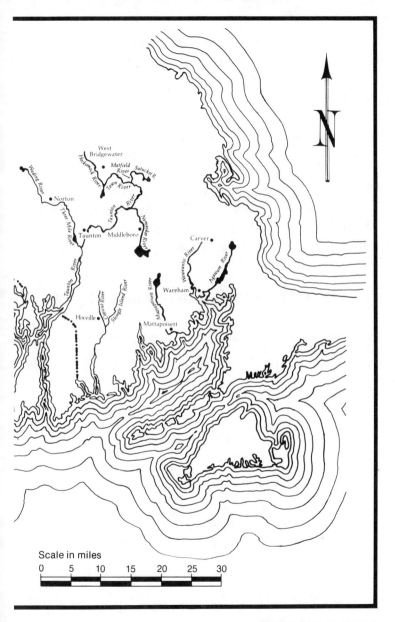

The rivers in the southeastern watersheds have remained surprisingly undeveloped despite their close proximity to large urban areas. They offer many miles of canoeing amid relatively unspoiled surroundings.

The Blackstone, Chinuret, Matfield, Nemasket, Satucket, Taunton, and Town Rivers can be canoed whenever they are not frozen. Parts of the Agawam, North, Pawcatuck, and Wood Rivers are also runnable throughout the canoeing season.

The cleanest and clearest river is the Agawam, followed at some distance by the Nemasket. The award for the darkest clean river (or the cleanest dark river) goes to the Mattapoisett. The Taunton was the most polluted, but in recent years it has been substantially cleaned up.

Wampanoag Commemorative Canoe Passage
MA

The Wampanoag Commemorative Canoe Passage follows inland waterways used by the Wampanoag Indians, who lived in southeastern Massachusetts. It connects the Massachusetts and Narragansett Bays.

From Massachusetts Bay, the canoe passage follows the North River past Hanover and heads south along Henning Brook to Furnace Pond in Pembroke. Then it crosses over to the Taunton River watershed via Little Sandy Pond. It goes through Stetson Pond and the twin Monponsett Ponds, and ultimately reaches Robbins Pond in East Bridgewater via Stump Brook. From Robbins Pond it follows the Satucket, Matfield, and Taunton Rivers.

See chapter 7 for descriptions of those portions of the canoe passage that follow the North River at the Massachusetts Bay end, and this chapter for the Satucket, Matfield, and Taunton Rivers from Robbins Pond to the city of Taunton: a total of almost 41 miles. The connecting link of about 12 miles is described in "Wampanoag Commemorative Canoe Passage," a booklet available free from the Plymouth County Development Council, Box 1620, Pembroke, MA 02359 (781-826-3136).

Pawcatuck River RI, CT

The Pawcatuck River drains much of southern Rhode Island. It rises under the name of the Queens River in West Greenwich and flows south to Usquepaug Village in South Kingstown. It is known as the Usquepaug River from here through the Great Swamp to the outlet from Worden Pond; then it is called the Charles River until it meets the Wood River south of Alton. From there it is the Pawcatuck as it flows south to the sea at Watch Hill, Rhode Island. (For information on the river between Worden Pond and Bradford, see the Charles River description. See the Chipuxet description above for Worden Pond.)

This is a very pleasant and interesting trip through three Rhode Island management areas, where there is good warm-water fishing. There are campsites along the river in the Carolina and Burlingame Management Areas. It is 29.5 miles from Usquepaug to Westerly.

Wood River ➤ Westerly		15.25 mi
Description:	Flatwater, Class I-II	
Date checked:	1998	
Navigable:	Passable at all water levels	
Scenery:	Forested, rural, towns	
Maps:	USGS Carolina, Ashaway	
Portages:	4.75 mi R Bradford Dam 20 yd	
	11.25 mi R Potter Hill Dam 100 yd	
Campsites:	2.25 mi L Burlingame Management Area (state)	
	2.75 mi L Indian Acres Canoe Camp	

With occasional broad meanders, the Pawcatuck River winds past open fields and swamps from the confluence of the Charles and Wood Rivers to Westerly. There is an abandoned mill town at Burdickville near the beginning, but most of the river is remote, with relatively few houses.

Below the confluence of the Charles and Wood Rivers, which form the Pawcatuck, it is a mile to the broken dam at Burdickville. Run it on the right or carry 30 yards on the left. Then the river is wide, flat, and scenic. At the Burlingame Management Area, where the river runs due south, there is a campsite on the left bank. Then in about 0.5 mile, where the river runs due north, you reach Indian Acres Canoe Campsite. The river meanders for 2 miles to Bradford, where there is access at the RI 91/216 bridge (4.75 mi). About 50 yards past the bridge, portage 20 yards on the right around a broken 4-foot mill dam. Then there are 6.5 miles of flatwater past the RI 3 bridge (10 mi) to the dam at Potter Hill (11.25 mi). Take out on the right just before the bridge and carry 10 yards down Laurel Street, past the fish ladder at the 8-foot dam.

Below the Potter Hill bridge (11.25 mi) is a short stretch of rapids, then flatwater to Boom Bridge (13.25 mi). From there it is 1.25 miles to White Rock.

Caution! At White Rock there is an old debris-covered dam that shunts most of the river into a canal on the left. The current then becomes strong with some occasional rocks. The rapids are an easy Class II, but there are few places to land once you are in the canal. Keep to the right. After 500 yards the river flows through a breach in the canal wall and returns to the old stream bed. At the quick S-turn there are some Class II rapids, which present no problem to capable canoeists as long as the channel is not blocked by debris. If you wish to scout this area, stop on the left above the old dam.

The best takeout is just before the RI 78 bridge (15.25 mi), which can be reached from White Rock Road on the east bank.

Below Westerly 3 mi

The river flows between the towns of Pawcatuck and Westerly. **Caution!** Just below the Stillman Avenue bridge is an old breached dam which can be run on the left at certain water levels, when it may be Class II with large waves. Scout this in advance.

Just before the river empties into Little Narragansett Bay there will be one more dam to portage. This spot is marked by evidence of a boatyard. An old wooden building will appear to block the river and the right bank will have wooden retaining walls. Portage on the right.

After this portage the river merges with salt water and there is the danger of encountering large, fast powerboats. You can take out at a marina in Avondale, or in Little Narragansett Bay at the waterfront parking area at the summer resort community of Watch Hill, over a vertical seawall.

Wood River *RI*

The Wood River rises in western Rhode Island and flows south to Alton, where it joins the Pawcatuck. It is one of the most attractive streams in the area. It flows through the Arcadia Management Area. The most popular section of the river starts at the RI 165 bridge and runs for 13.25 miles to Alton. This section is always passable.

West Greenwich ➤ Pawcatuck River	16.5 mi
Description:	Lakes, flatwater, quickwater, Class I
Date checked:	1998
Navigable:	Above RI 165, high or medium water: January through May. Passable at all water levels below RI 165.
Scenery:	Forested, rural, towns
Maps:	USGS Hope Valley, Carolina
Portages:	6 mi L Barberville Dam 70 yd
	8.5 mi L Wyoming Dam 200 yd
	9.5 mi R Hope Valley Dam 100 yd
	13.25 mi e Woodville Dam 70 yd
	15.75 mi R Alton Dam 100 yd

From RI 3, head west on RI 165 for 5.25 miles to Escoheag Hill Road. Go north for about 1 mile to the first right. Take the dirt road down a steep hill to the river.

For the first 2.5 miles to RI 165, the river is narrow and shallow. Most of the way there is quickwater with sharp turns.

Another put-in point is on the south side of RI 165, 3.5 miles west of RI 3. There is also access at Browning Mill Pond (reached by taking Roaring Brook Road). Two miles of quickwater are followed by 1.5 miles of dead water to the Barberville Dam. The rapids below the dam are shallow and in low water you should extend the portage around the dam to avoid the rapids.

Below Barberville Dam (6 mi) there is good current, then a mile of flatwater to Wyoming Pond at Skunk Hill Road, where there is good access. It is 0.75 mile across the millpond to the dam at the junction of RI 3 and RI 138, a favorite swimming spot.

The river is shallow below the Wyoming Dam (8.5 mi); portage 300 yards down RI 3 to the next bridge and put in below a power station. In another mile, portage the Hope Valley Dam. Take out on the right, cross the road, and put in 25 yards downstream of the bridge, after passing an old mill. In one-quarter mile there is a 6-inch dam you can easily run. In another quarter-mile the Wood passes under I-95. Gain access from the south side of Switch Road (Hope Valley/Woodville Road) at a parking area just south of the I-95 viaduct. You may want to shuttle from Wyoming to this point, thereby skipping two portages. The river then flows through scenic woods before reaching marshland above Woodville Dam (13.25 mi). Portage the dam from river right and cross the bridge.

After Woodville Dam the river deepens. Turn left at a fork. The current is steady. Laurel is abundant in this area. Marsh and forested banks give way to 0.75 mile of ponding above Alton Dam (15.75 mi), where there is a state launching area on the right.

At Alton, a portage of 100 yards on the right is followed by 0.75 mile of flatwater to the confluence with the Pawcatuck River (16.5 mi).

Charles River RI

The Charles River is formed by the confluence of the Usquepaug River and the Chipuxet River (just downstream of Worden Pond). This description starts just below there and ends at the confluence of the Charles and Wood Rivers, which is the beginning of the Pawcatuck River.

The old mill towns along the way are much the same as they were in the 1700s. From the parking lot at the Kenyon Mill, walk up the hill and visit the mill store. In Shannock, the house on the high dam was built in 1709. A suggested 18-mile trip starts at the Worden Pond access and ends at the Bradford access at RI 91/216 on the Pawcatuck River.

Biscuit City Landing ➤ Wood River		8.75 mi
Description:	Flatwater, Class II	
Date checked:	1998	
Navigable:	High and medium water: January through June, after heavy rain	
Scenery:	Forested, towns	
Maps:	USGS Kingston, Carolina	
Portages:	0.75 mi L dam in Kenyon 20 yd	
	1.5 mi L high dam in Shannock 20 yd	
	1.75 mi R low dam in Shannock 100 yd	
	3.5 mi L dam in Carolina 70 yd	
Campsite:	4 mi L Carolina Management area (state)	

To reach the access off RI 2, take Biscuit City Road about 0.5 mile north of the railroad crossing in Kenyon to Worden Pond Road and go 1.5 miles to the landing at Worden Pond. The outlet of Worden Pond is to the west (left) after you put in. There is flatwater past the high, arched, concrete RI 2 bridge (0.5 mi) to the dam at Kenyon (0.75 mi). Portage on the left 50 feet. There is less than a mile of flatwater to the high dam at Shannock. The carry is on the left for 50 feet; put in under the bridge. A short distance beyond is the low dam, which has been run, but this is not advised. The carry here is on the right. This dam is built at an old Indian fishing falls, and a fight over usage once occurred here between the Pequot and Narrangansett Indian tribes. A plaque is on the right bank. There is flatwater to Carolina (3.5 mi), where there is a dam at RI 112 which crosses the river on three bridges.

Below the left-hand bridge at Carolina is a Class II chute in high water that should be scouted. It is followed by 0.25 mile of easy

Class II rapids that are very scratchy in low water. At Richmond (5.25 mi) there is access off RI 91 next to a dam which is runnable in the center.

Below the Richmond dam (5.25 mi) there is a good current for 1.25 miles to a wooden bridge (6.5 mi). It is 2.25 miles to the confluence with the Wood River (8.75 mi).

Chipuxet River *RI*

The Chipuxet River rises in Exeter near Slocum and flows south through the Great Swamp to Worden Pond and then to the Pawcatuck River, which flows into Little Narragansett Bay. The entire river can be run throughout the year, but may require some dragging and skirmishes with overgrown brush.

Hundred Acre Poad ➤ Biscuit City Landing	9.75 mi
Description:	Flatwater, quickwater
Date checked:	1998
Navigable:	Anytime except during drought
Scenery:	Forested, wild
Maps:	USGS Slocum, Kingston

Put in at the bridge on Wolf Rocks Road just above the pond. It is about 1 mile through Hundred Acre Pond to the outlet at the south end, where there are some shallow riffles under the railroad bridge. Some dragging may be necessary to Thirty Acre Pond. RI 138 crosses 0.5 mile below Thirty Acre Pond at Taylor's Access (2 mi), an alternate put-in. The Chipuxet then flows through the Great Swamp, one of Rhode Island's natural treasures. To shuttle, go west on RI 138, south on RI 2, and left on Biscuit City Road.

One-half mile below Taylor's Access is a railroad bridge, with Worden Pond 2 miles farther. Exercise caution on Worden Pond, as it is shallow and gets choppy in a southerly wind. It is possible in bad weather to paddle left to cottages that line the east shore. In good weather, keep the island to your left as you paddle southwest to Stony Point. The route goes around Stony

Point and southwest to the next point. An old seaplane hangar can be seen in the cove to your right. Follow the south shore of the point until you reach the outlet, which can be difficult to spot, where you will re-enter the swamp (6.75 mi). Beware of overhanging poison ivy.

Here the river is narrow, winding, and enclosed by brush. You have to barge through. In approximately 0.25 mile you will approach a dock and pump house at the Great Swamp Management Area and the large impoundment where osprey are often sighted. Not long after the impoundment area you exit the swamp at the confluence with the Usquepaug (Queens) River (10 mi). At this point the river is known as the Charles River.

In 0.75 mile the river runs near railroad tracks. When the tracks come into view, look for a sign on a tree on the right that says Boat Landing. This will point you to a backwater leading to the Biscuit City landing and parking area. Access by car is off RI 2 on Kenyon School Road.

It is also possible to proceed another mile downriver, under RI 2, to the mill in Kenyon (12 mi). Take out on the right above the dam in the mill parking lot, reached by car by continuing south on RI 2 from Biscuit City and taking the first right after it crosses the river. Between Kenyon and Shannock there are three dams.

Pettaquamscutt River   *RI*
(locally called Narrow River)

The Pettaquamscutt River rises in North Kingston and after a short distance flows into Pausacaco Pond and then to tidewater. The upper reaches of the river, which are too small for motorboats, and the pond offer some very pleasant paddling.

Gilbert Stuart Road ➤ Mouth	6 mi
Description:	Tidal, marsh
Date checked:	1998
Navigable:	Passable at all water levels
Scenery:	Wild, forested, marsh, settled
Maps:	USGS Wickford, Narrangansett Pier

Put in from Gilbert Stuart Road, where there is parking for about 10 cars. Carry the canoe down a path to the river. The river is about 10 feet wide and runs for about 300 feet before opening to a pond 0.25 mile in diameter. Keep left going downriver to pass through another narrow channel into a second pond, which takes on the essence of a river. The river is more developed now, but it is lovely.

The river narrows slowly and after about 2 miles reaches an underpass (Lacey Bridge) where people fish from the bridge. Development below the bridge increases. Then suddenly a fragile marsh appears on the left. Look for osprey nests 2 feet in diameter atop telephone poles. Pass under Middle Bridge, another fishing spot. Eventually the river turns left and becomes tidal. To the right is the 600-acre Pettasquamscutt Wildlife Cove Refuge.

Powerboats can be a problem in the tidal area in the summer. This is also a popular spot for kayakers to go out into the surf. The tide at the mouth is 3 feet. Tides are about the same as Newport, or about 3.5 hours earlier than Boston.

Blackstone River *MA*

The Blackstone meanders 46 miles from Worcester, Massachusetts, to Pawtucket, Rhode Island, through urban developments, historic villages, farmlands, and forests. Once one of the most heavily industrialized rivers in New England, the river is being cleaned up (although a certain amount of pollution is to be expected) and developed as a park, the Blackstone River Valley National Heritage Corridor.

The Blackstone does have many isolated scenic stretches away from roads and mills. The area around Rice City Pond has been set aside as a state recreation area. There are also some challenging rapids. Parts of the canal that handled commerce between Worcester and Providence are still intact.

Worcester ➤ Rockdale   11 mi

Description:	Flatwater, quickwater, Class I, II, III, IV
Date checked:	1998
Navigable:	Medium to high water: April, May
Scenery:	Settled, towns, rural
Maps:	USGS Worcester South, Milford, Grafton
Portages:	0.75 mi L dam
	2 mi R rapids at Millbury (optional)
	2.75 mi e dam at power substation
	4 mi L dam
	5 mi e dam (optional)
	6 mi L dam
	8 mi e Fisherville dam
	9 mi R Farnumsville dam

The upper Blackstone is very enjoyable to paddle in spite of its degraded (but improving) water quality and the many dams. There is good current throughout, with some whitewater. The entire Blackstone in Massachusetts and Rhode Island will become the Blackstone River Valley National Heritage Corridor. There are signs for it along the Mass. Turnpike (I-90) and I-390.

The first practical access is just northwest of the Millbury Street/Ballard Street intersection in Worcester. There is ample parking at the mill.

Take the left channel at a small dam (0.75 mile) and portage. Quickwater follows below the US 20 (1 mi) and I-90 (1.25) bridges. Mixed flatwater and quickwater continue to Millbury Center (2 mi), where a short stretch of Class II begins adjacent to a mill building. At 2.25 miles the Blackstone turns left beneath a railroad bridge and drops in a stretch of Class II-IV rapids, which culminates in a narrow rocky channel beneath the South Main Street bridge. To portage this section, take out to the right of the railroad bridge and follow the tracks to the road crossing. It is possible to run the Class II portion and exit on the left bank above the South Main Street bridge; scout this area first. The portage follows Maple Street along the southerly bank of the river about 0.5 mile to the next bridge crossing.

Portage the dam located at a power substation (2.75 mi) on either side, and Singing Dam (4 mi), so called because of the strange rhythm made by the river flowing over it. Put in at the base of the dam or along a dirt road just beyond. The breached dam in Wilkinsonville (5 mi) is runnable, but the portage is probably better. Approach the Saundersville Dam on the left, and portage down the steps. The dam runoff can be entered from the eddy at the base.

At 6.5 miles the Blackstone divides in two. Cronin Brook joins the left branch; the right branch, a remnant of the Blackstone Canal, passes under the Pleasant Street bridge, then breaks into a 200-yard stretch of quickwater. Run the breached dam. At 8 miles the Blackstone becomes Fisherville Pond, where the Quinsigamond River enters on the left. The Quinsigamond is a pleasant 4-mile flatwater trip from the junction of MA 122 and MA 140 to Fisherville Pond. Carry over the stepped dam at Fisherville Mill to avoid the rapids to the left. To run the chute along the left bank below the dam, take out on the left bank just above the dam and carry down the steep slope just below the dam and enjoy the short Class II rapids in the old tailrace.

Portage, right, around the dam in Farnumsville (9 mi). From here is it a pleasant 2 miles to the takeout in Rockdale (11 mi). Access to this takeout is behind the chemical company on Sutton Street in Rockdale, one block west of MA 22.

Northbridge ➤ Blackstone	12.75 mi
Description:	Lake, flatwater, quickwater, Class I-II
Date checked:	1998
Navigable:	Passable at all water levels
Scenery:	Forested, towns
Maps:	USGS Grafton, Uxbridge, Blackstone
Portages:	3 mi R dam on Rice City Pond 100 yd
	12 mi L dam above Blackstone Gorge 100 yd
	(12.75 mi dam)

To reach the put-in, go east on Church Street from MA 122 between Northbridge and North Uxbridge. Put in at the bridge. There are 2.25 miles of quickwater and many turns to Rice City Pond (named for the large stands of wild rice growing in it). At the southern end (3 mi) the river divides; both branches spill over dams. Pass under the right-hand bridge. Avoid the left-hand bridge because there is a 6-foot waterfall under it. There is access at a picnic area by the bridge. This section is a portion of the Blackstone Canal. The river below the right-hand dam winds for 1.75 miles with quickwater around sharp corners to MA 16, just above which there is a mill on the right.

One-quarter mile below MA 16 (4.75 mi), the Mumford River enters on the right. The Blackstone meanders for the next two miles past the mouth of the West River (6 mi) to the MA 122 bridge (7.25 mi). The river straightens somewhat for the next 3.25 miles to the bridge at Millville. Here the river divides. There are very short Class II rapids on each side, with the left side being sportier.

A little more than 1.5 miles below the Millville bridge (10.5 mi) is a large dam more easily portaged on the left. Below the dam the river flows through Blackstone Gorge. This is an isolated, granite gorge with 600 yards of Class IV-V rapids that are difficult and dangerous in high water. They begin just below the dam and run through an S-turn that begins to the left. They end with a turbulent chute which is best run in the middle. Scout this section from the left bank.

At the end of the gorge, the Branch River (12.5 mi) enters on the right. You can begin a trip on the Branch River along RI 146A in North Smithfield, Rhode Island, to avoid the gorge. Below the gorge the outflow from the hydroelectric diversion returns to the Blackstone on the left, followed closely by the takeout, also on the left. Note the old Tupperware mill complex on the left. Portage, right, under the third of three closely spaced bridges to avoid a 5-foot dam (12.75 mi).

The top of the gorge can be reached by traveling south on Staples Lane (a private way shown as Rolling Dam Road on some maps) or west on County Road, both off MA 122 in Blackstone. There is a small park at the gorge with a hiking trail and limited parking. Below the gorge, the takeout is behind the old Tupperware mill at a baseball field and park. It can be reached via Old Mendon Street south of MA 122.

The river in Rhode Island, with 10 dams below the gorge, becomes increasingly urban but is clean enough to support trout in downtown Woonsocket. Some of the dams are quite dangerous. Obtain the "Blackstone River Canoe Guide" from the Blackstone River Valley National Heritage Corridor (One Depot Square, Woonsocket, RI 02895) for complete details.

Taunton River *MA*

The Taunton River basin, 530 square miles, is the second largest drainage area in Massachusetts. The river has one of the flattest courses in the state, with only a 20-foot difference along the 40-mile length of the main stem. Its mouth is at Fall River. It forms a part of the Wampanoag Commemorative Canoe Passage, a twisting series of waterways that connect Massachusetts Bay to Narragansett Bay.

The Taunton is the coming together of several streams. Southwest of Brockton the Hockomock flows into the Town River. Southeast of Brockton the Satucket flows into the Matfield. In Bridgewater the Matfield and Town Rivers join to form the Taunton River. Below the city of Taunton the river is tidal, and many large cabin cruisers are berthed here.

Although there are many towns in the region through which the Taunton flows, it manages to avoid most of them. It flows along the edge of some fields, but most of the way the river is lined with thick woods and tangled underbrush. This is a nice, if not environmentally ideal, river for exploration.

MA 104 ➤ Taunton		21.25 mi
Description:	Flatwater, Class I	
Date checked:	1998	
Navigable:	Passable at all water levels	
Scenery:	Forested, rural, towns	
Maps:	USGS Bridgewater, Taunton	
Portage:	0 mi R dam below MA 104 20 yd	

East of Bridgewater, MA 104 crosses the Taunton River near some old factories. Just below the bridge there is a dam that backs up water on both the Matfield and Town Rivers. Portage 20 yards on the right. The Winnetuxet River enters on the left after 3.25 miles. Many bridges cross the river. The second one is partially collapsed (3.75 mi). The fourth is a railroad bridge beside a brick factory, and then, just below a power line, is the mouth of the Nemasket River (6.75 mi) on the left.

Under the fifth bridge, Titicut Road (7.75 mi), are some Class I riffles. Then comes MA 18/28 (8.25 mi). Just above the next two bridges are riffles that are flooded out in high water. Then you pass under MA 25 (no access) and US 44 (12.75 mi).

The biggest rapids, but still only Class I, are under the Church Street bridge, an old stone structure that constricts the flow of the river into several narrow passages. Many canoeists on the Taunton River lack whitewater skills, and this is where they run into trouble. The waves are biggest, and the current trickiest, in high water.

Pass below a bridge beside a factory in East Taunton at 15.25 miles, where there are many long, overgrown stone-wall embankments lining the riverbank. After considerable winding, the river flows under MA 24 (no access). In the city of Taunton there are several more bridges beyond a closed girder bridge (19.75 mi) next to US 44. The first bridge below the two railroad bridges is MA 140 (21.25 mi), and the Mill River enters on the right just beyond it.

Canoeing beyond Wier Village is not recommended. Beware of tidal influence, strong winds on open water, underwater obstructions, and powerboat wakes.

At high tide there are no rapids as you pass through Taunton. High tide occurs about 2.5 hours earlier than Boston; low tide about one hour earlier. The tide varies between 2.5 and 3.5 feet.

Hockomock and Town Rivers MA

The Hockomock River flows south from Brockton and, with the addition of Quisset Brook, meets the Town River, which then flows generally eastward to Bridgewater, where it joins the Matfield River to form the Taunton River.

The Hockomock is a small, meandering stream that flows for much of its length through meadows and along the edges of fields. Most of the Hockomock Swamp is owned or controlled by the

Massachusetts Division of Fisheries and Wildlife. Its meanders are very tight. Windfalls have not been cleared, making paddling above MA 106 difficult. It would be an interesting area if it were brushed out.

The Town River flows out of Nippenicket Pond in Bridgewater and within a mile is joined by the Hockomock. This upper section is overgrown, but it is regularly paddled and brushed out. The river below the confluence with the Hockomock is noticeably wider. A good trip at high or medium water is the 8 miles of the Town River from Nippenicket Pond in Bridgewater to the High Street dam in the same town. At low water, the five miles between the Scotland Street bridge and the High Street bridge in Bridgewater are recommended. You may want to skip the 4 miles of river below the High Street dam to MA 104 because of pollution and debris.

Nippenicket Pond (Bridgewater) ➤ High Street Dam	8 mi
Description:	Flatwater, quickwater
Date checked:	1999
Navigable:	High and medium water: March through May
	Low water: E of MA 24 only
Scenery:	Marsh, rural, settled
Maps:	USGS Brockton, Taunton, Whitman, Bridgewater
Portages:	4 mi R old stone bridge (high water only) 10 yd
	5 mi e Forest Street bridge (high water only) 20 yd
	6 mi L dam at War Memorial Park 10–100 yd

Put in at Nippenicket Pond at the state fishermen's access landing off MA 104, just west of MA 24. At the northern end of Nippenicket Pond, go to the left of the point with stonework and hug the shore. The river exit (1.25 mi) is within 200 yards. The river meanders through alders and willows, but the channel can be followed in high to medium water. It is often marked with surveyor's ribbon.

The meeting with the Hockomock (2 mi) is shortly before the MA 24 bridge (no access) and the Scotland Street bridge (3 mi). To reach the river at Scotland Street, go east on MA 106 from MA 24.

Take the first right (Lincoln Street), bear right onto Elm Street, then bear left onto Scotland Street. Parking is minimal here.

After the Scotland Street bridge the river is wider, deeper, and more sluggish. There is an old stone bridge and three road bridges before you reach the first dam. About 0.25 mile below the stone bridge there is a ridge with large pines on the right bank, which makes a pleasant lunch spot. The Forest Street bridge has been constructed with low supporting timbers and must be carried at high water.

Take out on the left side of the pond at War Memorial Park (6 mi). Access to the park is southwest on River Street from the junction of MA 28 and MA 106. To continue, carry to the main river below the spillway. If the water is high or too low, put in past the MA 28 bridge; do not run the canals. There is dangerous low stonework from an old bridge under the MA 28 bridge. It is flatwater below the MA 28 bridge for 2.5 miles through the marshes to the dam at High Street. To reach the takeout, follow Main Street for 1 mile past the MA 18/28–MA 104 junction and turn right onto High Street. There is also a fishermen's access with parking off Ash Street.

High Street ➤ MA 104   4 mi

This section is not recommended. This description is not current. From the High Street dam, portage 100 yards from the right-hand channel across the island and put in below the left-hand dam. Low water may require a longer carry. After 200 yards of quickwater the two channels rejoin. The river is flat as it passes north of Bridgewater in a little valley. Debris in the river becomes more noticeable, especially near a shopping center adjacent to the MA 18 bridge. The river passes under Haywood Street (3 mi) before entering the dead water at the confluence of the Matfield and Town Rivers. Follow the right shore and continue south down the Taunton River for 0.5 mile to the bridge on MA 104 (4 mi).

Satucket and Matfield Rivers *MA*

The Satucket River flows into the Matfield in East Bridgewater. Both rivers form a part of the Wampanoag Commemorative Canoe Passage. In Bridgewater the Matfield and Town Rivers join to form the Taunton River.

The Satucket is a small river that winds past active farms and through woods. Fallen trees can be a problem. The water is clean but dark. The Matfield is a dirty river, and its turbid water is in marked contrast to that of the Satucket at the confluence.

The woods and meadows along the river are very attractive and seemingly isolated, although they are experiencing real estate development.

Robbins Pond ➤ MA 104		8.25 mi
Description:	Flatwater	
Date checked:	1998	
Navigable:	Passable at most water levels	
Scenery:	Forested, rural, towns	
Maps:	USGS Whitman, Bridgewater	
Portage:	4.5 mi e dam at Plymouth Street 100 yd	

To put in, follow Pond Street northeast from MA 106 to the outlet of Robbins Pond. The Satucket River winds around pastures on the left. Beware of barbed wire and a low bridge. Poor Meadow Brook (0.5 mi) may be passable from MA 27 in Hanson.

After the Washington Street bridge (1.75 mi) the river is noticeably wider. Past Bridge Street (3.25 mi), where there is good access, the river reaches the backwater of the Plymouth Street Dam. If you can pass under the MA 106 bridge, take out on the left just above the dam and portage past all the buildings. If the water is high, take out on the right, go around the fence 100 yards above the bridge, portage along MA 106 to the right of the factory, and put in from the parking lot.

Below the dam (4.5 mi) the river winds in a small wooded valley. After 1.5 miles the Satucket River flows into the Matfield in a wide marsh. The Matfield enters on the right and is noticeably dirtier. After passing under two bridges, the Matfield goes under some power lines and joins the Town River to form the Taunton River.

Past a small dump and a peninsula on the left, the Taunton River flows for 0.5 mile south to the MA 104 bridge (8.25). It is easy to miss this turn. Take out above the bridge on the right.

Nemasket River *MA*

The Nemasket flows north from a series of ponds in Lakeville through Middleboro to the Taunton River. It is one of the prettiest rivers in eastern Massachusetts. Because Assawompset Pond and its connecting ponds are the water supply for Taunton, you must put in downstream of them.

Vaugh Street Bridge ➤ Taunton River	11 mi
Description:	Flatwater, quickwater
Date checked:	1998
Navigable:	Passable at all water levels
Scenery:	Forested, rural, towns
Maps:	USGS Assawompset, Bridgewater
Portages:	3.25 mi R dams at Municipal Light Plant 50 yd
	5.25 mi e dam at Oliver Mill Park (low water) 30 yd

Put in at the Vaugh Street bridge. Vaughn Street is 1.1 miles south of I-495 at Exit 4, MA 105, and the bridge is to the left about 1 mile. The river meanders through marshes to the municipal light plant. Do not go under the bridge but take out on the right, carry across the road, and put in by the fish ladder.

There is 0.75 mile of quickwater below the dam, then a rocky Class I drop as the river passes through a breach in an old canal wall. The dam at Oliver Mill Park just before the US 44 bridge (5.25 mi) must be carried in low water. The park is an ideal place to put in for easy trips that continue on the Taunton River.

Below US 44 the river winds past a sewage-treatment plant and through forests and marshes for 4.5 miles to the Taunton River. The two bridges, Plymouth Street (7.25 mi) and Murdock Street (8 mi), can be reached by following roads on either side of the river north from US 44. Be careful of the S-approach to the Plymouth Street bridge in high water and use the center span. You may have to carry this bridge. Murdock Street is a fair access point.

There are large meanders under a power line as you approach a railroad bridge and the confluence with the Taunton River (10 mi). The first takeout from the Taunton River is 1 mile downstream at Titicut Street (11 mi), south of the Bridgewater State Prison and reachable from MA 18/28 via Plymouth Street.

Wading and Three Mile Rivers *MA*

The Wading River flows from Lake Mirimichi off MA 106 in Foxboro southeast through Mansfield and into Norton, where it meets the Rumford River. At that point it becomes the Three Mile River, which flows through Taunton. These small, isolated streams wind through woodlands, swamps, and small millponds.

These rivers are passable for a total of 18 miles from Lake Mirimichi to MA 140 just outside Taunton.

The Wading River is a small stream that offers all types of canoeing in early spring (late March) through the summer (some spots will have to be portaged), and usually into the late fall. The area from Barrowsville Pond to the first bridge at MA 140 offers the best canoeing on the river. It is a good spot for the beginning canoeist who lives in the greater Providence area and wants to spend either a whole day or an afternoon paddling on this river, which is 45 minutes from downtown Providence. It's a popular river with the local paddlers in the spring high water, although outside of the immediate area it is basically unknown.

Barrowsville Pond ➤ MA 140   3.5 mi

Description:	Pond, quickwater, Class I, II
Date checked:	1998
Navigable:	Medium to high water
Scenery:	Forested, settled, towns
Maps:	USGS Wrentham, Attleboro, Norton
Portage:	1 mi dam at end of pond; low bridge

Starting at Barrowsville Pond, at Power Road, there is a 0.5-mile paddle across the pond itself to the outlet at the southeastern corner. Portage around the dam. The river then passes under Barrows Road and runs next to a mill on the right. Here the water starts to become quick; watch for rocks. The next 0.5 mile to a millpond is quick, easy, Class I water. At the millpond are the remains of an old colonial gristmill; the waterway on which the wheel was used has widened sufficiently to create a Class II stretch, which can be run in high water. This rapid should be scouted from the left. This area is a good playing spot that can be portaged back around and run several times before continuing downstream. In high water the waves can become as high as 3 to 4 feet, and there is a turn that will require some planning. In low water, this rapid becomes scratchy. Directly below is a large pool with a footbridge that is too low to run and will have to be portaged. The next 0.5 mile to the chute is just quickwater.

Upon reaching the chute, scouting is not usually required (except in low water), as this chute is as straight as an arrow and generally free of obstructions. This is a good run in high water (Class II) and a short portage in low. The next mile to the bridge at MA 140 is easy quickwater, with an occasional fallen tree and midstream boulder. At the bridge at is a 2-to-3-foot ledge, with a midstream boulder directly at the bottom of the chute. This should definitely be scouted. High water makes this boulder difficult to miss, as it is only a canoe's length away from the bottom of the chute. Takeout is possible on the other side of the bridge, just before the gauge station on the left. There is ample parking on either side of the bridge, which is usually fairly full.

MA 140 ➤ Taunton River   7 mi

After this point, the river continues through a swamp and becomes overgrown. It is very hard to follow the river as it winds through a maze of trees, and it is definitely not recommended at any time or level. Although the river before MA 140 is fairly clean and the scenery attractive, the stretch below the swamp starts to become noticeably polluted, increasingly so the closer you get to Taunton. The scenery becomes unattractive. The height of ugliness is the sewage-treatment plant in Taunton.

Copicut and Shingle Island Rivers *MA*

Map: USGS Fall River East

These two rivers in Dartmouth are part of the drainage of the East Branch of the Westport River. The mile on the Copicut River from Cornell Pond on Hixville Road to the confluence with the Shingle Island River is quite attractive. The mile on the Shingle Island River below the confluence to Lake Noquochoke is reported to be overgrown. Paddling at high water is recommended.

Mattapoisett River *MA*

The Mattapoisett is a small stream that rises in Snipatuit Pond and flows to Buzzards Bay. The water is very dark, and for most of the distance the river meanders with a good current through brushy swamps. The brush is clipped, and there is a clear passage. There is an annual canoe race every May or June, in which contestants use homemade canoes. There are occasional houses, farms, and cranberry bogs.

Snipatuit Pond ➤ Mattapoisett		12.25 mi
Description:	Lake, flatwater, quickwater	
Date checked:	1999	
Navigable:	High water: above MA 105, early spring	
	Passable at most water levels below MA 105	
Scenery:	Forested, rural	
Maps:	USGS Snipatuit Pond, Marion	
Portages:	7.75 mi e complex of dams 10 yd	

Neck Road in Rochester crosses the north end of Snipatuit Pond, and it is 1.75 miles from there to the southeast corner of the pond (to the left of a farm) where the river begins. After about 0.25 mile in woods the stream enters a meadow.

A recommended put-in is at Snipatuit Road (2.75 mi), where there is a complex of ponds associated with a fish hatchery. Class I rapids lead to Hartley Road (3.25 mi). The stream is unobstructed as it flows across the bottom of an empty millpond to the remains of Rounseville Dam (4.25 mi), which is runnable at high water.

At MA 105 the river opens up, but soon closes again. The river from here on has enough water to be canoeable all year. One and a half miles below MA 105 (4.25 mi) you reach New Bedford Road (5.75 mi), and 1.5 miles after that you enter an old millpond. The broken dam is easily run in high water. Below Wolf Island Road (7.75 mi), there is a cranberry bog on the right and a dam that must be portaged. The river re-enters the bushes, passes through two old bridge abutments (9.75 mi), and finally breaks out into the clear at the Acushnet Road bridge.

The rest is easy. The river passes under I-195, and there are some Class I rapids before you reach a stone bridge (12 mi), a good takeout. The fish weir just above the MA 6 bridge (12.25 mi) can be run, and at low tide there is some quickwater below the bridge.

Weweantic River MA

The Weweantic River rises in East Carver, provides a portion of the boundary separating Carver and Middleboro, and flows south toward Wareham. It flows through the Great Cedar Swamp and other marshy areas, through heavily wooded areas, and around cranberry bogs.

To reach Popes Point bridge, take MA 58 south to the first right (Meadow Street), 1 mile south of Carver Center. Take the second right (1.75 mi) onto Popes Point Road. From Popes Point bridge, the river winds a lot. In 1.5 miles you will come to a pump house at a fork in the river; go left. In 700 feet you will see power lines. Keep the power lines to the south. This is a very swampy area and the channel is not obvious at high water. Bear left at the fork by the power lines. When portaging the old mill just above the East Street bridge, be alert for metal spikes. To reach the East Street bridge by car, head southwest on Meadow Street, bearing right to the end. Turn right on Rochester Road to East Street.

Below East Street the river takes a sharp left. There are rocks at low water. The Weweantic is a narrow winding river at this point, with good tree cover. In 1.5 miles you come to an old flume with uprights. Go through the middle. You will see cranberry bogs in this area. The river then reaches the MA 58 bridge and passes through cranberry bogs for another mile. Passage is more difficult below the

Gibbs Cranberry Bog Dam, and it is recommended only at high water. After 1.5 miles you will go under MA 25 and then MA 28. The river then widens and reaches a small pond. Take out at the hydroelectric dam at the end of the pond. To reach the dam's dirt access road, go left on MA 28 from MA 58, then right on Carver Road.

It is five to six hours from Popes Point to East Street, another 2.5 to three hours to MA 58, and another 2.5 to three hours to the hydroelectric dam.

Agawam River MA

This river flows south through cranberry country to Buzzards Bay. It is a small stream with unusually clear water and a fairly dependable flow as it leaves Halfway Pond in Plymouth. This flow is subject to interruption in the fall, however, because the river is dammed in several places to provide water to flood the cranberry bogs when there is danger of frost.

The first 3.5 miles to Glen Charlie Pond are the most attractive. The scenery is varied: cranberry bogs, ponds, pitch pine forests, and a winding stream. Large sections of the two lakes at the end are developed, especially on the east shores.

The river is a delight in November after the cranberry-picking season, when the bogs are a dark maroon color. There are a few places where bogs are right next to the river, and you can collect overlooked cranberries from the canoe.

Halfway Pond ➤ Wareham		8 mi
Description:	Lakes, flatwater, quickwater, tidal	
Date checked:	1998	
Navigable:	High or medium water: spring and fall	
Scenery:	Forested, rural, settled	
Maps:	USGS Sagamore, Wareham	
Portages:	0.25 mi R low bridge 10 yd	
	0.25 mi L diversion dam 20 yd	
	1.25 mi L reservoir dam 20 yd	
	3.25 mi L dam on Stump Lake 10 yd	
	5 mi L dam on Glen Charlie Pond 10 yd	
	5.25 mi R dam 10 yd	
	7 mi R dam on Mill Pond 20 yd	

Begin at Halfway Pond, which is east of Myles Standish State Forest in Plymouth. The river leaves the south end of the pond and in 200 yards passes a dirt road. Soon there is a small cranberry bog on the right, and then the first carry. In a short distance the stream passes through a cranberry bog for 0.5 mile, requiring a carry around a diversion dam. At the end of the bog (0.75 mi), the canoe must be dragged along some boards in a large culvert. Soon the stream opens into a reservoir.

Below the reservoir dam (1.25 mi) is another large cranberry bog, which extends along the river for 0.75 mile. Then there is a very nice half-mile quickwater run through an open pitch pine forest. Just before you enter Stump Lake (2.5 mi) there is an old bridge that canoes can be dragged over.

Stump Lake has many surprises just below the surface. In spite of the crystal-clear water, the submerged stumps are not easy to spot. Below the dam (3.25 mi) a short stretch of quickwater leads to Glen Charlie Pond. Pass a number of houses and a wide bay on the left, and continue more or less straight to the dam (5 mi).

Shortly after Glen Charlie Pond is another dam (5.25 mi), some quickwater, and then Mill Pond. Follow the left shore 1.5 miles to the dam.

At the end of Mill Pond (7 mi), carry across the westbound lane of US 6/MA 28 and run quickwater beneath the bridge carrying the eastbound lane, below which you reach tidewater. The river swings to the right through salt marshes and passes under US 6 (8 mi), just past which there is good access on the right.

Bass River MA

The Bass offers diverse scenery along its route. From its mouth at West Dennis Beach, it passes north into a series of wide ponds separated by narrows. In the ponds canoes will be influenced by southwest winds. In the narrows, there are short stretches of tidal current. At the mouth, saltbox houses give way to moored yachts. The middle section is bordered by conservation land, some of the last undeveloped property on the Cape. The uppermost pond usually has warm-water swimming by mid-May.

West Dennis Beach ➤ Mill Pond	7 mi

Description:	Flatwater, quickwater, tidal
Date checked:	1998
Navigable:	All year
Scenery:	Settled, forested, marsh, cranberry bogs
Map:	USGS Dennis

A southwest wind will help paddlers putting in at the mouth and paddling to Mill Pond. It is also advisable to put in one or two hours before high tide, which at the mouth is one hour behind Boston.

Put in on the west side of the Loring Avenue culvert next to the West Dennis Beach traffic circle. Park by the side of the rotary or in the beach parking area. Boat, canoe, and kayak launching from the beach is prohibited. This section runs west between residential docks and low sand dunes before turning right into the main channel. Paddling north toward the tall MA 28 bridge (2 mi), you'll see how well you judged the wind and tide. Under the bridge, the Bass slackens as it enters the first of six wide areas. After passing the dead-end cove on the right, paddle straight ahead toward the Bass River Country Club (2.5 mi). Take the channel on your right, keeping the country club on your left as you enter the second and largest wide area.

Here you can explore Grand Cove on your right, adding 2.5 miles to your trip, or proceed with Salt Box Beach on the left to a sharp left bend past a public landing (good access) and under the Great Western Road bridge (3.5 mi). You have now reached South Dennis by paddling north from West Dennis (navigational logic endemic to New England)! The town conservation land on the right, 0.5 mi before the US 6 bridge (4.5 mi), is a superb picnic spot. A large rock in the river has a cylindrical hole in it, which natives claim was used by the Vikings as a mooring. Native Americans used this area as a fishing village.

From here the Bass constricts into its 500-yard-long narrows, where tidal influence is greatest. Tides here are four hours later than at the mouth. Current under the US 6 bridge forms 3-foot standing waves twice a day, halfway between high and low tides, which weaken to nothing at full high and low. Careful timing, as indicated above, will give you favorable current.

Above US 6 (4.5 mi) tidal influence is minimal. The Bass widens into Kelleys Bay on the right and Dinahs Pond on the left. Continue by taking the channel between them. Another constriction leads to Follins Pond (5.25 mi). Keep to the left shore until the pond is behind you and a creek that forks (6 mi) is ahead. The narrow channel on the right leads to Mill Pond. Avoid the wider channel on the left, which soon ends in a small pond. The right channel leads to a shallow creek that passes through a stone-lined culvert under North Dennis Road (6.25 mi). The culvert is narrow enough to allow paddlers to grip both walls and pull the canoe through. The upper reaches of the Bass take on a wilderness quality. The quiet backwater slowly opens up into Mill Pond, which is far enough from the ocean to contain very little salt. Its dark waters and shallow bottom make Mill Pond one of the first warm swimming spots of the year. Outward Reach Road (7 mi) comes down to the pond shore on the right, making an ideal takeout.

Scorton Creek MA

Ploughed Neck Road ➤ Scorton Neck   4 mi
Description: Tidal
Date checked: 1998
Map: USGS Sandwich

Put in at the mouth of the creek at Cape Cod Bay. Go 0.1 mile east of the railroad crossing on MA 6A, north on Ploughed Neck Road for 0.8 mile to North Shore Boulevard, and right almost to the end of the road. Turn right between cottages to reach the put-in. Parking is limited.

For an alternate put-in, go south of the MA 6A bridge and east of Ploughed Neck Road to the former state bird farm entrance. You have to buck the tide if you put in here: there are sandbars at the bridge at low tide.

Do not plan on crossing the dunes to the beach. Pull up canoes on the east shore of the creek mouth and walk around to the end of the dunes.

There are 4 miles of creek to explore, with good bird-watching.

CHAPTER 7

Atlantic Coastal Watersheds

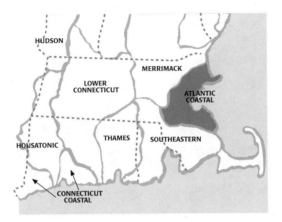

ATLANTIC COASTAL WATERSHEDS

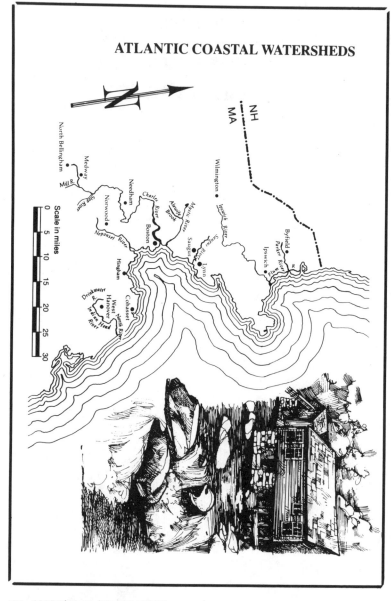

NH
MA

North Bellingham

Medway

Mill R.

Stop River

Norwood

Needham

Charles River

Alewife Brook

Boston

Neponset River

Wilmington

Mystic River

Ipswich River

Saugus River

Saugus

Lynn

Ipswich

Byfield

Parker River

Plum Island River

R.

Hingham

Drinkwater R.

West Hanover

Cohasset

North River

Indian Head River

Scale in miles

0
5
10
15
20
25
30

The rivers in this section drain eastern Massachusetts and flow eastward to the Atlantic Ocean. Due to their close proximity to population centers, the most desirable rivers are heavily used, and both public and private agencies work continuously to protect their scenic attractiveness and recreational access.

The canoeing season extends from early spring to late fall. Only the Drinkwater and Indian Head Rivers, described as part of the North River, require high water for easy passage.

Good rapids, though short, are to be found at all seasons at the Cohasset Tidal Rips. There are some rapids on the Drinkwater and Indian Head Rivers, but they are not likely to satisfy a whitewater enthusiast's desire.

In addition, two sections of tidewater not associated with rivers are included; they have some special interest for canoeists.

SOUTH RIVER *MA*

The South River rises mysteriously in the swamps and ponds in the northwest corner of Duxbury and flows 14 miles to meet the North River virtually at the mouth of the latter.

Marshfield ➤ North River		8 mi
Description:	Flatwater, tidal	
Date checked:	1998	
Navigable:	Year-round	
Scenery:	Forested, settled	
Maps:	USGS Duxbury, Hanover, Scituate	

Put in at the Willow Street bridge off MA 139/3A. Parking is limited along Willow Street. Watch for poison ivy. You can also put in down the steep bank at the MA 139/3A bridge just above Willow Street, at Veterans' Memorial Park. In high water you may have to portage the Willow Street bridge (low clearance), so you might as well put in there.

Leaving Marshfield, the river meanders through acres of salt marsh. Shorebirds, gulls, hawks, cormorants, bay ducks, egrets, heron, and osprey are common in this area. Farther along you come to the sand dunes of Humarock, with permanent settlement on the east bank.

The river narrows under the Julian Street bridge (5 mi), causing the tidal current to be very strong and difficult to paddle against. Check the tide table before you set out.

Once under the Sea Street bridge (5.5 mi) the river widens even more and becomes an estuary. Watch for strong winds and rough water in this final stretch. The creeks offer a more protected route and interesting exploration. The South River empties through a narrow gut between Trouant Island and a sand spit extension of Fourth Cliff. This gut and the river mouth are very dangerous waters and not safe for small boating. A portage over the cartway to Trouant Island will take you to Macombers Creek, which flows into the North River and avoids the confluence of the two rivers and the unpredictable mouth.

North River MA

This river has a freshwater and a tidal section. It is formed in Pembroke by the confluence of Indian Head River and Herring Brook. The lower North River is the tidal portion. Herring Brook and the Indian Head River require high water for paddling; the North River is passable at high or low tide, with high tide preferred.

The upper reaches have much to offer. The swamps are home to varied wildlife and are awash in color throughout the paddling season. The lower portions, tidal in nature, are wonderfully attractive too.

West Hanover ➤ MA 3A   15.75 mi

Description:	Lakes, flatwater, Class I-II, tidal
Date checked:	1998 (North River only—upper section not current)
Navigable:	High water: recommended for freshwater sections, early spring
	Medium water: scratchy in freshwater sections, spring and late fall
Scenery:	Forested, settled
Maps:	USGS Whitman, Hanover, Weymouth, Scituate
Portages:	1.25 mi L 2d King Street bridge 30 yd
	2.75 mi R dam on Factory Pond 10 yd
	4 mi L dam in South Hanover 100 yd
	5.5 mi e dam at Elm Street 30 yd

The first put-in is from MA 139 in West Hanover. After the King Street bridge (0.5 mi) there is 0.25 mile of Class II rapids that are scratchy in medium water. You may have to portage the next King Street bridge (1.25 mi) in high water because of low clearance. The dam at the outlet of Forge Pond can be run, and it leads to a narrow, shallow Class II rapid. Halfway down at an old bridge is a dam with a 1-foot drop that can be lined. There is a bridge across Factory Pond just before it hooks around to the left. Portage the dam (2.75 mi) on the right beside the factory. Flatwater continues as the stream passes under a bridge and through a swampy area with some small, passable debris dams. At the South Hanover Dam (4 mi), take out at the culvert on the left if the water is high.

Below the dam in South Hanover there are 100 yards of Class II rapids, with flatwater for 0.25 mile to a shorter Class II drop that is runnable if not blocked. After another 0.5 mile of mostly flatwater there is a Class II drop at an old dam site beside a factory up on the left bank. The river soon enters the deadwater behind the dam at Elm Street, where there is good access.

Below Elm Street (5.5 mi) the Indian Head River enters the tidal marshes. There is good access from Riverside Drive about 0.25

mile below Elm Street. Indian Head Drive may be unmarked, as is the launch area. There is plenty of parking, and access to the river is easy.

A short paddle downstream takes you to the "crotch" where the Indian Head and Herring Brook join to form the North River. The lower sections of the North River are subject to a strong tidal current. At its mouth the tides are the same as Boston, but upstream, at the MA 53 bridge in Hanover, they are as much as three hours later.

The North River snakes for 10.5 miles to Massachusetts Bay. It is continuously bordered by marshes, and several markers identify the sites of colonial shipyards. There are five road crossings between Elm Street and the ocean. The first two are MA 53/139 and, a few hundred yards farther, Washington Street in Hanover. Access is difficult at these bridges. The next crossing is MA 3 (no access). About 1 mile below MA 3 is a nice picnic spot at Blueberry Island on the south side of the river. The next road crossing is Bridge Street in Norwell, where there is good access. The final bridge is MA 3A (15.75 mi) where there is access through marinas. A final access is available from the Driftway in Scituate about 0.75 mile back up the First Herring Brook on your left, about 1 mile below MA 3A.

The open ocean is 1.75 miles below MA 3A at New Inlet, where the North and South Rivers meet and flow into the ocean. The very strong tidal currents in New Inlet may present a hazard, especially with an outgoing tide and/or a strong offshore breeze.

Cohasset Tidal Rips MA

Situated between Cohasset Harbor and the Gulf (an estuarine waterway lying to the south), the Rips is frequently used for whitewater instruction and practice by canoeists and kayakers. It is located on the south side of Cohasset Harbor just seaward of the Border Street bridge.

Beginning at high tide, the water flows out for nine hours. As the level of Cohasset Harbor drops, a short, narrow, and turbulent rapid is exposed. At its most difficult stage, near low tide, it is Class

VI and too rough for open canoes. Kayakers attempting it must know what they are doing, for there is a danger of both boat and body getting injured on the ledges.

The best conditions for practice in canoes begin when the rapids reverse midway on the incoming tide. Within the three hours preceding high tide, the rapids build up to a wide Class II pitch with heavy waves and strong eddies. The current begins to lessen about one hour before high tide, when the flow reverses again. Tide times are about the same as Boston.

Boston Harbor Islands MA

Boston Harbor contains some 30 islands, 17 of which are cooperatively managed as a state park by the Department of Environmental Management (DEM) and the Metropolitan District Commission (MDC). The Boston Harbor Islands were designated in 1996 by President Clinton as a National Recreation Area (part of the national park system). After arriving by ferry at Georges Island, you can take the free water taxi to Bumpkin, Gollops, Lovells, Peddocks, and Grape Islands.

The islands feature sandy beaches, flowering meadows, historic forts, hiking paths, birds, and wildlife. During the summer months special programs are run on many of the islands.

Ferry service is available from Long Wharf in Boston, Hewitts Cove in Hingham, and Squantum Point Park in Quincy. Fares are $8.00 for adults, $7.00 for seniors, and $6.00 for children under 12.

In addition, Higham Bay is sufficiently sheltered so that islands are easily accessible to paddlers in moderate weather and most stages of the tide.

Contact Boston Harbor Islands State Park visitor services (781-740-1605) for more information about the islands, ferry schedules, special programs, or camping permits.

Neponset River MA

The Neponset meanders from Foxboro to Dorchester Bay. After more than 10,000 years of human habitation, the Neponset is not a pristine river system, but it still provides nearly 150,000 people with clean drinking water and offers diverse natural, historic, and recreation areas. Despite the large number of people who live and work near the Neponset, it is sometimes referred to as the "Hidden River" because it can be so hard to find. The Neponset Watershed Association, 2438 Washington Street, Canton, MA 02021 (781-575-0354) is working to protect and restore the Neponset and the surrounding watershed, and has recently published an explorer's guide to the Neponset Watershed.

Norwood ➤ Hyde Park	9.5 mi
Description:	Flatwater, Class I
Date checked:	1995, 1997
Navigable:	High and medium water: January through May and after heavy rain. It is passable at all water levels below Exit 11 off I-95
Scenery:	Forested, settled, urban
Maps:	USGS Norwood, Blue Hills

With the exception of a few riffles on the lower part of the river, canoeing on the Neponset is all flatwater. The river is passable all year below Norwood.

The most upstream put-in is the Bade Canoe Launch in Norwood. (Park in the back left corner of the parking lot at Groundwater Technologies, 100 River Ridge Drive). The river is relatively narrow here and may be scratchy for the first half-mile during late summer. During drought conditions, start at Neponset Street or Paul's Bridge.

Just before you come to the Neponset Street Canoe Access, the East Branch comes in on the right. The East Branch carries as much as and sometimes more water than the upper section of the main stem.

One mile after crossing under I-95 (for the second time) you will pass Signal Hill on your right. It may be obscured by foliage. The light-aircraft traffic comes and goes from the Norwood Airport on the left.

Three-quarters of a mile below Signal Hill, Purgatory Brook enters on the left. On your right you will see your first buildings since the Bade Canoe Launch. About 500 feet below the

Dedham Street bridge is a small stretch of quickwater. Just below the railroad bridge Pecunit Brook enters on the right.

Below the MA 128 bridge (5 miles) the river enters the northern section of the Fowl Meadow, an extensive area of wildlife habitats. The Paul's Bridge Canoe Access is another 2.5 miles below. Just downstream of Paul's Bridge you emerge from Fowl Meadow and cross into the urban stretch of the Neponset. Mother Brook, the first man-made canal in the United States, enters on your left 1.75 miles below Paul's Bridge.

Below Mother Brook, your progress is blocked by the Tileston and Hollingsworth Dam, which has no public portage. From here you have to paddle back to Paul's Bridge and put in below the T&H Dam.

The next put-in point below the T&H Dam is at Ryan Playground in Mattapan Square. Heading downstream from the playground, you will pass through wild rice fields that cover the small islands in the middle of the river. The Central Avenue bridge will be just ahead. Only experienced paddlers should continue past this point, since there are stronger currents followed by a large drop at the Lower Mills Dam.

Below the Lower Mills Dam the Neponset widens in an estuary and ends at Boston Harbor. If you paddle on these open waters, use caution. Watch for wind and high waves.

Charles River *MA*

The Charles River is the major recreational waterway in the Boston area. The winding, 80-mile river passes many towns, offering some good canoeing, sailing, fishing, and picnic areas.

Cleanup campaigns, storm-drain diversion projects, and tighter pollution laws have all helped to make the Charles a cleaner river. The water, however, will always be dark. The brown color is primarily due to tannins in surrounding border vegetation and is not a sign of pollution. Nearly 20 dams and 90-odd bridges have slowed the flow of the river so that it can be extremely sluggish. In the summer the water tends to stagnate behind the dams, but they do help to maintain a canoeable water level in some reaches of the river.

The Army Corps of Engineers has preserved 8,500 acres of flood plain as part of a flood plain management system. The Metropolitan District Commission is active in the recreational development of the lower 40 miles of the river and has published a folder detailing their many recreational facilities on the Charles and other local waterways. This is free from MDC Headquarters, 20 Somerset Street, Boston, MA 02108.

The Charles River Watershed Association (2391 Commonwealth Avenue, Auburndale, MA 02166) is a nonprofit organization dedicated to the welfare of the river. CRWA publishes a newsletter for its members about water-management issues in the watershed. It also sponsors the region's largest canoe and kayak race, the Run of the Charles, each April.

North Bellingham ➤ MA 109		14.5 mi
Description:	Flatwater, Class I-II	
Date checked:	1998	
Navigable:	High water: recommended above MA 115, March, April	
	Medium water: rapids above MA 115 bony, late April to June, fall	
	Low water: some spots thin below MA 115	
Scenery:	Forested, rural, settled	
Maps:	USGS Franklin, Holliston, Medfield	
Portages:	1.25 mi R Caryville Dam	
	3.25 mi R dam	
	5.25 mi L Medway Dam (difficult) 200 yd	

The portion of the Charles starting at Medway is especially beautiful, and is recommended. There are occasional rapids in an attractive setting, mostly woods and meadows with an occasional house. There are no portages in this section.

The source of the Charles is north of Echo Lake in Hopkinton. The river above North Bellingham is small and steep in some sections; other sections are fenced in and unattractive. Passage beneath one of the I-495 crossings is not possible in high water. Do not attempt a dangerous portage across the interstate highway.

In Medway, put in from the bridge on Sanford Street (Lincoln Street in Franklin), which crosses Village Street next to a convenience store in Medway.

In North Bellingham, begin on the left bank from the parking lot behind a mill on Maple Street. After some Class I rapids at the start, in 1.25 miles you reach a small pond behind a dam. Carry right. In 2 miles there is another pond and dam, with the third dam 2 miles beyond that.

Portage the Medway Dam (5.25 mi) on the left. Carry past the industrial buildings through a new parking lot, cross Sanford Street, and carry down 200 yards to the end of River Street. Then carry across a shallow canal and an island to the river.

Immediately below the Sanford Street bridge (5.25 mi), the river enters a steep valley where there are some easy Class II rapids. Partway down is an old, washed-out, runnable dam. The current slackens to flatwater at the Populatic Street bridge (5.5 mi), where there is good access. After 1.5 miles the river enters Populatic Lake (7 mi). Follow the left shore 200 yards to the outlet.

Below Populatic Lake the river is noticeably wider and deeper. After 1.25 miles Mill River (8.25 mi) enters on the right through a culvert. The Mill may be canoed in high water for 2 miles, from just below City Mills Pond off Main Street in Norfolk. After the Mill River culvert there is easy access on the right bank from River Road.

Just beyond the Mill River there are Class I rapids at the Myrtle Street Bridge. Passage under the left span is recommended, as the right span has submerged boulders. Rockville Rips (8.75 mi) at the Pleasant Street bridge in Millis begins at a broken dam with narrow channels that require quick maneuvering. The left is recommended at high water, the right at medium water. The bridge is 15 feet downstream. The left and center spans offer clear passage, but the right contains submerged boulders. Quickwater is followed by flatwater to the MA 115 bridge.

Below the MA 115 bridge (9.5 mi) is a short section of quickwater. Passage is left of center. The remaining 5 miles to MA 109 are mostly flat, with meadows lining one or both of the banks. The Forest Street bridge (11 mi) provides good access.

The Stop River enters at 13.5 miles. In high or medium water it is canoeable for 2.5 miles from South Street in Medfield.

MA 109 ➤ Needham   16.5 mi

Description:	Flatwater
Date checked:	1998
Navigable:	Navigable at all water levels
Scenery:	Forested, settled
Maps:	USGS Medfield, Natick
Portages:	10.5 mi R South Natick Dam
	(16.5 mi) Cochrane Dam

One of the loveliest parts of the river is above South Natick Dam, offering a large bird population including heron and owls. Large meadows in Medfield and Millis give way to wooded banks and smaller meadows in Dover and Sherborn. Land on the north side at Rocky Narrows is owned by the Trustees of Reservations. In Natick the river borders the Massachusetts Audubon Society's Broadmoor Sanctuary. The river meanders in the large meadow between MA 109 and MA 27, making wind a factor. The section between Broadmoor Sanctuary and South Natick Dam can be scratchy in low water.

There are many sharp meanders past the mouth of Bogastow Brook (2.5 mi) on the left to the MA 27 bridge (3.5 mi), where there is access from the southbound lane. In 2 miles the river passes through Rocky Narrows, an interesting feature. The ledge on the right bank offers a nice view and pleasant lunch spot. In 1.5 miles you come to the Bridge Street bridge (7 mi), where there is good access. Take out on the right at the South Natick Dam (10.5 mi) in a small park area below the dam, on the right from the parking lot.

In the next few miles the river wanders erratically, so a map is handy. After 5.5 miles there is a road bridge, followed closely by a railroad bridge. Take out on the left at an MDC parking area just above the dam (16.5 mi) at South Street in Charles River Village, Needham.

Needham ➤ Norumbega Park 18.25 mi

Description:	Flatwater, Class II
Date checked:	1998
Navigable:	Navigable at all water levels, except at beginning
Scenery:	Forested, urban
Maps:	USGS Natick, Newton
Portages:	13.5 mi L Silk Mill Dam
	13.75 mi R Metropolitan Circular Dam
	15.5 mi L Cordingly Dam
	15.75 mi L Finlay Dam

Put in below Cochrane Dam, which is at the west end of South Street in Needham. In high water there are 400 yards of Class II rapids below the dam, which are often used for whitewater training. If the water is low, or if you want a flatwater trip, put in downstream. At the Chestnut Street bridge (0.5 mi) are more short rapids that are shallow in low water.

Below Chestnut Street in Needham, the Charles flows generally eastward and passes under MA 135 (3 mi) and MA 128/I-95. Soon it swings in a big loop through Dedham. The Dedham Loop can be bypassed by following Long Ditch, which leaves on the left below MA 128/I-95 and rejoins the Charles at the railroad bridge below Dedham. It is 0.75 mile long and cuts off 5.25 miles of river.

Below the lower end of Long Ditch (9.75 mi) the river flows through an attractive marsh (the Great Plain, as in Great Plain Avenue in Dedham) before it reaches the industrial area above the two dams in Newton Upper Falls. Portage the first one (13.5 mi) across the grassy area on the left and put in before Echo Bridge. Portage the second (13.75 mi) on the right and carry down Quinobequin Road under MA 9.

The 1.5 miles from Newton Upper Falls to Newton Lower Falls are close to MA 128. Portage Cordingly Dam (15.5 mi) on the left through the parking lot of the Walnut Street industrial area. At the put-in there are a few whitewater rips, followed in a few hundred yards by the Finlay Dam, which must be carried on the left over the street. It is 2.5 miles from Newton Lower Falls past MA 128 to the MA 30 bridge (18.25 mi) at Norumbega.

Norumbega Park ➤ Charles River Dam	14.75 mi
Description:	Lakes, flatwater
Date checked:	1998
Navigable:	Navigable at all water levels
Maps:	USGS Natick, Newton, Boston South
Portages:	2.75 mi R Moody Street Dam 300 yd
	3.75 mi R Bleachery Dam 100 yd
	5.75 mi R Watertown Dam 50 yd

Just below the intersection of MA 128/I-95 and the Massachusetts Turnpike (I-90), the Charles widens into an impoundment formed by the Moody Street Dam. The scenery in this area is as beautiful as any to be found on the river. Unfortunately, traffic noise and motorboats intrude.

A historic point of interest in this section is the stone tower on a hill in the Charles River Reservation about 0.5 mile below the put-in. Although placed to mark the spot where Norsemen supposedly settled in 1543, subsequent research has disproven the theory.

The put-in may be reached by following the signs to MA 30 from MA 128 or the Massachusetts Turnpike, and then by following the signs to the duck-feeding station across from the Marriott Hotel. The put-in is at the extreme left. An alternate put-in is available at Recreation Road off MA 128. The Charles River Canoe and Kayak Club offers rentals at the put-in.

The river narrows dramatically at the Prospect Street bridge (2 mi), below which the banks become more urban. Take out on the right at the Moody Street Dam (2.75 mi). Carry across Moody Street and across the bridge to Riverbend Park. Follow the path and put in below the footbridge.

The Bleachery Dam (3.75 mi), which lies 100 yards below a wooden railroad bridge, can be lined under certain conditions. If portage is necessary, carry 100 yards along the right bank. The Rolling Stone Dam (4.75 mi) has been breached and can be run easily on the left. A short stretch of quickwater follows. The Watertown Dam (5.75 mi) is marked by a modern, steel-beam footbridge that lies forty yards upstream. The dam is easily portaged on the right

Below the Galen Street bridge in Watertown (6 mi) the Charles begins to widen. Boat traffic increases in this area. It is possible to paddle the entire basin, with Cambridge on the left and Boston on the right, through the locks (14.75 mi), and out into Boston Harbor.

Mystic River *MA*

The Mystic River flows from Upper Mystic Lake in Winchester roughly southeast to the ocean. It is short, easily canoeable, and flat. The upper river is urban but generally pleasant; the tidal portion is heavily industrial, polluted, and filled with heavy shipping. For further information, contact the Mystic River Watershed Association, 276 Massachusetts Avenue #510, Arlington, MA 02174.

Mystic Lake ➤ Boston Harbor		9 mi
Description:	Flatwater, tidal	
Date checked:	1998	
Navigable:	Passable at all water levels	
Scenery:	Settled, urban	
Maps:	USGS Lexington, Boston North	
Portage:	1.25 mi R dam	

In high or medium water it is possible to start on the Aberjona River and paddle about 1 mile from Winchester Center to Mystic Lake, with a carry around the USGS weir. Usually the Mystic Lakes will provide a better start.

From the entrance of the Aberjona River into Upper Mystic Lake at its northeast corner, it is about 1.25 miles south to Lower Mystic Lake; portage 50 yds right through the Medford Boat Club facilities. It is another 0.25 mile to the river's exit at the southeast corner of Lower Mystic Lake. In 0.25 mile you come to the MA 60 bridge (2 mi), and in another 0.25 mile the Harvard Avenue bridge. Alewife Brook enters on the right in another 500 yards.

In the next mile the Mystic River is largely contained by parkways. It passes beneath seven bridges before it reaches Medford Center (4 mi). Be careful of motorboats in this area. Below Medford Center is the basin formed by the Amelia Earhart Dam in Everett. An expanded greenbelt lines the river.

The Malden River enters just above the dam; it is broad, with marshes, two small undeveloped islands, and commercial development, and can be paddled for 1.75 miles.

Bring a boat horn. At Amelia Earhart Dam give two long and two short blasts to be put through the lock into the tidal part of the river. In 2.5 miles pass under the Mystic-Tobin Bridge and see Old Ironsides and the Charlestown Naval Shipyard National Park. The Charles River enters on the right, and you are in Boston Harbor (9 mi).

Saugus River MA

The Saugus River rises at Lake Quannapowitt in Wakefield and meanders a total of 13 miles through densely populated Wakefield, Lynnfield, Saugus, and Lynn to its mouth at Broad Sound. This description covers the lower 4.7 miles from the Saugus Iron Works National Historic Site to the ocean.

The Saugus River's present condition reflects its many human "uses" over the last 350 years. These include the filling of wetlands, increased sewage and chemical pollution from industrial and residential sources, and the withdrawal of water from the river. Yet the river's condition has improved over the last 10 years due to concerned citizens, improved stewardship by industry, the Clean Water Act, and the efforts of the Saugus River Watershed Council.

Iron Works Site ➤ Vitale Park	4.5 mi
Description:	Flatwater, tidal
Date checked:	1997
Navigable:	Passable at most water levels
Scenery:	Urban
Map:	USGS Lynn

Put in at Bridge Street. You can usually pass under the Hamilton Street bridge (1 mi). Do not portage over the busy road.

Continuing downstream, you will see the spire of the Saugus Town Hall on the right. As the tidal influence increases, the vegetation begins to change from freshwater species to salt-tolerant plants.

Pass the Pirates Glen Rock on your left. According to local legend, in the 1600s pirates would travel upriver to secretly trade gold and silver for shackles and chain. They would then meet and socialize at Pirates Glen, which is located north of this rock outcrop.

Pass the Stocker Playground (2.25 mi), which is on the left. This is a good access point (off Winter Street, ample parking) if you want to go first one way, then the other.

At the Boston Street bridge (2.75 mi) if the tide is too high you may have to portage. Take out on the south side (right) and put in on the north side (left). Below Boston Street the river splits. You may go straight (east) or left (south) around Oxbow Island (3 mi).

Pass a salt-marsh peninsula called Ballards Landing (4 mi) on your right, and the Saugus lobster fleet. Take out at the old public landing located 0.1 mile west of Vitale Park, which is reached via Ballard Street.

Vitale Park ➤ Broad Sound

This section ends at the mouth of the Saugus River. It is heavily traveled by pleasure craft and commercial fishing boats. Not recomended for canoes.

Little River and Alewife Brook *MA*

Little River is a small, seldom-visited stream with more wildlife than one would expect in such an urban setting. Alewife Brook, which connects Little River to the Mystic River, is not recommended.

Little Pond ➤ Mystic River		2.5 mi
Description:	Flatwater	
Date checked:	1997	
Navigable:	Passable at most water levels	
Scenery:	Urban	
Map:	USGS Boston North	

The put-in is at Little Pond, accessible by a public trail (50 yards) off Brighton Street between Larch Circle and Sandrick Road in Belmont. The river leaves the middle of the eastern shore. The beginning of the trip has forested banks which soon give way to an industrial park. The Little River goes under a footbridge (1 mi), then under the MA 2 bridge to join Alewife Brook. Alewife Brook is flanked by concrete banks and a hurricane fence. The trash level has improved in recent years. The entire length of the waterway can be safely negotiated.

Ipswich River MA

The Ipswich River, one of the most beautiful rivers in Massachusetts and perhaps the most canoed river on Boston's North Shore, originates in marshland in northern Burlington. The river forms at the meeting of Maple Meadow Brook and Lubber's Brook, approximately 0.5 mile west of I-93. It then meanders for 45 miles in northeastern Massachusetts, before emptying into the southern end of Plum Island Sound. It runs through many miles of wetlands in an area dotted with drumlins and other glacial formations.

Housing developments and urban areas are scattered all along the river, but they are separated by long sections of woods, swamps, and meadows. In particular, the 8.75-mile section from I-95 eastward through Bradley Palmer State Park is especially attractive because large segments of the river corridor are protected by the Audubon Society and local, county, and state agencies, as well as through easements obtained by the Essex County Greenbelt Association.

From source to mouth there is a varying amount of debris in and along the river. The section along MA 62 in North Reading is the most cluttered.

Wilmington ➤ Howe Station		12.5 mi
Description:	Flatwater	
Date checked:	1997	
Navigable:	Passable at most water levels	
Scenery:	Forested, settled	
Maps:	USGS Wilmington, Reading, Salem	
Portage:	7.25 mi L dam in Peabody 20 yd	

The going is slow in this section, with wide meanders, alders, fallen trees, and many small bridges. Ducks, geese, and other birds are common.

Put in from the bridge on Woburn Street, which parallels I-93 west of Exit 27 (Concord Street). The river is very small as it passes through Hundred Acre Swamp before I-93 (0.5 mi). Then it winds for 7 miles, passing under MA 28 and then Haverhill Street in North Reading (4.5 mi) about halfway to the dam in Peabody. The river becomes more isolated as it flows in wide wetlands past the MA 114 bridge (10.25 mi). There is good access at the MA 62 bridge (12.5 mi).

Howe Station ➤ Willowdale Dam	11.75 mi
Description:	Flatwater, quickwater
Date checked:	1997
Navigable:	Passable at most water levels
Scenery:	Forested, settled
Maps:	USGS Georgetown, Ipswich
Portage:	11.75 mi R Willowdale Dam

This is the most popular section of the Ipswich River for canoeing, with a fair current and many meanders. The river flows under several bridges, among them I-95 (3 mi), US 1 (5.25 mi), and MA 97 (6.25 mi), before it reaches Wenham Swamp. As it does (just after a railroad bridge), the Salem-Beverly Waterway Canal leaves on the right. In flood stages Wenham Swamp resembles a lake, and following the river channel may be difficult. The river turns north through an area where the shores are protected. You will pass Massachusetts Audubon's Ipswich River Wildlife Sanctuary, and skirt the northern end of Bradley Palmer State Park. Nature trails wander along the left bank. Where the river swings east again, the valley narrows. Take out on the left at Foote's Canoe Livery, on Topsfield Road, just above the dam.

Willowdale Dam ➤ Ipswich   5 mi

Description:	Flatwater, Class I
Date checked:	1997
Navigable:	Passable at most water levels
Scenery:	Forested, settled
Map:	USGS Ipswich
Portage:	5 mi L dam

Put in at the Winthrop Street bridge just downstream of Willowdale Dam. Access is not easy. You may want to put in at Foote's above the dam, and portage the dam on the right. Below Winthrop Street the river becomes a deep, slow-moving stream, canoeable even in August. Some shallow spots and rock dams may require wading/lining at low water. Two miles from Winthrop Street are the handsome three-arch Mill Street bridge and Norton's Mills. Immediately below, the Miles River enters on the right. The 3 miles from Norton's Mills to Ipswich are all smooth water. The houses become more numerous and you know there is a village ahead.

The best place to take out above the 3-foot Sylvania Dam in Ipswich is a Conservation Commission canoe landing on the left, at the end of Peatfield Street. The dam is entirely confined within vertical retaining walls and cannot be portaged at the site. You can also land on the right bank at the town park below the 1640 Whipple House. It is a 200-foot carry to South Main Street, MA 1A.

Ipswich ➤ Atlantic Ocean   3.5 mi

Below the dam, the river is unpleasant until you reach the Choate bridge, an ancient stone arch. The dam is approximately the head of the tide. Rapids begin at the County Street bridge and extend 100 feet downriver at half and low tides.

As the river widens, wind can be a problem. In favorable weather on a rising tide, one can paddle north inside Plum Island to the mouth of the Merrimack. Beware of strong tidal currents and rips in the last 3 miles to the sea. The tidal difference is 8.5 to 10 feet, with high tide about the same as Boston and low tide 20 minutes later.

Parker River MA

The Parker rises in Boxford and is fresh water as it flows through Georgetown and Groveland until Central Street in Byfield (a village in the town of Newbury), where it becomes tidal. The freshwater section is canoeable between Thurlow Street in Georgetown and River Street in Byfield Center, and also between Larkin Road and Central Street in Byfield.

Below Central Street, the tidal river meanders through beautiful salt marshes on its way to Plum Island Sound. The Parker River, along with its tributaries the Mill River and the Little River, are the major freshwater inputs to the sound.

The Parker River National Wildlife Refuge, a nationally known birding destination, encompasses most of Plum Island (a barrier island) and a good portion of the salt marshes on either side of Plum Island Sound. Dams and lack of public access restrict paddling along other portions of the river.

For more information about the river, contact the Parker River Clean Water Association, P.O. Box 798, Byfield, MA 01922 (978-462-2551).

Georgetown ➤ Byfield		2.5 mi
Description:	Lake, flatwater	
Date checked:	1998	
Navigable:	Passable at most water levels	
Scenery:	Forested, towns	
Maps:	USGS Ipswich, Newburyport	

You can paddle this largely undeveloped section, which flows through the Crane Pond Wildlife Management Area, in either direction. The upstream put-in is on Thurlow Street in Georgetown, with a downstream access along the power line at River Street (the gate is intended to keep out motor vehicles, not paddlers). Although there are several existing fire rings, camping is not permitted in the Wildlife Management Area.

From Thurlow Street, the river's clear channel meanders through open meadows and then widens into Crane Pond, a natural depression and alewife breeding pond. The river flows out of the pond almost directly opposite the input, flows through meadows, passes through steep banks with hemlocks, and enters a forested section. It then widens into a millpond with a takeout along the power line.

Byfield Millponds   1 mi

Description:	Flatwater (millponds)
Date checked:	1998
Navigable:	Passable at most water levels
Scenery:	Forested, towns
Maps:	USGS Ipswich, Newburyport

From Larkin Road, the river flows slowly through a beautiful marsh past the Byfield Water District's well fields, which supply most of Byfield with drinking water. The river water seeps through porous soils to recharge the underground aquifer. Just past the well fields, Wheeler Brook enters from the south. This section, rich in wildlife, is an ideal short paddle for families. Takeout is at Central Street, to the right of the milldam.

Byfield ➤ Newbury Old Town   9 mi

Description:	Tidal
Date checked:	1998
Navigable:	Passable at most water levels
Scenery:	Salt marsh, towns
Map:	USGS Newburyport

The tidal section of the Parker is passable from Central Street in Byfield for 9 miles to Plum Island Sound. This section is most easily paddled three hours before and after high tide, which is about an hour later than Boston. Low tide presents a different perspective from down in the tidal channels; paddle on the incoming tide to avoid being stranded by a lack of water.

In addition to the Parker River, it is also possible to paddle the tidal portions of its tributaries the Mill River (from the south, draining much of Rowley) and the Little River (from the north, draining parts of Newburyport and Newbury).

Access to the tidal portion of the Parker is available at Middle Road (just north of Governor Dummer Academy), at US 1 in Newbury, and on US 1A in Newbury Old Town at the town landing (resident sticker required, or else $100 fine). The Mill River may be accessed from a pullout just south of Governor Dummer Academy on US 1. The Little River is accessible from Newman Road, with parking available at the Trustees of Reservations' Old Town Hill, just to the east.

Plum Island River and Plum Island Sound

The Plum Island River, which flows from the waters of the Merrimack, is the river that makes Plum Island an island. Flowing south, it is joined by the Parker River, at which point it becomes known as Plum Island Sound.

At the highest tides, the sound covers the high marshes and appears to be quite a large bay. A number of tidal creeks perforate the marsh on both sides and make for interesting exploration by canoe or kayak. The Rowley River and Ipswich River both empty into the southern portion of the Plum Island Sound.

For information about local protection efforts, contact the Parker River Clean Water Association (see address on page 199) and the Friends of the Parker River National Wildlife Refuge, P.O. Box 184, Newburyport, MA 01950.

Merrimack River ➤ Ipswich River		8 mi
Description:	Tidal	
Date checked:	1998	
Navigable:	At all but the lowest tides	
Scenery:	Salt marsh, barrier island, towns	
Maps:	USGS Newburyport, Ipswich	

The Plum Island River may be reached from the Plum Island Turnpike bridge or via the Parker River at the US 1A bridge (town landing; resident sticker required). The southern portion of Plum Island Sound and the Rowley River are accessible from the Ipswich beaches along the road to Great Neck or at Cranes Beach. The Wildlife Refuge itself forbids launching of boats.

The tide on the Plum Island River from the Plum Island bridge to the Parker (4 mi) is not strong, and it is possible to paddle against the tide. The best time to paddle this section is within 3 hours of high tide, which is almost an hour later than Boston.

When paddling at lower tides, especially around the full and new moons, be careful not to become stranded on the mud flats.

The tide on Plum Island Sound and on the Parker is very strong and difficult to paddle against. In the summer there may be many motorboats and sailboats, and the channel is marked with buoys. **Caution!** The currents can be dangerous. Skilled paddlers can begin a trip at the north end, paddle the outgoing tide to the Ipswich beaches, and beat the tide. You must wait at least an hour after the tide turns to begin the return trip on the incoming tide.

Merrimack Watershed

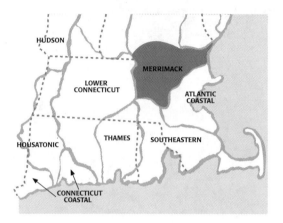

MERRIMACK WATERSHED

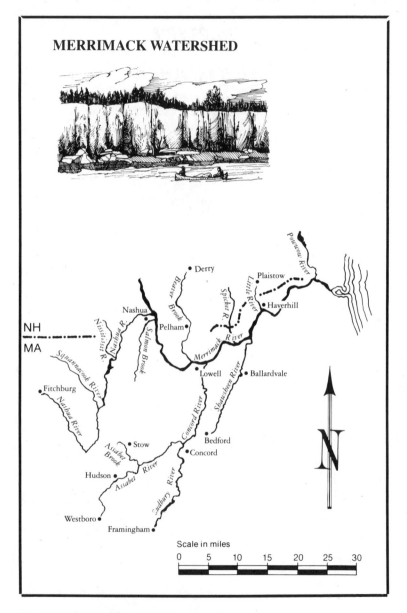

The Merrimack Watershed sprawls across central New Hampshire and northeastern Massachusetts. It encompasses, and is situated next to, large population centers. There are many rivers to enjoy throughout the watershed.

The Merrimack is already a large river when it enters Massachusetts. Many of its frequently canoed tributaries lie in New Hampshire and are described in the AMC River Guide: New Hampshire/Vermont. *Only tributaries that flow at least in part through Massachusetts are described in this book. However, the entire main stem description is included.*

Further information about the river is available from the Merrimack River Watershed Council, P.O. Box 1377, 56 Island Street, Lawrence, MA 01842 (978-681-5777).

Merrimack River NH, MA

The Merrimack River begins in Franklin, New Hampshire, at the confluence of the Pemigewasset and Winnipesaukee Rivers. It flows south into Massachusetts and then turns east and runs into the sea at Newburyport.

Except in the large cities, the banks are still rather nice from a distance. Suburban sprawl usually does not reach the river's edge. From Franklin to Concord, the river has a sandy bottom. The closer you get to the sea, however, the muddier the river becomes.

Almost all of the river is runnable throughout the paddling season. It should he avoided at high water, however, when the current is fast—the landings are difficult and the approaches to the dams can be dangerous.

Most of the big drops have been harnessed for power. When the river's natural flow is low, the water level is affected by the demand for electricity. Low water has the biggest impact below Franklin and below Amoskeag Dam in Manchester. Information on daily flows can be obtained by calling the dispatcher at the Public Service Company of New Hampshire (603-634-3616).

The Merrimack is close to many large population centers, and frequent launching ramps provide access to all sections of the river.

Franklin ➤ Concord	24 mi
Description:	Flatwater, quickwater, Class I (Class II-III in early spring)
Date checked:	1998
Navigable:	Passable at all water levels; dam controlled, peak power generation on Pemigewasset River
Scenery:	Forested, settled
Maps:	USGS Penacook 15, Concord

Put in on the Pemigewasset River below Eastman Falls Dam if you want to begin with a one mile of Class II rapids. If you prefer a half-mile of quickwater, begin on the Winnipesaukee River behind the high school in Franklin.

From the confluence of the Pemigewasset and Winnipesaukee Rivers, there are Class I rapids for the first 0.5 mile. Then there is a moderate current to Boscawen (10.5 mi), where the first bridge (closed) is located. Another 4.5 miles of meandering river bring you to Penacook, the US 4 bridge off Exit 17 of I-93 (poor access), and the mouth of the Contoocook River on the right.

In the mouth of the Contoocook River (15 mi) is an island joined to the mainland by two railroad bridges which are a monument to Hannah Duston. In 2 miles there is another bridge, with a launching ramp downstream on the right. From that point it is 1 mile to Sewall Falls Dam, which has been breached and no longer needs to be portaged. Beware of assorted debris and a new set of standing waves now rated as Class III. Consider scouting the run. A nice sand beach on the right shore just above the dam offers a fine landing place. The dam itself is old; take care when using it as a vantage point.

Below Sewall Falls Dam (18 mi) is a Class III rapid that is 0.25 mile long and rocky in low water. In another 3.5 miles there is a railroad bridge and an I-93 bridge. Just upstream is a launching ramp that can be reached from Exit 16. The remaining distance to the Bridge Street bridge (24 mi) was shortened in 1976 when a new channel was cut across a meander. A new launching ramp is on the right bank near the cloverleaf of I-393, 1 mile above Bridge Street.

Concord ➤ Manchester		18.25 mi
Description:	Flatwater, quickwater	
Date checked:	1998	
Navigable:	Passable at all water levels	
	Dam controlled; good flow all year	
Scenery:	Forested, settled	
Maps:	USGS Concord l5, Suncook, Manchester North	
Portages:	5 mi L Garvin's Fall Dam 100 yd	
	10.5 mi L dam at Hooksett 0.25 mi	
	(18.25 mi R Amoskeag Dam 200 yd)	

The best put-in is on the right, from Fort Eddy Road, just below I-393. Other put-ins are just above the Bridge Street bridge, the Manchester Street bridge, and the US 3 bridge, all on river left. After 2.25 miles of meandering you pass under a railroad bridge, below which there is some turbulence. You quickly come to Garvin's Falls Dam (5 mi). Portage on the left. There is a short Class II rapid below it.

In the next 5.5 miles to the dam at Hooksett, pass the mouth of the Soucook River (5.75 mi) and the Suncook River (8.75 mi). About 0.25 mile above Hooksett Dam there are two nice boat-launching ramps on the left. With care you can paddle in low water as far as the abutment on the left (10.5 mi). Portage past the parking area to another launching ramp below the dam.

There is some turbulence around the bridge abutments below the Hooksett Dam, then 7.25 miles of smooth water to Manchester. The Amoskeag Bridge and the Manchester skyline are visible a long distance upstream. Take out at the bridge on the right to portage Amoskeag Dam. Look for the concrete steps by the river and the Holiday Inn.

Manchester ➤ Nashua	17.75 mi
Description:	Flatwater, quickwater, Class II-III
Date checked:	1998
Navigable:	Passable at most water levels; watch for wind
	Dam controlled; peak power generation
Scenery:	Forested, settled, urban
Maps:	USGS Manchester North, Manchester South,
	Nashua North

Gauge readings at Amoskeag Dam in Manchester can be obtained by calling the Public Service Company dispatcher (603-634-3616). Flood stage is anything over 21,000 cubic feet per second. Spring runoff typically produces 12,000 to 15,000 cfs. Early-summer levels run around 5,000 cfs, and dry summers bottom out at 1,200 to 1,300 cfs. At 5,000 to 12,000 cfs, the two most difficult rapids, Goffs Falls and Griffins Falls, are easy-to-moderate Class III; at high water they wash out. The Merrimack moves a lot of water with a constant current of strong quickwater rather than through rocky drops.

There is a mile of Class II rapids through Manchester. On the left bank the walls of old factories rise straight up from the river, and on the right there is a limited-access highway. In high water, keep to the right.

Past two highway bridges and shortly below the rapids, the Piscataquog River (2 mi) enters on the right in South Manchester. At 1.5 miles there is a riffle, and soon the I-293 bridges comes into sight.

There is a put-in at the Manchester Holiday Inn, off Exit 6 of I-295. Land under the I-293 bridges (4.25 mi) to scout the Class III drops, Griffins Falls and Goffs Falls, which can be run on either side but not in the middle. This spot can be reached on the right via a dirt road. In another 0.75 mile there is a railroad bridge with a ledge just above it. It too can be run on either side, but not in the middle, where there is an island. This ledge can be inspected in advance from dirt roads on either side.

Below the railroad bridge (5 mi) there is smoothwater for 1.25 miles to a short Class II drop, and then more smoothwater for 2 miles to a longer Class II rapid just below a big power line. After 2.25 miles of smoothwater, the Souhegan River (10.5 mi) enters on the right. Almost 3 miles downstream of the confluence with the Souhegan, on the right, are the best-preserved remains of the old lock and canal system. In another mile there is a Class II rapid, followed by 3.25 miles of easy paddling to the NH 111 bridge (17 mi) in Nashua just below the mouth of the Nashua River on the right.

Nashua ➤ Lowell	14 mi
Description:	Flatwater, quickwater
Date checked:	1998
Navigable:	Passable at all water levels
Scenery:	Forested, settled, towns
Maps:	USGS Nashua South, Lowell

From the NH 111 bridge in Nashua, it is only 1 mile to the south end of town, where Salmon Brook enters on the right. The river is now all smoothwater. It passes between tilled fields and meadows for some distance, finally entering a section with wooded banks before it reaches the next bridge, MA 113, at Tyngsboro, Massachusetts, 5 miles below. There are more signs of human habitation in the next 4 miles to North Chelmsford, where Stony Brook enters on the right. In another 3 miles you arrive at Lowell. Take out at the public launching ramp above the dam.

The river is followed by the railroad. Watch for interesting old stone bridges and culverts spanning small tributaries.

Lowell Portage at Pawtucket Falls 1.25 mi

Pawtucket Falls is not as canoeable as the people rescued from it evidently thought.

Lowell ➤ Lawrence	10.5 mi
Description:	Flatwater, quickwater, Class I
Date checked:	1998
Navigable:	Passable at all water levels
Scenery:	Forested, towns, urban
Maps:	USGS Lowell, Lawrence
Portage:	(10.5 mi L dam 0.25 mi)

The most convenient start below the dam is at the second bridge upstream on Beaver Brook. Other access points are at the Aitken Street bridge, Raymond J. Martin Park, and, in Methuen, on Riverside Drive just off MA 110. The river runs swiftly past factories, the mouth of the Concord River (1.5 mi), and over the riffle at Hunts Falls (2 mi). During the remainder of the distance it gradually slows and passes under I-93 (8 mi) to Lawrence (10.5 mi). Day-trippers should take out at any of the many canoe access points, while through-trippers should land on the left to carry the dam.

Lawrence ➤ Newburyport   27.75 mi

Description:	Flatwater, quickwater, tidal
Date checked:	1998
Navigable:	Passable at all water levels; tidal
Scenery:	Forested, towns, urban
Maps:	USGS South Groveland, Ayers Village, Haverhill, Newburyport West and East

Put in at the ramp on the left behind the factories. The river has riffles for the first 3 miles, then becomes wide and smooth. After 1 mile the Spicket River enters on the left and the Shawsheen on the right. I-495 crosses at 1.5, 5.75, and 7.25 miles. In the bend to the north between the last bridges, the river becomes tidal. The last of four small bridges is Rock Village (16.25 mi), with a picnic area on the right. The mouth of the Powwow is at 21 miles, and I-95 at 22 miles. Deer Island and several other islands lie in the river between this bridge and the US 1 bridge (24.75 mi). The last 3 miles are wide and heavily used by large boats. Salisbury Beach Park is on the left and Plum Island on the right. Paddling beyond the breakwater is not recommended.

The tidal rise and fall at the Merrimack River entrance varies between 8.5 feet and 9.5 feet. High tide is about five minutes later than Boston and low tide 10 minutes later. At Newburyport, the respective differences increase to 15 minutes and 55 minutes, with corresponding increases farther up the river.

Nashua River *MA, NH*

The Nashua River has two principal branches, the South Branch, rising near Worcester, and the North Branch, formed by the junction of the Whitman and Nookagee Rivers in West Fitchburg. The two branches meet at Lancaster Common and flow north to the Merrimack River at Nashua, New Hampshire. The South Branch is dammed at Clinton to form the Wachusett reservoir, which supplies water to Boston. There is, therefore, usually little or no flow through the old riverbed between Clinton and the junction with the North Branch at Lancaster Common, so this branch has now become the principal headwater of the river.

The Nashua River has enjoyed a major restoration in the last 25 years. The industrial pollution is gone now. Birds, wildlife, and fish are returning, and paddling the Nashua River is now an enjoyable experience. For further information on the river contact the Nashua River Watershed Association (NRWA), 592 Main Street, Groton, MA 01450. It prints a river guidebook that locates the frequent access points and points of interest.

Leominster ➤ Lancaster   10.5 mi

This section is clear, but extra caution must be taken because of numerous sweepers and strainers.

Description:	Quickwater, Class I, II
Date checked:	1998
Navigable:	High water: spring into mid-June
Scenery:	Forested, settled, towns
Maps:	USGS Fitchburg, Shirley, Clinton
Portage:	2 mi L dam

Put in at the Searstown mall. The paddling is easy through an open valley not far from the birthplace of Johnny Appleseed. The first dam is hard to see around a right-hand turn. Land on the left to carry. One Class II rapid is under a power line around a double island. There is one last riffle before the MA 117 bridge, although the current continues, and curves and snags still trouble unskilled paddlers. Takeout at Lancaster Canoe Launch is at the Main Street bridge, or a little farther to the railroad trestle on river right.

Lancaster ➤ Ayer   10.5 mi

Description: Quickwater
Date checked: 1998
Navigable: Passable at most water levels; generally
                        runnable anytime
Scenery: Forested, settled, towns
Maps: USGS Clinton, Shirley, Ayer
Portage: (10.5 mi L dam)

Here the river sharply reverses itself and starts its northward swing. Below the confluence with the South Branch (0.5 mi) the river is much larger, with a strong current and fewer meanders. It passes under MA 117 (2 mi) by the mouth of the Still River on the right, and under MA 2 (8.5 mi) and finally approaches the dam at the Ayer Ice Company. Do not approach the dam on the right. Portage over a low cement wall on river left just above the dam.

Ayer ➤ East Pepperell   11 mi

Description: Flatwater, quickwater
Date checked: 1998
Navigable: Passable at most water levels
Scenery: Forested, towns
Maps: USGS Ayer, Pepperell
Portage: (11 mi R dam 0.5 mi)

Nonacoicus Brook enters on the left in 1 mile, and the Squannacook River enters on the left at 3 miles, just below the MA 2A bridge. It flows easily past MA 225 (5.5 mi) and MA 119 (8.25 mi), where it enters the extensive ponding behind the dam at East Pepperell. The Stony Wading Place was here before the bridge was built. The old dam remains are barely visible at low water. Ruins of the 1841 Oliver Howe paper mill are adjacent to the Groton Canoe Launch here on the right.

The Pepperell Pond is one of the more beautiful and interesting segments of the entire river. Although less than 3 miles in length as the crow flies, the maze of oxbows, islands, backwaters, and meanders make it possible to spend an entire day here. A survey by a wildlife biologist hired by the NRWA confirmed that this area is unique in the diversity of its plant and animal life.

Waterfowl and other birds are particularly abundant. Conservation restriction and public land purchases will ensure that the Pepperell Pond will remain protected.

The Nashua River has repeatedly been cited by the EPA and many other state, regional, and federal agencies for its remarkable progress. The growing NRWA greenway program has thus far protected approximately 60 percent of the riverbank.

The long portage is best made by car 0.5 mile to the covered bridge on the Nashua River. Alternately, people continuing during medium water may put in at the Mill Street bridge on the Nissitissit River just to the north and run down the last mile of it to the Nashua. Or you may put in on the Nissitissit behind Lower Industrial Park off MA 111, 0.25 mile from the Nashua.

East Pepperell ➤ Mine Falls	9.75 mi
Description:	Flatwater, quickwater
Date checked:	1998
Navigable:	Passable at all water levels
Scenery:	Forested, settled, towns
Maps:	USGS Pepperell, Nashua South
Portages:	5.25 mi e old dam at Ronnells Falls
	(9.75 mi R Mine Lot Falls [difficult] 0.25 mi)

On April 19, 1775, when the men of Pepperell had gone to Concord to answer the alarm, the women dressed in their husbands' clothing and armed themselves with whatever they could find. They patrolled the Mill Street bridge in East Pepperell and arrested a Tory, Captain Leonard Whiting of Hollis, who was bearing dispatches to the British in Boston.

From the put-in below the dam in East Pepperell it is only 0.75 mile to the junction of the Nissitissit. The current is moderate as far as the broken dam at Ronnells Mills, just below the NH 111 bridge. Besides the obvious problems, some spikes still protrude. This section can be run on river right, but only with scouting and good safety precaution.

The main flow of the river is on the right, which is free of debris from the old dam. At high water this is a short Class III run.

There is convenient access on the right above or the left below the dam.

From here to the first dam 1 mile west of Nashua the current slows. The takeout at Mine Lot Falls is a 700-foot carry, so you might be better advised to take out at the Horrigan Conservation Area off NH 111, about three-quarters of the way down.

Mine Lot Falls ➤ Merrimack River   5.5 mi

Description:	Flatwater, quickwater, possible rapids
Date checked:	1998
Navigable:	Passable at most water levels
Scenery:	Forested, settled, urban
Map:	USGS Nashua South
Portages:	3.75 mi L dam (difficult footing) 200 yd along railroad track

Portage Mine Lot Falls on the right. This is the dam that forms the Nashua Canal.

The first rapids below the dam should not be run. A good path leads high above the river, with a trail down over boulders to the river almost at the end of the rapids, about 0.25 mile.

Below the rapids the river wanders peacefully in a big loop to the left under the Everett Turnpike and a prize-winning pedestrian bridge.

Just before the last loop, a factory comes into sight on the right, with a solid line of factories around the next bend. Water from the canal exits under these factories. Below the stone-arch Main Street bridge is another dam that can be portaged on either side, although the right is shorter, and the bank is steep in either case.

The river is quickwater for the remaining 1.75 miles to the Merrimack. The chief obstruction is shopping carts.

Alternate Canal Trip   3 mi

Portage into the canal on the right (east) side of the Nashua River. The canal is sluggish and pleasant, passing under the same turnpike and pedestrian bridges as the river.

At the far end, the canal goes down the drain and emerges from underneath the factory. You can carry to the right down the railroad track and then straight ahead, bearing right to the Standard Hardware parking area by the river. A more desirable carry is under a power line 0.5 mile upstream, where the river is only a short distance down the bank through the bushes.

River Canal Circle Trip   about 6 mi

Put in the canal from the parking area behind the high school. There is also a convenient takeout for people coming downstream, better than at Mine Falls. Paddle left upstream toward the dam, where a carry can be made with some effort over to the river. Continue downstream to where the factory comes into view. There is a culvert on the right (the upstream end of the oxbow shown on the maps). Carry up to the canal and paddle back to the start.

Squannacook River *MA*

The Squannacook rises in Ash Swamp in Townsend and flows into the Nashua River in Ayer. It was designated a Scenic River by Massachusetts in 1984. It is a pretty stream with good current nearly all the way. Fallen trees may be a problem.

West Townsend ➤ Nashua River	14.75 mi
Description:	Flatwater, quickwater, Class I, II
Date checked:	1998
Navigable:	High water
Scenery:	Forested, towns
Maps:	USGS Townsend, Shirley, Ayer
Portages:	2.75 mi R low dam
	6.25 mi L dam
	10.25 mi L Vose Mill
	11.5 mi R dam

There are many possible runs on the Squannacook. For the upper, put in from a side road leading north from West Townsend (continuation of NH 123 to Mason) below a dam.

A quarter mile downstream is an easily runnable ledge. Just above Townsend at a right turn is Black Rock (1.75 mi), a huge boulder overhang. This area is public property (Howard Park).

Below the railroad trestle, within sight of the MA 119 bridge (2.5 mi), there is a 4-foot dam, easily portaged on the right. About 200 yards below, an old dam at a blind left corner creates a wave. Below MA 13 a good current continues with beautiful hemlock-covered banks at many points. An old bridge abutment (4.75 mi), the access from Meetinghouse Road, marks the beginning of a swampy section that is not long but difficult to get through. Below the swamp is the ponding from the dam at Townsend Harbor (6.25 mi). At ordinary water levels it is possible, by lying flat in the canoe, to turn left above the dam and go through the sluiceway. Pass beyond the historic gristmill on the other side of the road. Take out there and slide the canoe down a narrow, steep path back into the river.

The river runs very swiftly on the left beside the mill, then gradually slows down. The river is larger and deeper than before. At a large pool, a picnic area is on the left. Stop on the left and scout the rapid below. This is a good takeout place for flatwater canoeists. To reach it, take the road from the high school on MA 119 to West Groton. A large Department of Fisheries and Wildlife sign marks the dirt road to the river. This road is closed to vehicles.

A gauging station is at the first drop. Just around the corner to the left is another ledge, and below it is the third and most difficult drop, which has large standing waves. At a reading of 4 feet, the best route is in the middle for the first two drops and at the extreme left for the final one.

Begin the carry where you see houses on the left bank. Or carry up to the road at the water-supply building, which is reached by a paved road on the left above Vose Mill. Paddle into the big bay on the left, just above the mill.

Take out on the right to carry the dam (10.25 mi). Quickwater leads to another millpond. Do not go beneath the MA 225 bridge at West Groton; take out at the small clearing just to the right. From here, cross the road and carry down a short, steep slope to the put-in below the dam (11.5 mi). Watch for poison ivy.

Below West Groton the river regains its twisty, narrow character. A convenient takeout is about 0.25 mile upstream on the Nashua River at the MA 2A bridge.

Nissitissit River *NH, MA*

The Nissitissit rises in Lake Potanipo in Brookline, New Hampshire, and flows southeast into the Nashua River in Pepperell, Massachusetts. Although the entire river may be run in high water, the section from the source to the NH 13 crossing is not recommended.

This is a trout stream with clear water. Sharp turns, beaver dams, and fallen trees may present difficulties.

Brookline ➤ West Hollis		4.5 mi
Description:	Quickwater, Class I	
Date checked:	1998	
Navigable:	High water	
Scenery:	Forested, rural	
Map:	USGS Townsend	

The first good put-in point is behind the fire station in Brookline off NH 130 in the town center. If the water looks too low, put in 2 miles farther downstream at the wooden Bohannon's Bridge, which has a short Class II drop just above. There is good parking here. From Bohannon's Bridge you will be out of sight of civilization for about 2.5 miles, winding through Campbells Meadows.

There is a good takeout spot with parking on conservation land on the left bank at West Hollis. To reach this point, take Brookline Road from MA 111 just before it crosses the river in Pepperell.

West Hollis ➤ Pepperell   3.5 mi

Description:	Quickwater, Class I
Date checked:	1998
Navigable:	High water
Scenery:	Forested
Map:	USGS Pepperell
Portages:	1.25 mi e small dam
	3.5 mi R dam in Pepperell

The 2 miles to the Prescott Street bridge are the the river's most scenic. Much of the land is in the Nissitissit Wildlife Management area. You can put in at this bridge; there is limited roadside parking. Below this point the stream is first quick and then shallow by the ruins of a colonial mill, and eventually quiet as you enter the millpond above the dam. There is a carry of a few hundred feet to MA 111. Take out on the right on private land.

Pepperell ➤ Nashua River   1 mi

The rapids below the dam can be run. Most of them are Class II and end shortly below the MA 111 bridge. The Mill Street bridge (0.25 mi) is the access before the Nashua River. From the confluence, it is another 4.5 miles to the NH 111 bridge on the Nashua River.

Beaver Brook *NH, MA*

Beaver Brook is a charming and pleasant, winding stream that flows from Beaver Lake in Derry to the Merrimack River at Lowell. There is a good current for most of that distance with some small beaver dams, minor rapids, and occasional carries. The brook flows through several suburban communities. Increasingly the settled areas intrude on the water, but portions of this brook still offer near-wilderness.

Derry ➤ West Windham   7 mi

Description:	Flatwater, quickwater
Date checked:	1999
Navigable:	High water: March and April
Scenery:	Forested, towns
Maps:	USGS Derry, Windham
Portages:	4 mi R dam at Kendall Pond 100 yd
	7 mi R dam at West Windham 40 yd

The original put-in on NH 28 is not recommended because of major sewer-pipe construction and numerous deadfalls along the river. Beaver Brook's source is Beaver Lake in Derry. It begins as a narrow brook with drops that were once exploited for mills. It quickly flattens out and passes through the Derry golf course (former meadowlands). This section is impractical for canoeing. If you don't mind urban encroachment, a good start can be had from Route 28 near the hospital in Derry. The brook is still small here and can be blocked by downed trees; be prepared to do some carry-overs. An alternative put-in is off Gilcrest Road in Londonderry (2.5 mi). Gilcrest Road can be reached by taking Exit 4 off I-93 onto NH 102 toward Londonderry, and then taking the first left. Gilcrest crosses Beaver Brook just before intersecting with Kendall Pond Road. In less than 1 mile, Beaver Brook enters Kendall Pond (3.5 mi).

Approximately 0.5 mile across the pond (4 mi) is the outlet, where there are a dam and a bridge. Take out on the right and put in on the right across the bridge. There are a few small rapids and quick current for the next hundred yards or so. The river flattens out and is a pleasant paddle for the next few miles past beaver dams and through meadows and hemlock groves. It eventually backs up in a millpond behind the dam in West Windham near the junction of NH 128 and NH 111 (7 mi). Portage the dam at West Windham on the right. The NH 128 bridge is just below it. Portage on the right, across the road. Beware of snowmobile bridges just past the dam. For the next 3 miles the stream winds through meadows and may have logjams and beaver dams.

West Windham ➤ Second NH 128 bridge   3 mi

Description:	Quickwater, Class I
Date checked:	1999
Navigable:	High water: March, April, wet fall
	Check the USGS water gauge at the 2 NH 128 bridge (located just down stream on river right). A reading of 6.5' and above makes for good canoeing
Scenery:	Forested
Map:	USGS Windham

This section is the start of the best parts the river has to offer for canoeing. The river widens and the bottom is gravelly. Numerous rocks give you a chance to practice reading water. The current starts off quick, so be alert. There are many small riffles and some beaver dams before reaching the NH 111 bridge (1.75 mi). The river flattens out a bit in the 0.25 mile to the next bridge, and then it's 1 mile more to the second NH 128 bridge (3 mi). You can take out on the left before the bridge. In the last mile there are two easy portages around a huge pine tree across the brook and a beaver dam.

Second NH 128 bridge ➤ Collinsville   10.5 mi

Description:	Flatwater, quickwater, Class II
Date checked:	1999
Navigable:	High water: March, April, wet fall
Scenery:	Forested, towns
Maps:	USGS Windham, Lowell
Portages:	0.75 mi L broken dam
	3.75 mi L small dam
	(10.5 mi R dam in Collinsville)

This section of Beaver Brook is more demanding than the section above. It has a few rapids (many strainers in high water) and two interesting stone-arch bridges. Considerable new home construction near the water intrudes on the natural beauty of some sections, but near-wilderness prevails in others.

Quickwater and small riffles prevail for about 0.5 mile. A white house on the right marks a left turn at a broken dam, about 0.5 mile from the put-in. **Caution!** Take out on the left and scout before attempting to run it. This is a Class II-II+ rapid in almost all water levels. Although the blocks are jagged, it can be run in the middle by experienced boaters. You can easily avoid the rapid by lining or portaging on the left. The second of two closely spaced bridges (Tallant Road) offers good access upstream on the left (1.25 mi). The river quiets down for 1.5 miles until it reaches a small rapid marked by an old bridge abutment (2.75 mi). The bridge is now closed. A mile below are the remnants of a small concrete dam (3.75 mi); you can lift over it. If you want to shoot the narrow sluiceway in the middle, make sure it is clear before you attempt it. The sluiceway is a common spot for strainers to develop from trapped branches; run it in the middle. The next mile or so usually has downed trees to carry over.

One-half mile past the second dam, a steel-beam bridge (4.25 mi) on NH 111A has good access on the left upstream of the bridge. **Caution!** This bridge has decreasing clearance as you go under it. It must be portaged (left) in high water.

It is 0.75 mile to a stone-arch bridge and another 0.5 mile to the bridge on Old Bridge Street (5.5 mi), opposite the shopping center on NH 38 in Pelham.

From the shopping center it is 0.75 mile to the Willow Street bridge, and from there the brook winds for 4.25 miles through meadows. There are some Class II rapids above the dam and bridge at Collinsville (l0.5 mi) in Dracut. Take out 150 yards above the dam, on the right at a grassy launching area.

Collinsville ➤ Merrimack River	3.5 mi.
Description:	Flatwater, quickwater, Class II
Date checked:	1999
Navigable:	Passable at most water levels; rapids require medium water
Scenery:	Forested, towns
Portages:	2.5 mi R dam 50 yd
	3 mi L dam 400 yd

If you are continuing downstream, land on the left to portage the dam. Although the water quality and trash detract somewhat, this is still a worthwhile trip.

Class II rapids run below the dam for 0.25 mile, with a couple of small ledges that are exciting at high water. The river then resumes its small, meandering character, passing under farm bridges at 1 mile and 1.25 miles. The next bridge (2.25 mi) offers good access. Around the corner and within sight of Parker Avenue is a 10-foot dam.

The next dam is confined entirely between two factories. Take out at a Dracut municipal structure on the left, 200 yards above the dam, where the ponding brook narrows again. Access is difficult below the dam, and it is only 0.5 mile to Martin Street, which is a recommended put-in for the Merrimack River below Pawtucket Falls.

Concord River MA

The Concord is formed by the confluence or the Assabet and Sudbury Rivers at Egg Rock in Concord. The water in the Concord and its tributaries has, at various times in the past, been used to power mills and factories, flood the Middlesex Canal, and supply water to Boston. Now some of the dams have been washed out, the canal is dry, and Boston relies upon the Quabbin Reservoir for water. The Concord has wide, marshy flood plains, many of which are included in the Great Meadows National Wildlife Refuge. This is the finest, most peaceful, tranquil, quietwater paddling in the metro-Boston region. There is nothing better than canoeing at sunrise in the GMNWR in the spring.

For a complete description of the river, its history, and its wildlife, refer to Ron McAdow's excellent book *The Concord, Sudbury and Assabet Rivers*, published by Bliss Publishing.

Concord ➤ North Billerica   10.75 mi

Description:	Flatwater
Date checked:	1998
Navigable:	Passable at all water levels
Scenery:	Forested, rural, settled
Maps:	USGS Concord, Billerica
Portages:	(l0.75 mi R dam at Talbot Mills—difficult in high water)

From the Lowell Road bridge in Concord, 200 yards below the confluence of the Assabet and Sudbury Rivers, the Concord flows northeast. The river passes under the Old North Bridge replica. This area is a part of the Minuteman National Historical Park. The river flows northeast for 2 miles and then swings north, with Balls Hill on the left. The GMNWR is on the right shore. You may occasionally see personal watercraft (jet skis) zooming around here. In another 2 miles you come to the MA 225 bridge (4.75 mi). This is a fine section for observing herons. The river continues past the MA 4 bridge (6.5 mi), the US 3 bridge (7.75 mi), the MA 3A bridge (9.5 mi), and the North Billerica bridge (l0.25 mi) to the dam at Talbot Mills (11 mi). This broad, deep section is used by motorboats and even water-skiers. Most slow down for canoes, though.

If you are continuing on to the Merrimack, the portage around this dam is difficult. There is no easy entry into the water below the dam due to industrial fencing. Scout this area before arriving at the dam. In low water, portage the dam over its edge.

North Billerica ➤ Lowell   4.5 mi

Description:	Flatwater, Class II
Date checked:	1998
Navigable:	Passable at most water levels
Scenery:	Urban
Maps:	USGS Billerica, Lowell
Portages:	3 mi e 10 ft dam—difficult
	(4.5 mi R 20 ft dam—difficult)

This section has year-round whitewater but is not recommended for canoeists. Passage around the three dams between Talbot Mills and the Merrimack is difficult. It is possible to paddle safely the first three miles on flatwater, beneath the I-495 bridges. Beyond a railroad bridge the current becomes strong and the river spills over a zigzag dam. The portage is difficult. Rapids continue for 0.75 mile down a steep-sided valley past factories. Below the next bridge keep right at an island. Scout this section from the right bank. Where the river breaks out of the gorge, the rapids culminate in a ledge that has a Class III+ hole. The next 0.75 mile has two stretches of whitewater with a difficult drop over a ledge.

Assabet River MA

The Assabet River begins at the Assabet Reservoir in Westboro and flows northeastward to Concord, where its confluence with the Sudbury creates the Concord River. It offers a number of short, fairly attractive trips.

For a complete description of the river, its history, and its wildlife, refer to Ron McAdow's excellent book *The Concord, Sudbury and Assabet Rivers*, published by Bliss Publishing.

Westboro ➤ Hudson	11.25 mi
Description:	Flatwater, quickwater, Class I
Date checked:	1998
Navigable:	High and medium water: March, April
Scenery:	Forested, rural, towns
Maps:	USGS Shrewsbury, Marlboro, Hudson
Portages:	3.75 mi R dam at Northboro 10 yd
	4.75 mi R dam at Woodside 15 yd
	(11.25 mi L dam at Hudson—difficult 200 yd)

In its upper stretches the Assabet is still a small stream. Most of this portion is runnable all year, but shallow places below the dam in Northboro and through Chapinville make the springtime preferable. The scenery includes frequent views of marshes and farms, with only a few interruptions from road crossings and dams.

From the put-in at Davis Street, there are 2.75 miles of winding, marshy river to the dam in Northboro. This dam, the site of a fulling mill from 1751, should be portaged on the right. If the water is high enough, run the riffles under the US 20 bridge; otherwise carry around over US 20. Riffles continue below this bridge under an old mill that drew its power from a dam on Cold Harbor Brook, which enters from the left. The main river is clear of obstructions. Just below, the river widens into a pond above the Woodside Dam. Just above are the stone Wachusett aqueduct and a low bridge on a side road. Portage the dam itself (4.75 mi), and the low bridge if necessary, on the right. Riffles continue below, as the river runs navigably under another mill and between stone walls.

For the next 6.5 miles the banks alternate between marsh and farmland. The river is occasionally overhung and obstructed. Pass a number of bridges, including those of I-495. The portage around the dam in Hudson (11.25 mi) is complicated by fences and concrete retaining walls. Carry on the left side through gas stations to a put-in just below the MA 85 bridge.

Hudson ➤ Maynard   8.5 mi

Description:	Flatwater, quickwater, Class I
Date checked:	1998
Navigable:	Passable at all water levels
Scenery:	Forested, marshy, towns
Maps:	USGS Hudson, Maynard
Portages:	3.3 mi L dam at Gleasondale 100 yd
	5.5 mi (lift over Barton Road into Boons Pond—optional)
	(8.5 mi L first dam at Maynard 15 yd)

Put in at the South Street parking lot in Hudson, just below the MA 85 bridge. It is quickwater for the first mile under Forest Street and past old factories, cemeteries, and rail beds to Main Street (1 mi). The Cox Street bridge is at 1.25 miles. Duckweed mats are often found in this area or down by Boons Pond.

Below Cox Street the Assabet enters marshland. The river widens and curves around a large farm on the right. Pass the Hudson Wastewater Treatment Plant. Gleasondale Dam (3.5 mi) follows. Portage left along a lightly worn path to a road. Turn right on the road, cross the river, and slide the boats down a short steep bank on the right, just after crossing the bridge. This portage passes through private property; please be considerate and courteous. The shallow rapids below may have to be walked in low water, then you come to the MA 62 bridge.

In another mile the Assabet splits around an island and widens as a round-roofed structure resembling an airplane hangar appears on the right. This marks the approach to Boons Pond outlet on the right (5.5 mi). Boons Pond is a delightful picnic spot and side trip and may be reached by paddling 70 yards in the shallow, marshy outlet and portaging (10 yd) Barton Road. A sandy beach is 800 yards due east, directly across the pond. Cars may be parked near the beach as an alternate takeout.

The Assabet continues past the outlet and turns sharply left, narrowing between the stone embankments of an old railroad bridge. After a few more turns, you come to Boon Road bridge (6 mi) and the river makes a wide, straight path for Maynard. A golf course appears on the left before the Tuttle Hill bridge with good access (8.25 mi). Portage the dam above Maynard (8.5 mi) on the left.

Maynard ➤ Concord   8.5 mi

Description:	Flatwater, quickwater, Class I-II
Date checked:	1998
Navigable:	High or medium water: March through May
	Low water: rapids in Maynard impassable
Scenery:	Forested, settled
Maps:	USGS Maynard, Concord
Portage:	2.25 mi L second dam in Maynard 50 yd

The rapids in Maynard provide good training for novice whitewater boaters. The remainder of the run is smooth and runnable all year.

Put in on the right bank from a dirt road next to the Pace Company. There are 1.5 miles of easy Class II rapids through Maynard. These can be malodorous and impassable in low water. Below the MA 27/62 bridge in Maynard Center the rapids end, followed by 0.75 mile of flatwater to the second Maynard dam (2.25 mi). Portage on the left.

Below Maynard, swift current and two quick crossings of MA 62 give way to another flatwater section above the broken dam in West Concord (4 mi). The gatehouse has been washed out, so the dam is runnable on the far right. **Caution!** Scout for obstructions. The next 2 miles contain a mixture of slow and moderate current, and highway and railroad bridges. After MCI Concord and the MA 2 bridge (6 mi), the river has high banks on the left and meadows on the right.

Spencer Brook, which enters on the left 1.25 miles below MA 2, was often spoken of by Thoreau. This brook can be explored a short distance, but tall marsh grasses overhang the canoe and the abrupt turns make passage difficult. **Caution!** Just past Spencer Brook there is a large rock in mid-river called Gibraltar and several other rocks that must be avoided. The river then makes two graceful curves with wooded banks, A short distance above the junction with the Sudbury River is the site of the hemlocks made famous by Hawthorne in *Mosses from an Old Manse.* These were on the right bank at the foot of Nashawtuc Hill, but they are now largely replaced by willows.

The Assabet joins the Sudbury to form the Concord River at Egg Rock. The Assabet is the senior partner in the Concord, with more flow than the Sudbury. The next takeout is 200 yards down the Concord River at the Lowell Street bridge (8.5 mi).

Assabet Brook *MA*

This tributary of the Assabet River is also known as Elizabeth Brook. It provides a short, pleasant run on a narrow stream. The water is moderately clear, in contrast to the darker main river. There are a number of obstructions necessitating short portages.

Stow ➤ Maynard	4.5 mi
Description:	Lakes, quickwater, Class I
Date checked:	1998
Navigable:	High or medium water: April through July
	Low water: rapids in Maynard impassable
Scenery:	Forested
Maps:	USGS Hudson, Maynard
Portages:	1.25 mi R dam on Wheeler Pond 20 yd
	3.5 mi R dam on Fletcher Pond 20 yd

Put in at the MA 117 bridge about a mile west of Stow. The stream, with a good current at this point, splits immediately around an island. The woods give way to marshier banks. The Stow Country Club is on the right. The brook leads into half-mile-long Wheeler Pond. Portage the outlet dam (1.25 mi) on the right, and, if necessary because of low clearance, the stone bridge on Wheeler Road just below. In another marshy 0.5 mile you reach the MA 62 bridge, shortly below which lies Fletcher Pond. After the portage at this outlet dam (2 mi), are 1.75 miles of river with good current and occasional riffles. Watch out for culverts. The brook passes the Assabet Country Club—with another low bridge—just before joining the Assabet River (3.75 mi). A takeout is possible at the bridge 0.25 mile down the Assabet or at the dam (4.5 mi) just above the MA 117 bridge in Maynard.

Sudbury River *MA*

The Sudbury joins the Assabet in Concord to form the Concord River. Canoeing above Saxonville (northeast Framingham) is impractical due to the size of the stream, frequent obstructions, and reservoir-use restrictions. There is generally enough water below Framingham, however, to float a canoe despite the reservoirs.

For a complete description of the river, its history, and its wildlife, refer to Ron McAdow's excellent book, *The Concord, Sudbury and Assabet Rivers*, published by Bliss Publishing.

Framingham Center ➤ Concord 20.25 mi

Description:	Lake, flatwater, quickwater
Date checked:	1998
Navigable:	Passable at most water levels
Scenery:	Settled, forested
Maps:	USGS Framingham, Natick, Maynard, Concord
Portages:	2 mi e low dam 10 yd
	3.5 mi R dam at Saxonville

Put in at Winter Street. Parking is available on the street. The river is broad and sluggish, with many bridges. Three miles below the put-in, portage the Fenwick Street dam on the right. The next mile to Saxonville is more pondlike. Portage the Saxonville Dam (4.5 mi), the last dam on the Sudbury, on the right, where there is a good access point.

Below Saxonville, high, wooded banks give way to wide meadows. From Saxonville to North Billerica on the Concord there are 27.5 miles of unobstructed flatwater. Saxonville can be reached by taking Edgell Road, the right fork off Central Street, north from MA 9 in Framingham Center.

There is 0.25-mile of quickwater between steep embankments below the dam. The river turns left and passes under the Danforth Street bridge (4.5 mi—good access) and another bridge. This is the halfway point along the length of the Sudbury. The remains of a stone bridge built in 1673 are at 7 miles. There are four more bridges before the MA 117 bridge (16.5 mi), which is 0.5 mile before the river enters Fairhaven Bay. This lovely area is Broad Meadows, part of the Great Meadows National Wildlife Refuge. The GMNWR headquarters are on the left (look for a concrete boat ramp) a short distance below the historic wooden Sherman's Bridge (14 mi).

Fairhaven Bay (16 mi) is a half-mile-long lake on the border between Concord and Lincoln. The river is wider as it leaves the bay. Just below a railroad bridge is the Old South Bridge (19.25 mi), originally built around 1660. After passing the site of an old railroad bridge (20 mi), the Assabet joins the Sudbury to form the Concord. The next takeout is 200 yards down the Concord River at the Lowell Street bridge (20.25 mi).

Spicket River NH, MA

The Spicket River rises in Island Pond in Hampstead and flows south to reach the Merrimack at Lawrence. The upper and lower parts are not practical to paddle, but the middle section offers a more pleasant quickwater run than might be expected in such a settled area.

Town Farm Road ➤ Methuen, MA		8 mi
Description:	Quickwater	
Date checked:	1998	
Navigable:	High water: March and April or after rain	
Scenery:	Wooded, settled	
Maps:	USGS Ayers Village, Lawrence	

Start at Town Farm Road, just below an alder swamp, or at NH 97, 1 mile south. The brook is small and wriggles back and forth among the trees, sometimes up to the backyards of houses. The least attractive section is near the trash from the shopping center along NH 28 (5 mi). After another mile the river parallels I-93. The river passes under the interstate ramp (7 mi) and under a railroad bridge. Take out on the left above the highway bridge.

Shawsheen River MA

There are a number of Shawsheen enthusiasts. It is little traveled and has some good wildlife. Detailed information can be obtained from the Shawsheen Watershed Association, 121 Pond Street, Tewksbury, MA 01876.

Bedford ➤ Ballardville

Description:	Flatwater, quickwater, Class I
Date checked:	1998
Navigable:	High water: April
	Medium water: May and June
Scenery:	Forested, settled
Maps:	USGS Concord, Billerica, Wilmington, Lawrence
Portages:	1+ mi R rapids below MA 62 bridge (rough)
	250 yd (15.25 mi R dam)

In high water, put in at the Great Road shopping center at MA 4/225 in Bedford. The stream is small and somewhat obstructed by branches until the Page Road bridge. The rapids below the MA 62 bridge must be carried on the right in low water. The river then becomes slow and meandering past the US 3 bridge (2 mi) to the Middlesex Turnpike (3 mi). Flatwater leads to the MA 3A bridge (4.5 mi), where the low bridge may require a portage right. The Shawsheen flows for the next 3.25 miles to the MA 129 bridge through wooded or marshy banks. There is a gauge on river right at the bridge; 2.5 is low but runnable. A minor rapid lies below the bridge past the ruins of the Middlesex Canal viaduct (7.75 mi). The best passage is right of the center granite tower. Land on the left past the ruins to see the historic marker there. In the next mile pass a railroad bridge, the low Whipple Road bridge, and the mouth of Content Brook.

The MA 38 bridge is a convenient place to launch or take out (10 mi). There are some minor rapids and fast current in the next 2 miles, past a triple-barreled culvert on a minor road. The river then meanders again and passes under I-93 (no access), followed by 2 miles of marshy flow to the dam at Ballardville. Take out right above the dam.

Ballardville Dam ➤ Stevens Street Dam   3.25 mi

Description:	Flatwater, quickwater
Date checked:	1998
Navigable:	Medium water: May and June
Scenery:	Forested, marsh, settled, urban
Portage:	2.75 mi R broken dam (beware water entering below dam)

Carry around the left side of the building to the parking lot. Put in below the unrunnable dam, where the Shawsheen is a narrow channel. It soon opens up and in 0.25 mile makes a sharp turn into a heavily wooded area. The stream entering left is the remains of the old river channel. The stream from Pomps Pond enters right.

The woods begin to thin out and houses appear as the channel enters a meadow area. The channel turns left between two stone pillars. Good access is available left on Center Street (2 mi). Quickwater flows under a stone-arch railroad bridge in this area. The remains of the next dam (2.75 mi) can be run after scouting, or portage right. A hanging pipe at the Essex Street bridge (3 mi) may cause trouble in high water.

After a sharp left turn, take out on the right at the 12-foot Stevens Street dam, at the Andover post office. Below this point conditions at the two small dams make canoeing dangerous, and portaging there is extremely bothersome.

Little River   NH, MA

Map:	USGS Haverhill

This stream is runnable from Plaistow, New Hampshire, to within a mile of the Merrimack River in Haverhill, Massachusetts, at which point it runs into a culvert. It is a small quickwater stream that is canoeable only at high water.

Begin the run from Main Street in Plaistow (NH 121A), just east of NH 125. In 0.5 mile the stream passes beneath Westville Road, and within another 0.5 mile beneath two bridges, the second of which is NH 125. It passes under NH 121 (1.5 mi) just above the state line. The stream remains small until it passes under I-495 (3 mi) and enters the backwater of a dam in Haverhill. Much of this is paralleled by railroad tracks. The best takeout points in Haverhill are at a playground (5 mi) on the right 150 yards past a railroad bridge and 0.5 mile above the dam, or at Benjamin and Apple Streets just above the dam.

Powwow River NH, MA

This small stream in southeastern New Hampshire has two sections that offer pleasant canoeing in largely isolated areas.

Kingston ➤ Powwow Pond   4 mi
Description: Pond, flatwater, quickwater
Date checked: 1985
Navigable: High water: stream
Scenery: Marsh, forested
Maps: USGS Haverhill 15, Exeter
Portage: (4 mi dam and rocky stream 2 mi)

The first section begins in Kingston, New Hampshire. Put in just below the outlet of Great Pond where NH 111 and NH 125 cross the river. One-and-a-half miles of narrow stream in a picturesque marsh give way to more open water above Powwow Pond, where there are many cottages. Take out at the east end of the pond to the left of a railroad bridge (4 mi). A short dirt road leads out to NH 107A.

Portage by car 2 miles via MA 107A to Chase Road. Put in from the dirt road on the left just before the river.

Chase Road ➤ Tuxbury Pond   4.5 mi
Description: Pond, flatwater, quickwater
Date checked: 1985
Navigable: Medium water
Scenery: Marsh, forested
Map: USGS Newburyport West

From Chase Road there are 2.5 miles of narrow stream through thick woods, then another mile of more open stream below the first bridge. It is a mile across the pond to the dam at the outlet, just across the state line in Amesbury, Massachusetts.

Lake Gardner ➤ Merrimack River		2.5 mi
Description:	Flatwater, tidal	
Navigable:	Navigable except in low water	
Scenery:	Urban, settled	
Map:	USGS Newburyport West	
Portages:	0 mi R Lake Gardner dam 20 yd	
	0.5 mi R small dam, falls below 500 yrd	

Carry over the earthen part of the dam. Within the next 0.75 mile there are three low bridges, a small broken dam (to be rebuilt), an unrunnable falls, and a tunnel through town. Take out below the third bridge and above the footbridge to avoid the hidden falls below. Carry across busy Market Street, then down Mill Street opposite an impressive old mill.

For the next 1.5 miles, plan to go with the outgoing tide. Industrial shores soon give way to woods and marsh. In 1 mile are the NH 110 and I-495 bridges. In another 0.5 mile, just below the Main Street bridge, is the Merrimack. Go right, around the large marina, and up the Merrimack 100 yards to the town ramp to take out. If swift currents make this impossible, take out at the steep-banked Alliance Park, on the left at the confluence.

Appendix A

Safety Code of American Whitewater
(FORMERLY THE AMERICAN WHITEWATER AFFILIATION)

The following code, adopted in 1959 and revised in 1998, is reprinted with the permission of American Whitewater, P.O. Box 636, Margaretville, NY 12455.

I. Personal Preparedness and Responsibility

1. Be a competent swimmer, with the ability to handle yourself underwater.

2. Wear a life jacket. A snugly fitting vest-type life preserver offers back and shoulder protection as well as the flotation needed to swim safely in whitewater.

3. Wear a solid, correctly fitted helmet when upsets are likely. This is essential in kayaks or covered canoes, and recommended for open-canoeists using thigh straps and rafters running steep drops.

4. Do not boat out of control. Your skills should be sufficient to stop or reach shore before reaching danger. Do not enter a rapid unless you are reasonably sure that you can run it safely or swim it without injury.

5. Whitewater rivers contain many hazards which are not always easily recognized. The following are the most frequent killers.

   A. **HIGH WATER** The river's speed and power increase tremendously as the flow increases, raising the difficulty of most rapids. Rescue becomes progressively harder as the water rises, adding to the danger. Floating debris and strainers make even an easy rapid quite hazardous. It is often misleading to judge the river level at the put-in, since a small rise in a wide, shallow place will be multiplied many times where the river narrows. Use reliable gauge information whenever possible, and be aware that sun on snowpack, hard rain, and upstream dam releases may greatly increase the flow.

B. **COLD** Cold drains your strength and robs you of the ability to make sound decisions on matters affecting your survival. Cold-water immersion, because of the initial shock and the rapid heat loss which follows, is especially dangerous. Dress appropriately for bad weather or sudden immersion in the water. When the water temperature is less than 50 degree F., a wetsuit or drysuit is essential for protection if you swim. Next best is wool or pile clothing under a waterproof shell. In this case, you should also carry waterproof matches and a change of clothing in a waterproof bag. If, after prolonged exposure, a person experiences uncontrollable shaking, loss of coordination, or difficulty speaking, he or she is hypothermic and needs your assistance.

C. **STRAINERS** Brush, fallen trees, bridge pilings, undercut rocks, or anything else that allows river current to sweep through can pin boats and boaters against the obstacle. Water pressure on anything trapped this way can be overwhelming. Rescue is often extremely difficult. Pinning may occur in fast current, with little or no whitewater to warn of the danger.

D. **DAMS, WEIRS, LEDGES, REVERSALS, HOLES, AND HYDRAULICS** When water drops over an obstacle, it curls back on itself, forming a strong upstream current which may be capable of holding a boat or swimmer. Some holes make for excellent sport. Others are proven killers. Paddlers who cannot recognize the difference should avoid all but the smallest holes. Hydraulics around man-made dams must be treated with utmost respect regardless of their height or the level of the river. Despite their seemingly benign appearance, they can create an almost escape-proof trap. The swimmer's only exit from the "drowning machine" is to dive below the surface when the downstream current is flowing beneath the reversal.

E. **BROACHING** When a boat is pushed sideways against a rock by strong current, it may collapse and wrap. This is especially dangerous to kayak and decked-canoe paddlers; these boats will collapse and the combination of indestructible hulls and tight outfitting may create a deadly trap. Even without entrapment, releasing pinned boats can be extremely time-consuming and dangerous. To avoid pinning, throw your weight downstream toward the rock. This allows the current to slide harmlessly underneath the hull.

6. Boating alone is discouraged. The minimum party is three people or two craft.

7. Have a frank knowledge of your boating ability, and don't attempt rivers or rapids that lie beyond that ability.

   Develop the paddling skills and teamwork required to match the river you plan to boat. Most good paddlers develop skills gradually, and attempts to advance too quickly will compromise your safety and enjoyment.

   Be in good physical and mental condition, consistent with the difficulties that may be expected. Make adjustments for loss of skills due to age, health, or fitness. Any health limitations must be explained to your fellow paddlers prior to starting the trip.

8. Be practiced in self-rescue, including escape from an overturned craft. The Eskimo roll is strongly recommended for decked boaters who run rapids Class IV or greater, or who paddle in cold environmental conditions.

9. Be trained in rescue skills, CPR, and first aid, with special emphasis on recognizing and treating hypothermia. It may save your friend's life.

10. Carry equipment needed for unexpected emergencies, including footwear that will protect your feet when walking out, throw rope, knife, whistle, and waterproof matches. If you wear eyeglasses, tie them on and carry a spare pair on long trips. Bring cloth repair tape on short runs, and a full repair kit on isolated rivers. Do not wear bulky jackets, ponchos, heavy boots, or anything else which could reduce your ability to survive a swim.

11. Despite the mutually supportive group structure described in this code, individual paddlers are ultimately responsible for their own safety, and must assume sole responsibility for the following decisions:

A. The decision to participate on any trip. This includes an evaluation of the expected difficulty of the rapids under the conditions existing at the time of the put-in.

B. The selection of appropriate equipment, including a boat design suited to their skills and the appropriate rescue and survival gear.

C. The decision to scout any rapid, and to run or portage according to their best judgment. Other members of the group may offer advice, but paddlers should resist pressure from anyone to paddle beyond their skills. It is also their responsibility to decide whether to pass up any walk-out or takeout opportunity.

D. All trip participants should consistently evaluate their own and their group's safety, voicing their concerns when appropriate and following what they believe to be the best course of action. Paddlers are encouraged to speak with anyone whose actions on the water are dangerous, whether they are a part of your group or not.

II. Boat and Equipment Preparedness

1. Test new and different equipment under familiar conditions before relying on it for difficult runs. This is especially true when adopting a new boat design or outfitting system. Low-volume craft may present additional hazards to inexperienced or poorly conditioned paddlers.

2. Be sure your boat and gear are in good repair before starting a trip. The more isolated and difficult the run, the more rigorous this inspection should be.

3. Install flotation bags in noninflatable craft, securely fixed in each end, designed to displace as much water as possible. Inflatable boats should have multiple air chambers and be test-inflated before launching.

4. Have strong, properly sized paddles or oars for controlling your craft. Carry sufficient spares for the length and difficulty of the trip.

5. Outfit your boat safely. The ability to exit your boat quickly is an essential component of safety in rapids. It is your responsibility to see that there is absolutely nothing to cause entrapment when coming free of an upset craft. This includes:

   A. Spray covers that won't release reliably or that release prematurely.

   B. Boat outfitting too tight to allow a fast exit, especially in low-volume kayaks or decked canoes. This includes low-hung thwarts in canoes lacking adequate clearance for your feet and kayak foot braces that fail or allow your feet to become wedged under them.

   C. Inadequately supported decks that collapse on a paddler's legs when a decked boat is pinned by water pressure. Inadequate clearance with the deck because of your size or build.

   D. Loose ropes that cause entanglement. Beware of any length of loose line attached to a whitewater boat. All items must be tied tightly and excess line eliminated; painters, throw lines, and safety rope systems must be completely and effectively stored. Do not knot the end of a rope, as it can get caught in cracks between rocks.

6. Provide ropes that permit you to hold on to your craft so that it may be rescued. The following methods are recommended:

   A. Kayaks and covered canoes should have grab loops of 0.25"+ rope or equivalent webbing sized to admit a normal-sized hand. Stern painters are permissible if properly secured.

   B. Open canoes should have securely anchored bow and stern painters consisting of 8-10 feet of 0.25"+ line. These must be secured in such a way that they are readily accessible but cannot come loose accidentally. Grab loops are acceptable, but are more difficult to reach after an upset.

   C. Rafts and dories may have taut perimeter lines threaded through the loops provided. Footholds should be designed so that a paddler's feet cannot be forced through them, causing entrapment. Flip lines should be carefully and reliably stowed.

7. Know your craft's carrying capacity, and how added loads affect boat handling in whitewater. Most rafts have a minimum crew size which can be added to on day trips or in easy rapids. Carrying more than two paddlers in an open canoe when running rapids is not recommended.

8. Cartop racks must be strong and attach positively to the vehicle. Lash your boat to each crossbar, then tie the ends of the boats directly to the bumpers for added security. This arrangement should survive all but the most violent vehicle accident.

III. Group Preparedness and Responsibility

1. Organization. A river trip should be regarded as a common adventure by all participants, except on instructional or commercially guided trips as defined below. Participants share the responsibility for the conduct of the trip, and each participant is individually responsible for judging his or her own capabilities and for his or her own safety as the trip progresses. Participants are encouraged (but are not obligated) to offer advice and guidance for the independent consideration and judgment of others.

2. River conditions. The group should have a reasonable knowledge of the difficulty of the run. Participants should evaluate this information and adjust their plans accordingly. If the run is exploratory or no one is familiar with the river, maps and guidebooks, if available, should be examined. The group should secure accurate flow information; the more difficult the run, the more important this will be. Be aware of possible changes in river level and how this will affect the difficulty of the run. If the trip involves tidal stretches, secure appropriate information on tides.

3. Group equipment should be suited to the difficulty of the river. The group should always have a throw line available, and one line per boat is recommended on difficult runs. The list may include: carabiners, prussick loops, first-aid kit, flashlight, folding saw, fire starter, guidebooks, maps, food, extra clothing, and any other rescue or survival items suggested by conditions. Each item is not required on every run, and this list is not meant to be a substitute for good judgment.

4. Keep the group compact, but maintain sufficient spacing to avoid collisions. If the group is large, consider dividing into smaller groups or using the "buddy system" as an additional safeguard. Space yourselves closely enough to permit good communication, but not so close as to interfere with one another in rapids.

   A. A point paddler sets the pace. When in front, do not get in over your head. Never run drops when you cannot see a clear route to the bottom or, for advanced paddlers, a sure route to the next eddy. When in doubt, stop and scout.

   B. Keep track of all group members. Each boat keeps the one behind it in sight, stopping if necessary. Know how many people are in your group and take head counts regularly. No one should paddle ahead or walk out without first informing the group. Paddlers requiring additional support should stay at the center of a group and not allow themselves to lag behind in the more difficult rapids. If the group is large and contains a wide range of abilities, a Sweep Boat may be designated to bring up the rear.

   C. Courtesy. On heavily used rivers, do not cut in front of a boater running a drop. Always look upstream before leaving eddies to run or play. Never enter a crowded drop or eddy when no room for you exists. Passing other groups in a rapid may be hazardous: it's often safer to wait upstream until the group ahead has passed.

5. Float plan. If the trip is into a wilderness area or for an extended period, plans should be filed with a responsible person who will contact the authorities if you are overdue. It may be wise to establish checkpoints along the way where civilization could be contacted if necessary. Knowing the location of possible help and preplanning escape routes can speed rescue.

6. Drugs. The use of alcohol or mind-altering drugs before or during river trips is not recommended. It dulls reflexes, reduces decision-making ability, and may interfere with important survival reflexes.

7. Instructional or commercially guided trips. In contrast to the common adventure trip format, in these trip formats a boating instructor or commercial guide assumes some of the responsibilities normally exercised by the group as a whole, as appropriate under the circumstances. These formats recognize that instructional or commercially guided trips may involve participants who lack significant experience in whitewater. However, as a participant acquires experience in whitewater, he or she takes on increasing responsibility for his or her own safety, in accordance with what he or she knows or should know as a result of that increased experience. Also, as in all trip formats, every participant must realize and assume the risks associated with the serious hazards of whitewater rivers. It is advisable for instructors and commercial guides or their employers to acquire trip or personal liability insurance.

   A. An "instructional trip" is characterized by a clear teacher/pupil relationship, where the primary purpose of the trip is to teach boating skills, and which is conducted for a fee.

   B. A "commercially guided trip" is characterized by a licensed, professional guide conducting trips for a fee.

IV. Guidelines for River Rescue

1. Recover from an upset with an Eskimo roll whenever possible. Evacuate your boat immediately if there is imminent danger of being trapped against rocks, brush, or any other kind of strainer.

2. If you swim, hold on to your boat. It has much flotation and is easy for rescuers to spot. Get to the upstream end so that you cannot be crushed between a rock and your boat by the force of the current. Persons with good balance may be able to climb on top of a swamped kayak or flipped raft and paddle to shore.

3. Release your craft if this will improve your chances, especially if the water is cold or dangerous rapids lie ahead. Actively attempt self-rescue whenever possible by swimming for safety. Be prepared to assist others who may come to your aid.

A. When swimming in shallow or obstructed rapids, lie on your back with feet held high and pointed downstream. Do not attempt to stand in fast-moving water; if your foot wedges on the bottom, fast water will push you under and keep you there. Get to slow or very shallow water before attempting to stand or walk. Look ahead! Avoid possible pinning situations including undercut rocks, strainers, downed trees, holes, and other dangers by swimming away from them.

B. If the rapids are deep and powerful, roll over onto your stomach and swim aggressively for shore. Watch for eddies and slack water and use them to get out of the current. Strong swimmers can effect a powerful upstream ferry and get to shore fast. If the shores are obstructed with strainers or undercut rocks, however, it is safer to "ride the rapid out" until a safer escape can be found.

4. If others spill and swim, go after the boaters first. Rescue boats and equipment only if this can be done safely. While participants are encouraged (but not obligated) to assist one another to the best of their ability, they should do so only if they can, in their judgment, do so safely. The first duty of a rescuer is not to compound the problem by becoming another victim.

5. The use of rescue lines requires training; uninformed use may cause injury. Never tie yourself into either end of a line without a reliable quick-release system. Have a knife handy to deal with unexpected entanglement. Learn to place set lines effectively, to throw accurately, to belay effectively, and to properly handle a rope thrown to you.

6. When reviving a drowning victim, be aware that cold water may greatly extend survival time underwater. Victims of hypothermia may have depressed vital signs so they look and feel dead. Don't give up; continue CPR for as long as possible without compromising safety.

For more information and detailed description on this topic, refer to Les Bechdel and Slim Ray's book, *River Rescue,* 3d edition (AMC Books).

V. Universal River Signals

These signals may be substituted with an alternate set of signals agreed upon by the group.

STOP: Potential hazard ahead. Wait for "all clear" signal before proceeding, or scout ahead. Form a horizontal bar with your outstretched arms. Those seeing the signal should pass it back to others in the party.

HELP/EMERGENCY: Assist the signaler as quickly as possible. Give three long blasts on a police whistle while waving a paddle, helmet, or life vest over your head. If a whistle is not available, use the visual signal alone. A whistle is best carried on a lanyard attached to your life vest.

ALL CLEAR: Come ahead (in the absence of other directions proceed down the center). Form a vertical bar with your paddle or one arm held high above your head. Paddle blade should be turned flat for maximum visibility. To signal direction or a preferred course through a rapid around obstruction, lower the previously vertical "all clear" by 45 degrees toward the side of the river with the preferred route. Never point toward the obstacle you wish to avoid.

I'M OK: I'm OK and not hurt. While holding the elbow outward toward the side, repeatedly pat the top of your head.

VI. International Scale of Difficulty

This is the American version of a rating system used to compare river difficulty throughout the world. This system is not exact; rivers do not always fit easily into one category, and regional or individual interpretations may cause misunderstandings. It is no substitute for a guidebook or accurate firsthand descriptions of a run.

Paddlers attempting difficult runs in an unfamiliar area should act cautiously until they get a feel for the way the scale is interpreted locally. River difficulty may change each year due to fluctuations in water level, downed trees, recent floods, geological disturbances, or bad weather. Stay alert for unexpected problems!

As river difficulty increases, the danger to swimming paddlers becomes more severe. As rapids become longer and more continuous, the challenge increases. There is a difference between running an occasional Class IV rapid and dealing with an entire river of this category. Allow an extra margin of safety between skills and river ratings when the water is cold or if the river itself is remote and inaccessible.

The Six Difficulty Classes

Class I: Easy. Fast-moving water with riffles and small waves. Few obstructions, all obvious and easily missed with little training. Risk to swimmers is slight; self-rescue is easy.

Class II: Novice. Straightforward rapids with wide, clear channels which are evident without scouting. Occasional maneuvering may be required, but rocks and medium-sized waves are easily missed by trained paddlers. Swimmers are seldom injured and group assistance, while helpful, is seldom needed. Rapids that are at the upper end of this difficulty range are designated Class II+.

Class III: Intermediate. Rapids with moderate, irregular waves which may be difficult to avoid and which can swamp an open canoe. Complex maneuvers in fast current and good boat control in tight passages or around ledges are often required; large waves or strainers may be present but are easily avoided. Strong eddies and powerful current effects can be found, particularly on large-volume rivers. Scouting is advisable for inexperienced parties. Injuries while swimming are rare; self-rescue is usually easy but group assistance may be required to avoid long swims. Rapids that are at the lower or upper end of this difficulty range are designated Class III- or Class III+, respectively.

Class IV: Advanced. Intense, powerful but predictable rapids requiring precise boat handling in turbulent water. Depending on the character of the river, it may feature large, unavoidable waves and holes or constricted passages demanding fast maneuvers under pressure. A fast, reliable eddy turn may be needed to initiate maneuvers, scout rapids, or rest. Rapids may require "must" moves above dangerous hazards. Scouting may be necessary the first time down. Risk of injury to swimmers is moderate to high, and water conditions may make self-rescue difficult. Group assistance for rescue is often essential but requires practiced skills. A strong Eskimo roll is highly recommended. Rapids that are at the upper end of this difficulty range are designated Class IV- or Class IV+, respectively.

Class V: Expert. Extremely long, obstructed, or very violent rapids which expose a paddler to added risk. Drops may contain large, unavoidable waves and holes or steep, congested chutes with complex, demanding routes. Rapids may continue for long distances between pools, demanding a high level of fitness. What eddies exist may be small, turbulent, or difficult to reach. At the high end of the scale, several of these factors may be combined. Scouting is recommended but may be difficult. Swims are dangerous, and rescue is often difficult even for experts. A very reliable Eskimo roll, proper equipment, extensive experience, and practiced rescue skills are essential. Because of the large range of difficulty that exists beyond Class IV, Class 5 is an open-ended, multiple-level scale designated by Class 5.0, 5.1, 5.2, etc. Each of these levels is an order of magnitude more difficult than the last. Example: Increasing difficulty from Class 5.0 to Class 5.1 is a similar order of magnitude as increasing from Class IV to Class 5.0.

Class VI: Extreme and exploratory. These runs have hardly ever been attempted and often exemplify the extremes of difficulty, unpredictability, and danger. The consequences of errors are very severe and rescue may be impossible. For teams of experts only, at favorable water levels, after close personal inspection and taking all precautions. After a Class VI rapid has been run many times, it's rating may be changed to an apppropriate Class 5.x rating.

Appendix B

Deerfield Agreement

Thanks to a little-noticed provision in a 1986 federal law, equal consideration must be given to environmental, recreational, and economic interests when a private hydroelectric dam can be relicensed. As it turns out, many dams across the U.S. are up for relicensing, and the impact on the rivers has been great. In fact, most changes in river conditions from the last edition of this guide to this one are due to changes in the way dams are operated, a result of the new relicensing guidelines.

The Deerfield is the most dramatic example. The "dryway" was a 3.5-mile stretch of rocky riverbed below the Monroe Bridge. Sporadically, New England Power released water, but it was otherwise dry.

The landmark agreement on the Deerfield guaranteed public use of the river and enhanced protection of river habitat, and provided a continuing supply of reliable, relatively clean energy.

The Deerfield experience was successful: the environmental movement, recreational users, and New England Power cooperated to find balanced uses for the river. NEP recognized its environmental responsibility, while environmental organizations recognized the need for power generation and the need for profitability.

The Deerfield agreement is a model for other hydro dam owners, conservation groups, and federal officials to look at when relicensing other dams in the coming years. It shows that parties with sometimes conflicting interests can come to a joint solution, for the benefit of the river and everyone who uses it.

Eating Wild

More than 150 species of edible wild plants can be found in Massachusetts, many of which grow along rivers. These include the well-known and well-loved fiddleheads of the ostrich fern, along with many other less-well-known but equally delicious species. The shoots of Japanese knotweed can be cooked and eaten like asparagus; the peeled young stalks are a great rhubarb substitute and on-the-river thirst quencher. Juneberry (shadbush) berries taste like a combination of cherries and almonds and are great for pies, muffins, or just stuffing your face right by the tree.

Euell Gibbons called cattails the "supermarket of the swamps" for their many edible parts, which include the starchy rhizomes, the hearts (like hearts of palm) underneath the outer leaves, and the immature bloom spikes; even the hypoallergenic pollen makes an attractive and nutritious addition to flour for pancakes, cookies, and other baked goods.

Black, wrinkled nannyberries look like raisins and taste like prunes spiced with cloves. Groundnut, a tuber-bearing vine in the pea family, produces tubers that grow an inch or two below the soil along the edge of damp riverbanks. They are delicious thinly sliced and fried in vegetable oil to make groundnut chips.

Riverside (a.k.a. Concord) grapes ripen in September and are usually smelled before seen; just follow your nose to find them. Bunches of grapes occasionally overhang the river and can be picked without leaving your boat.

Other edible species found along rivers include arrowhead, calamus, jewelweed, wild rice, and stinging nettle.

—Russ Cohen

Polluted Runoff

Our rivers and streams all are much cleaner, more attractive, and more enjoyable thanks to the Clean Water Act, which became law in the early 1970s. Factories no longer pour industrial waste into the rivers. Sewage is extensively treated before the effluent is discharged. These environmental victories might lead you to believe the job is done, that our rivers are clean. The improvement is great, but there is more to be done.

When pollution comes from a specific, localized source, it is often referred to as "point-source" pollution. Point-source pollution is easily traced to its source. Examples of point-source pollution include chemical pollution from factories, sewage pollution from a sewage plant, or gasoline leaking from an underground storage tank. Point-source pollution has been reduced if not eliminated from many rivers.

Pollution that comes from a diffuse source, or from multiple, poorly defined sources, is called "non-point-source" pollution. Non-point-source pollution is the water pollution from unknown or undefined sources that enters a river from runoff during a storm. A good example of non-point-source pollution is the runoff from parking lots.

With point-source pollution largely controlled, the biggest challenge facing us now in eliminating water pollution is how to address non-point-source pollution. It is a difficult problem, one that requires grassroots awareness to protect our rivers and other water supplies from accidental pollution.

Rivers Protection Act

Rivers are second only to our coastline as the commonwealth's most valuable natural features. Many of Massachusetts' best-known and most-loved places—the Charles River Esplanade, the historic Old North Bridge area in Concord, the thrilling scenery and white-water of the Deerfield valley, and the recovering Atlantic salmon fishery in the Connecticut and Merrimack—are in, on, or along our rivers.

Rivers, streams, and adjacent corridors also serve as key elements of our ecological infrastructure. These areas of undeveloped, naturally vegetated land are a major means of transport and absorption of natural as well as human-generated nutrients and waste products. They facilitate the movement of species from one area to another. A substantial portion of the state's rare and endangered species are dependent upon rivers, streams, and adjacent undeveloped land for habitat and/or migration corridors.

But Massachusetts has a long history of abuse and neglect of its river systems. Massachusetts' prominent role in the Industrial Revolution occurred largely due to and at the expense of its riverine resources.

The Rivers Protection Act, signed into law by Governor William Weld in 1996, gives rivers in Massachusetts extra protection. It authorizes local conservation commissions to regulate land-use activities within a 200-foot-wide riverfront strip along each side of the river. (The riverfront area is only 25 feet wide along rivers flowing through the most densely populated communities, including Boston, Cambridge, Chelsea, Fall River, Lawrence, Lowell, New Bedford, Springfield, Winthrop, and Worcester.)

The Rivers Protection Act is a giant step forward in the effort to safeguard the future integrity of our rivers and the open lands contributing to and dependent upon such systems.

Water Flow

You have almost certainly noticed that river levels fluctuate. Natural changes are predictable, usually with the seasons. But many changes in the river level are also due to human influence, from hydropower generation to withdrawals for drinking-water supply.

These man-made changes in water levels are not necessarily benign. In fact, water-supply withdrawals and diversions may cause serious damage to rivers and other water-dependent ecosystems, such as wetlands. The presence of water in sufficient amounts and periods of time is crucial to the continued survival of many plants and animals in these areas.

Droughts and other low-water events are especially stressful times for fish and other water-dependent organisms. Most of these species have evolved to withstand a certain level of stress resulting from naturally occurring drought periods. Water withdrawals and diversions for water supply or other purposes, however, can significantly increase the duration, frequency, and severity of drought conditions.

Artificially induced drops in water levels may lead to a marked decline in the quality and quantity of habitat for water-dependent species in rivers, streams, wetlands, and other hydric ecosystems. These impacts can result in the demise of sensitive (and often the most ecologically significant) species and a drop in overall species diversity, a key indicator of ecological health.

Instead of developing new water-supply resources and possibly further depleting rivers of their water, water-conservation measures are a more sensible and less expensive way to preserve natural habitats. Install a low-flow toilet in your bathroom, for example, and make sure none of your faucets drip.

SuAsCo Becomes Wild & Scenic

After three years of study and four years of congressional action (and inaction), the Sudbury, Concord, and Assabet Rivers finally received federal Wild & Scenic designation in April 1999. This status is important because it permanently protects the rivers from any kind of development or alteration.

Wild & Scenic designation protects a total of 16.6 miles of the Sudbury River, a 4.4-mile segment of the Assabet River, and 8 miles of the Concord River.

When he signed the bill designating SuAsCo Wild & Scenic, President Bill Clinton said, "The addition of these rivers to the National System recognizes their outstanding ecology, history, scenery, recreation values, and place in American literature. Located about 25 miles west of Boston, the rivers are remarkably undeveloped and provide recreational opportunities in a natural setting to several million people living in the greater Boston metropolitan area."

Ten of the Wild & Scenic river miles lie within Great Meadows National Wildlife Refuge, which was established to protect the outstanding waterfowl habitat associated with extensive riparian wetlands. Historic sites of national importance, including many in the Minute Man National Historical Park, are located near the rivers in Concord.

Each of the eight towns along the river segments voted in town meeting on the Wild & Scenic designation, and the votes were unanimous in all eight towns.

A conservation plan, built upon local and private initiatives, will protect the river segments through local zoning and land-use controls. The SuAsCo River Stewardship Council will have primary responsibility for implementing the conservation plan.

SuAsCo is a treasure. Go quietly and enjoy its tranquillity, its wildlife, its history, and its now permanently preserved character.

Great Blue Herons

You will see great blue herons (*Ardea herodias*) frequently as you paddle the rivers and streams of Massachusetts, Connecticut, and Rhode Island, and elsewhere. This large heron is commonly found standing at the edge of a pond or marshy pool, or in a marshy section of a river, watching for fish and frogs, its principal prey. It also feeds on small mammals, reptiles, and occasionally birds.

These birds stand as much as 4 feet tall, and have a wingspan almost 6 feet. You won't miss them, even though they invariably spook upon your approach. You will never get close to one! Most likely, you'll first see it lumbering off into the sky.

Great blue herons lay three to five pale, greenish-blue eggs on a platform of sticks lined with finer material, usually in a tree but sometimes on the ground. Most herons migrate for the winter, but some remain. Those that do overwinter often succumb to severe weather.

Enjoy these great birds. Even if you have seen dozens of them, they are still a delight.

Purple Loosestrife

In July you'll notice beautiful purple flowers on tall, sticklike plants. And if you see one, you will see many, because they're everywhere. You'll think they're beautiful—and they are—until you know the whole story.

Purple loosestrife is an alien life-form in North America. The plant, with its attractive purple blooms, landed on these shores more than 100 years ago, its seeds carried in the planking of ships. In the past century, it has advanced across the continent, partly due to its persuasive beauty, and, more importantly, because North America has no natural defenses against the plant's onslaught.

While it can seem benign on dry land, purple loosestrife causes great damage in wetlands. No waterfowl will nest, no fish will survive, and no animal will graze or burrow in a wetland area dominated by purple loosestrife. Neither will any of them feed on the plant.

It is so aggressive that it replaces all other plants in the wetland. Chemical control of the plant would not only be impractical, but it could damage the wetland environment.

Efforts to find a biological control are taking place across North America. The search took researchers to Europe where the plant originated. There, purple loosestrife has a variety of enemies to keep it in check. When the research was first started, about 120 types of insects were identified as living off purple loosestrife and then the number was narrowed to five insects that live exclusively on loosestrife. Researchers have concentrated on two species—a flower feeding beetle and a leaf-eating beetle.

Early test results are promising. Where the bug numbers were large enough, purple loosestrife took a beating. But it's going to take quite a few years of releases of insects for significant results to show. The goal is not eradication of loosestrife but to have some control over the spread.

Index

About the Appalachian Mountain Club

BEGIN A NEW ADVENTURE!

Join the Appalachian Mountain Club, the oldest and largest outdoor recreation club in the United States. Since 1876, the Appalachian Mountain Club has helped people experience the majesty and solitude of the Northeast outdoors. Our mission is to promote the protection, enjoyment, and wise use of the mountains, rivers, and trails of the Appalachian region.

Members enjoy discounts on
all AMC programs, facilities, and books.

Outdoor Adventure Programs

We offer more than 100 workshops on hiking, canoeing, cross-country skiing, biking, and rock climbing as well as guided trips for hikers, canoers, and skiers.

Facilities: Mountain Huts and Visitor Centers

The AMC maintains backcountry huts in the White Mountains of New Hampshire and visitor centers throughout the Northeast, from Maine to New Jersey.

Books and Maps

Guides and maps to the mountains, streams, and forests of the Northeast—from Maine to North Carolina—and outdoor skill books from backcountry experts on topics from winter camping to fly fishing. Call 800-AMC-HILL to request a complete catalog.

The Appalachian Mountain Club
5 Joy Street
Boston, MA 02108
617-523-0636

Find us on the web at **www.outdoors.org** to order books, make reservations, learn about our workshops, or join the club.